TAKE THE SLOW ROAD
SCOTLAND

CONWAY
Bloomsbury Publishing Plc
50 Bedford Square, London, WC1B 3DP, UK

BLOOMSBURY, CONWAY and the Conway logo
are trademarks of Bloomsbury Publishing Plc

First published in Great Britain 2018

A catalogue record for this book is available from
the British Library.

Library of Congress Cataloguing-in-Publication
data has been applied for.

ISBN: PB: 978-1-84486-538-3
ePub: 978-1-84486-539-0
ePDF: 978-1-84486-540-6

10 9 8

Designed by Austin Taylor
Typeset in Lato, Janda and Raleway

Printed and bound in Italy
by Printer Trento S.r.l.

Bloomsbury Publishing Plc makes every
effort to ensure that the papers used in
the manufacture of our books are natural,
recyclable products made from wood grown
in well-managed forests. Our manufacturing
processes conform to the environmental
regulations of the country of origin.

To find out more about our authors and books
visit www.bloomsbury.com and sign up for
our newsletters

MIX
Paper from
responsible sources
FSC
www.fsc.org   FSC® C015829

DEDICATION

For the skinny-dipping, confectionery-
conveying companions, the bored
back-seat drivers and gear-grinding gypsies,
the laughing layabouts and secret-sharing
surfers, the hand-holding hobos
and the natural navigators.

For friends and family.

For those who stick with it when things get tricky.

A sincere thank-you for being there.

TAKE THE
SLOW ROAD

SCOTLAND

Inspirational Journeys round the Highlands, Lowlands and
Islands of Scotland by Camper Van and Motorhome

MARTIN DOREY

CONWAY
LONDON · OXFORD · NEW YORK · NEW DELHI · SYDNEY

CONTENTS

WEST COAST 34

ISLANDS 84

CAUTION
Otters Crossing

SOUTH AND CENTRAL SCOTLAND 176

EAST COAST AND CAIRNGORMS 226

HIGHLANDS AND THE NORTH 292

ABOUT THIS BOOK

Hello.

Welcome to the slow road.

Don't rush. There is plenty of time. We have a lot of long, light evenings ahead of us. There are sights to see and people to meet. There are smiles to be smiled.

If we do this right the slow road could be everything that you have been looking for.

The slow road is open spaces, nights under the stars, warm evenings skinny dipping on white-sand beaches, early mornings waking to wet grass outside the van, dark nights staying up to search the sky for the aurora, warming your hands on open fires, laughing with friends, taking time for the kids, having fun.

The slow road is getting from A to B but always via Z.

It is making idle meandering your sole purpose. It isn't lazy, far from it, because you have a reason to be dawdling. Taking the slow road is perfecting the gentle, lost art of wandering. Call it bumbling, bimbling, pootling, tootling, sauntering or drifting if you like, but the end is the same:

Life lived away from the TV and the couch.
Life lived with a smile on your face.
Life lived in harmony.
Life lived with love.

Now get in the van.

7

HOW TO USE THIS BOOK

Now, don't take this the wrong way, but I need to tell you a little about how to get the most out of this book. That's because it has been written to work in two ways. First, I want you to be inspired enough from reading it in advance of your next adventure to rush to book your ferries, flights and motorhome and to hit the slow road. Second, I want you to be able to use this book while you are on the slow road. So it's just at home on your coffee table as on your dashboard.

The book is divided into geographical areas, with a number of driving routes within each. Each route is then divided into a little bit of writing about my experiences while researching the route. These include snippets of things that happened along the way, things you shouldn't miss or things that I found special

about the route. After that it's 'The Driving', which is all about how the route works. Next are the listings of places to stay on the route, including information on 'official' wild-camping spots, toilets and emptying points as well as nice campsites. After that it's the listings of what's in the area. This can include castles, ancient sites, nice beaches or anything that caught my eye along the way. Finally, each section has a quick-look information box that tells you a little of the useful stuff you'll need, such as which OS maps to buy, how long the route is, where to hire a motorhome nearby or how long the route is likely to take you.

All in all, *Take the Slow Road* has been designed to be the kind of book you'll want hanging about to nag you a little each time you flick through it. It should speak to you in a mildly insistent voice that says 'Get out the diary. Book it now!'

It has also been designed to give you lots of practical on-the-road advice, detailed directions and places to see while you are on your trip. That's the bit for when you're on the slow road, getting ideas and looking for direction. The maps should help you to plan routes, join routes together and drive them, and the pictures, I hope, will have you reaching out for the keys, packing your bags and dashing out the door.

Scotland is an awesome country. And I mean that in the true meaning of the word.

Have fun!

INTRODUCING SCOTLAND

Welcome to Scotland.

If anywhere is perfect for a road trip it is Scotland. It has great distances, great views, great people and some of the greatest landscapes in the United Kingdom. Scotland also has the UK's deepest lake, the highest mountain and the oldest building. It has eagles, red squirrels, wild cats, pine martens and capercaillies. Whales, dolphins, otters and seals swim in its seas. Huge, beautiful Caledonian pines grow alongside its byways and on its mountainsides, while rare machair grasslands thrive above the tideline of its most beautiful west coast and island beaches.

Scotland also has roads. Thousands of miles of them. Many of them are spectacular in the extreme. With the exception of some of the major routes, every road I have driven in the writing of this book (and that is a lot of roads) has something special about it. Heck, even the M74 passes through some interesting scenery.

Scotland has Britain's highest main road, highest classified road and the world's longest triple tower cable-stayed bridge, the Queensferry Crossing. It is a country of superlatives, where you can be at the most north-westerly tip of Europe or at the UK's most remote pub.

For motorhomers and camper vanners Scotland is a brilliant place to travel. Generally there is a positive and tolerant attitude towards 'wild camping' and parking up at beaches or in the countryside, even though the Land Reform (Scotland) Act 2003 (which allows wild camping in Scotland) and Scottish Outdoor Access Code do not make specific reference to sleeping in vehicles. So, the tolerance is down to an understanding that motorhomes and camper vans are 'good for business'. It is our responsibility to make sure it stays that way. There is more about this on page 18.

The camping scene is doing well in Scotland, too. While it isn't overrun with campsites, there are plenty enough in which to get a shower, fill up the tanks and plug in for a few days if you need to. The Caravan and Motorhome Club has around 30 Club Sites with many more Certificated Sites.

In the Outer Hebrides, motorhomers are well catered for too, with showers and chemical-toilet emptying points available for you to use in leisure centres, in public toilets and at public buildings. I have done my best to list as many of them as I can in these sections.

If you are self-contained there is no limit to how wild you can go in Scotland. The population is concentrated largely on the central lowland belt and on the east coast around Inverness, Perth and Aberdeen. This leaves large tracts of the country with fewer than one person for every 10 hectares (2011 census). And if you have time and don't mind slow, winding, sometimes difficult roads, you will love it.

But of course, that is what this book is about. It is about getting there slowly and taking time to enjoy the little roads, the views, the high passes and the very best of Scotland's incredible road network.

So forget about the timetable. Let thoughts of the mortgage and bills drift away behind you. Allow the road to take you to places you've not been before.

Put the old girl into gear and hit the slow road.

There is no better way to see Scotland.

HOW TO GET TO SCOTLAND

Scotland is relatively easy to get to. All you have to do is put your pedal to the metal and drive. That's if you have a camper van or motorhome. If you don't then it gets a little more complicated since you'll have to arrange transit between your airport or train station and your hire company (I assume you are hiring in Scotland).

Hiring a motorhome

I have listed motorhome hire companies local to each route, as well as listing them all together in the hire section. So if you'd rather fly to your destination and hire locally or hire from one of the major cities, anything is possible. For example, if you wanted to visit the Isles of Harris and Lewis it would be perfectly possible to fly to Stornoway and then get a lift or taxi to Harris Classic Campers at Seilebost.

Alternatively, you could just drive from home or from your preferred hire specialist and then take a ferry. Up to you. That's the beauty of the slow road.

Getting to Scotland from elsewhere in the UK

Driving There are two main routes from England, with a couple of scenic alternatives.

The M74 joins the M6 and takes you straight to Glasgow and Edinburgh.

The A1 takes the east-coast route via Berwick.

The A68 goes from Hexham/Newcastle and takes a scenic route via Jedburgh.

From Carlisle it is possible to take the beautiful A7 to Galashiels.

There is a widdly route that crosses the border from Kielder to Saughtree. This would be at your own risk though, it's untested, but from where I saw it, could be fun...

Train Glasgow and Edinburgh are served well by mainline services from London and other UK cities.

The Caledonian Sleeper connects Inverness, Aberdeen, Glasgow, Perth and Edinburgh with London and takes approximately 12 hours from Inverness.

Car ferry from Ireland Ferries run from Belfast and Larne to Cairnryan in Dumfries and Galloway, about 80 miles (130 kilometres) south-west of Glasgow.

Getting to Scotland from Europe

It is possible to fly to Scotland's major airports: Glasgow, Edinburgh, Aberdeen, Prestwick and Inverness.

Getting to Scotland from elsewhere in the world

Scotland's major airports are all served by direct flights from the USA, Middle East and Europe. Other destinations are served from European hubs, with direct flights to Scotland.

MAPS AND MAP READING

Maps have been an important part of planning this book. And just as important in the writing. Without them I'd have been wandering and writing aimlessly, unable to make decisions, unable to remember the twists and turns and unable to understand the essence of the land I was in, was writing about or was about to enter.

In short, without a map I would be lost.

Why I love maps

Maps give you incredible detail about the land you are in, and the larger the scale the better it will be: large-scale maps will tell you whether a road is a single track with passing places, is fenced, is more or less than 4m (13ft) wide – or even what direction the water in a pipeline might be flowing. All the clues are there if you know what to look for. Good maps hold the key to just about everything, allowing you to find your way and be fully informed. Maps make me want to get in the van and go.

Sadly, map reading is a skill that we are in danger of losing, thanks to the age of convenience. If we want to we don't have to think at all on our journeys, instead simply pressing a few buttons and then following directions blindly. This is fine if you are trying to find a postcode or navigate through an unknown city, but when it comes to following routes, looking for a place to spend the night, seeking out secret beaches, understanding features in the landscape or making last-minute diversions to unexpected places, only a good map will do.

So, if you decide to set out on any of the journeys I have laid out for you in this book, I implore you to take a map too. Don't rely on me or a satnav or your phone without the back-up of a decent-scale map to keep you on track. The orange OS map, 'Explorer', gives you 1:25,000 detail while the pink OS map, 'Landranger', gives you half that scale at 1:50,000.

While satnavs are fine and can help you to pinpoint your position, they often lack the kind of detail you need to understand exactly where you are or where you are going.

We are very lucky in the UK that our land is one of the world's most mapped places. There is more detail to be found on our OS maps than is found anywhere else in the world, giving us a 2-D picture of the landscapes that is second to none. Each day, Ordnance Survey makes 10,000 changes to its database of more than 500 million geographic features. That's an incredible amount of detail in such a small space.

What's wrong with your satnav? One of the things I dislike about satnavs is the fact that they take decision-making away from you. They lead you places without telling you anything about them. There is no wider context when it comes to a satnav. And that means you are out of control. You are no longer in charge of your own destiny and your journey is at the hands of whomever it was who wrote the algorithm for your software.

Satnavs also rely on electricity and battery power, as well as infrastructure, to work. But what if your battery goes on your phone, the satellite goes belly up or your car dies? Without a paper map to get you out you'll be lost. Perhaps in more ways than one.

How to fold an OS map Frankly, there is a knack to it, but really, you're on your own. I am not your mother.

WHERE AND HOW TO STAY IN SCOTLAND

It's all very well driving around Scotland, but sooner or later you are going to have to stop and take a nap. In a camper van or motorhome it should be pretty simple. You rearrange some cushions, perhaps push a lever, unroll some bedding or even press a button and, hey presto, your bed is ready. Everything you need is at hand and you'll be cosy all the way through until breakfast.

So all is sweet. But the question remains as to *where* you are going to park up to get that dreamy night's sleep.

Leave it nicer

Leave it nicer: your responsibility as a camper van or motorhome owner. Wherever it is you end up – on a remote beach, in a touring park or in the car park of a quayside pub – you have a responsibility to your fellow motorhome owners and to the world which you inhabit. That is to keep it tidy, to not make any mess and to be respectful.

- Tidy up your pitch when you arrive and before you leave.
- Don't drop grey waste anywhere other than in designated places.
- Use eco-friendly soaps, detergents and liquids.
- Empty your chemical loo at designated points only.
- Take your litter home.
- Recycle as much as you can.
- Buy and eat local to contribute to the local economy.
- Smile and be nice.

Touring parks and campsites

Scotland has a lot of campsites. From high-density touring parks to large, very well organised Caravan and Motorhome Club or Camping and Caravanning Club sites, every need is catered for. You can join either club to get discounted rates or you can simply turn up and, if necessary, join on site. Alternatively, you can use camping sites such as Cool Camping for sites with a difference or Pitch Up for online booking on the go.

> www.caravanclub.co.uk
> www.campingandcaravanningclub.co.uk
> www.pitchup.com
> www.coolcamping.com
> www.campsited.com

Certificated Locations While driving route 13 I came across a Caravan and Motorhome Club CL. This is a small site with a limited number of pitches. You can locate them with the handbook provided by The Caravan and Motorhome Club or The Camping and Caravanning Club or simply chance upon them as you drive. Either way, they offer a chance to camp in out-of-the way sites, often in interesting locations.

> www.caravanclub.co.uk
> www.campingandcaravanningclub.co.uk

Britstops Based on the France Passion scheme, Britstops have been working hard to put growers, pub and restaurant owners, beauty spots, activity centres and farmers in touch with motorhomers by offering free overnight stops in exchange for nothing more than a smile and a wave and, hopefully, some business. There are around 50 of these located in Scotland. I stayed on one near Montrose that was by a fabulous pub on a quayside. All we had to do to stay was buy a pint or two. Not a bad deal.

The guidebook at present costs £27.50 and thereafter camping is free, just follow the code of conduct.

> www.britstops.com

'Wild camping' spots A lot of people visit Scotland to exercise their right to 'wild camp' in a camper van or motorhome. Yet, however hard I look, the Land Reform (Scotland) Act 2003, which permits wild camping and defines it as 'lightweight, done in small numbers … well away from roads…' does not refer to motorised vehicles. The Scottish Outdoor Access Code does not refer to camper vans or motorhomes either. The inference is that the kind of 'wild camping' allowed is using tents, not your van: you have no right to wild camp in a camper van or motorhome in Scotland. In addition, the Road Traffic Act 1988 states that:

> you can drive a vehicle up to 15 yards off a public road for the purposes of parking, but this does not confer any right to park the vehicle. Most un-metalled roads, unfenced land and beaches are private property, and you don't have the right to park unless it's authorised by the landowner by verbal agreement or signage.

Sorry. That's one myth busted.

However. Informal camping or off-site camping takes place at many locations in Scotland 'without causing undue concern', according to the

The informal camping code

According to Scottish Natural Heritage (www.snh.scot):

- Avoid overcrowding by moving on to another location.
- Carry a trowel to bury your human waste and urinate well away from open water, rivers and burns.
- Use a stove or leave no trace of any campfire.
- Never cut down or damage trees.
- Take away your rubbish and consider picking up other litter as well.
- If in doubt, ask the landowner – following their advice may help you find a better camping spot.
- Access rights are not an excuse for anti-social or illegal behaviour.

guidance on 'Freedom Camping' from CAMPA, The Campervan and Motorhome Professional Association. This is good news. But it doesn't grant any rights.

You may find that at previously popular sites or at sites where there have been problems, notices discouraging overnight parking or camping have appeared. Don't disregard them. They exist, usually, because of persistent problems, mess, antisocial behaviour and littering.

If you are to camp off-site in your camper van or motorhome then please follow the simple rules of the informal camping code. If you can't, follow this: LEAVE IT NICER.

Loch Lomond and camping management zones In Loch Lomond and The Trossachs National Park, problems have been so persistent that the park authority has had cause to repeal the right and passed local bylaws requiring permits to wild camp at certain times of the year. This applies to camper vans and motorhomes as well as tented camping. At the time of writing the fees were £3 per night. Expect more of these.

www.lochlomond-trossachs.org

Island camping When the number of motorhomes reaches saturation point, particularly on small and beautiful islands, problems can occur. It is not your fault for going there or the islanders' fault for living in a beautiful place, but sometimes, if there are too many people all trying to do the same thing, things can get difficult. It seems that island or even individual grazing trusts are taking charge by setting

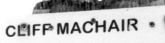

CLIFF MACHAIR

Is in a designated National Scenic Area.

We have had to put in fences to combat erosion.

Please help with this conservation by observing the following:

1. Strictly NO fires on the grass
2. Access the beach via the marked path.
3. Do not obstruct turning area.
4. Put £5 per vehicle or tent per night in the Honesty Box.
(This will be used to defray costs of erosion repair and control.)

Thank you.

Note Access to Cliff Machair and any overnight camping is entirely at your own risk. Valtos Grazing accept no liability for any accident or damage occuring to persons or property during your visit.

their own agenda, working hard to encourage visitors while reducing the impact where camping is restricted to one area of machair, and installing an honesty box to help pay for it. I am all for that and would happily pay for a loo, decent parking and a tap, such as is found at some spots on Lewis.

When problems occur because people have had no respect it makes me furious.

Islands deal with it in different ways:

On some islands, such as **Colonsay,** I have heard that informal camping in camper vans and motorhomes is not encouraged and people are required to demonstrate that they have a booking or place in which to camp when they arrive.

On **Arran,** when asking if I could pay to empty tanks and fill up with water I was told by a campsite owner that the residents 'despise' wild campers. Whether or not this is true is moot, but it does show that there are issues (or the campsite owner is annoyed because he feels he is losing business).

Either way, Arran is a special place with few 'wild' spots that are away from the beady eyes of residents. All local public toilets have shut or are on reduced hours, due to council cuts. Campsites are the only option when it comes to emptying tanks.

Barra and the Uists have their own code about wild camping, described in a leaflet that can be picked up at tourist information centres and various other places. This leaflet points out places where you can empty and charge tanks as well as places to shower. This is great and shows that there is some consideration and that we are welcome, but it must be managed and treated with respect.

The West Harris Trust has designated a number of areas where overnight parking/camping is permitted in order to control the number of people randomly camping in a small stretch. This works well, although there are still a few places where it is possible to camp outside these areas. There are also designated hook-up points and showers at Talla na Mara, a local restaurant and cultural centre. At Hushinish there are new designated spots being created to help alleviate the issues around wild camping and overcrowding.

www.westharristrust.org

Lewis also has a number of spots where it is possible to empty waste tanks and these are available from the tourist information office in Stornoway or Tarbert. There are also lists of car parks with toilets that can be used for wild camping.

WHAT TO TRAVEL WITH

Travelling through Scotland in a motorhome or camper van can be a wonderful experience, but it can also be demanding at times. Wild spots – and even pitches – are rarely flat, taps are rarely close enough to the road and camping shops rarely pop up when you need them.

That means you may need some kit. The following kit list will help to get you out of trouble and will help to give you the best motorhoming and camper-vanning experience.

Kit

Hoses and universal adaptors

Water is essential but it's not always easy to get it from the tap to the van. Carrying jerrycans is easy, but even so, a length of hose can get you out of all sorts of trouble. If you have a portable toilet or on-board toilet then a short length of hose can help you to clean it out. Keep it separate from the fresh-water hose. A set of Hozelock tap adaptors and a universal adaptor will mean you can always fill up.

> **KIT LIST**
> - 10m (33ft) of flexible fresh-water fill-up hose
> - set of universal tap-to-hose adaptors
> - 1m (3ft) length of hose for slopping out toilets

21

Levelling chocks and spirit level Some people can sleep on a slope, but I can't, so I *always* carry my levelling chocks. Recently I have acquired a mini two-plane spirit level that sits on the dashboard and tells me when I am getting close to level, but really a glass of water on a flat surface will do. And if you forget your chocks, a few copies of this book will do just as well.

KIT LIST
- 1 x set of Level Up levelling chocks
- 1 x spirit level

Electric cables and extensions If you have electric hook-up then you'll need a C Form or 16amp cable to go with it. A cable that is about 25m (80ft) in length is usually sufficient to reach any pitch. It may also be a good idea to carry a 13amp adaptor plug as well as a 13amp socket if your van doesn't have a 16amp socket.

KIT LIST
- 25m (80ft) 16amp cable
- 13amp plug adaptor
- 13amp socket (to 16 amp)

Wind-up torches and lamps Wind-up torches are incredibly useful because they don't need any maintenance and don't create any waste. Some lanterns will charge up from the 12V socket in the van, so can always be kept topped up at no cost. Both are useful if you have to do a midnight loo stop.

Spare gas canisters Camping shops can be few and far between in some parts of Scotland, so take a spare canister or two if you can. If you are running on LPG fill up *before* you head into the wild. Some stations do not supply it or may not have the right nozzle adaptor.

Solar panel If you are going off-grid then a solar panel can trickle a charge into your leisure battery to stop it from running down, especially if you are running a lot of stuff off it. However, if you don't want to go to the hassle of fitting a larger one, consider running phones, lamps and gadgets off a portable solar charger.

Midge spray Not every trip to Scotland is going to be plain sailing and at some point you are going to encounter midges. Fortunately, being in a camper van or motorhome means you'll be able to hide from the worst of it, but if you have to go out, carry spray as a matter of course. Avon's Skin So Soft is considered the best.

Maps maps maps I always carry a map of the whole of Scotland for route planning, as well as large-scale maps of the specific areas I am visiting – so I can get into the heart of the landscape.

OS 'Explorer' maps offer 1:25,000 scale and OS 'Landranger' maps offer 1:50,000 scale.

Wet-weather gear You never know in Scotland. One minute it could be dry, the next it could be wetter than a wet weekend in Weston-super-Mare. Be prepared for any weather and hope you don't have to use it.

Axe and firelighting equipment You may not always get the chance to have a fire but it's always worth carrying the kit to make it happen should the need arise. Just remember to avoid lighting fires in sensitive areas or on grass or where there is a danger of it spreading. If possible, take a fire pit too, then you can light up safely without damaging turf.

> **KIT LIST**
> • Axe
> • Firelighters/matches/fire steel
> • Firepit/wood/kindling

Toilet kit If you don't carry a portable toilet then sooner or later you may have to indulge in a nature wee (or worse). The Scottish Outdoor Access Code has specific information about this: do not urinate within 30m (100ft) of any open waters, rivers or streams. If you do have to defecate, do it as far as possible from rivers, streams, buildings and animals. Dig a hole and bury it. Carry a trowel or folding spade.

> **KIT LIST**
> • Trowel
> • Cheap toilet paper (it tends to break down more easily)

Kit for a motorhome or camper van If you are hiring a motorhome or camper van then it should come with all you need for a good trip, but it's always worth checking with the hirer before you turn up. It might not be possible to carry large items such as chocks with you when you hire so it's always a good idea to check and request essential items.

23

HIRING A MOTORHOME OR CAMPER VAN

Are you ready? Hiring a motorhome or camper van could result in one of the best holidays you ever have! We have included a list of Scotland's hire companies on page 346, but, in the meantime, here are some thoughts on the kind of vans and motorhomes you can hire. Which one will be best for you?

You can hire motorhomes and camper vans all over Scotland, which means you can choose your pick-up location and the way you like to travel.

Classic camper vans

Classic are cool! There is no doubt about that. And hiring one to pootle about in in Scotland is going to be a dream come true for many people. You'll get waves from everyone you pass, will be able to camp in comfort and will smile from ear to ear all day long.

The pros Classic VW campers are fantastic to hang out in. They look very cool and will bring smiles wherever you go. In lots of ways they are the ultimate in camping awesomeness with their good looks, happy ways and quirky workings. They are also small enough to go anywhere.

The cons They are a bit slow. They can be difficult to drive. They are not always ideal if you have more than four people to sleep or if you like a lot of space. But they are cool. Very cool.

Modern van-sized campers

If you like the size of a classic but don't want to be restricted by space and comfort, go for a new VW T5 or T6. They will often sleep four (with a pop-up roof) and can go fast. Camping convenience in a perfectly sized package.

The pros Fast and reliable. Convenient. Come with all the bits and pieces. Completely safe for a family of four or five.

The cons Often without a loo or shower. Space can be an issue for bigger families or when the midges strike or the weather breaks and you have to go indoors.

Motorhomes

In many ways a motorhome is the perfect vehicle in which to explore Scotland because they are self-contained. This means you can go off grid for days at a time as you have all you need: heating, lighting, toilet, shower, kitchen, beds, storage space. When you hire one, make sure you specify the number of sleeping berths and travelling seats required.

The pros Motorhomes are great for going off grid. With everything on board you have all you need. Can be good for big families, so long as there are enough seat belts.

The cons Big and bulky. Can be slow. Difficult to drive on some of Scotland's smaller roads. Hard to hide sometimes if you want to stealth camp!

DOS AND DON'TS

Everyone has an idea of what they can and can't do when out and about, right? But sometimes what we consider to be OK isn't for others. So here's a few thoughts about what you should and shouldn't think about when driving and camping in Scotland.

Midges

Yes, it's true: Scotland can have a midge problem during the summer months (May to September). However, it's not as bad as it seems and I wouldn't let it spoil a trip. Even if you go into an area where there are plenty of midges you'll be able to escape them by retreating into your camper van or motorhome. And that's the beauty of travelling this way: you always have an escape route.

Midge bites are annoying and itchy and can last for a few days. However, it is relatively easy to avoid them, if you know a bit about them:

• Midges come out from about May onwards, with the female biting midges being most prevalent from June onwards.
• Midges don't like direct sunlight, so sit in the sun, if it comes out.
• Midges don't like windy conditions and can't fly if the wind is above 7mph (11kph).
• Midges like damp, still conditions, so loch sides on still days are particularly risky.
• Midges particularly like dawn, dusk and times when there is cloud cover.
If you walk, midges often can't keep up with you, so staying on the move will help to stop them annoying you. If you are staying still for long periods then head nets can stop them from attacking you.

There are various forms of insect repellents that midges don't like. However, the long-favoured anti-midge formula is Avon's Skin So Soft moisturiser and spray, which contains insect-repelling ingredients. However, if you prefer a truly natural and native approach then you might need to look at bog myrtle oil. It is available online.

The best prevention against midges is to go inside your camper van or motorhome when there is no wind or sun at dusk and dawn.

Wild camping etiquette

I write about this a lot but it's as well to keep mentioning it because it's important. Camper vans and motorhomes have long been welcome in Scotland. But there are a lot of them. So, in order to keep it sweet and the welcome warm in the glens, I would ask everyone to be respectful, to clear up when they arrive and before they leave, to follow the Scottish Outdoor Access Code, to avoid parking where you stick out like a sore thumb, and to be polite and nice if someone asks you to move on.

Also, it can go a long way if you ask permission to stay overnight, spend money in local shops, eat out and generally contribute to the local economy when you are there. Be generous at honesty boxes and smile wherever you go. Thank you.

Driving

This book is called the slow road because it's about taking it easy, dropping down a gear and making time to enjoy the good things about travel. But that doesn't mean it's OK to cause tailbacks and be an annoyance to other drivers. If you drive too slowly then you can be guilty of the offence of 'inconsiderate driving' and, of greater importance,

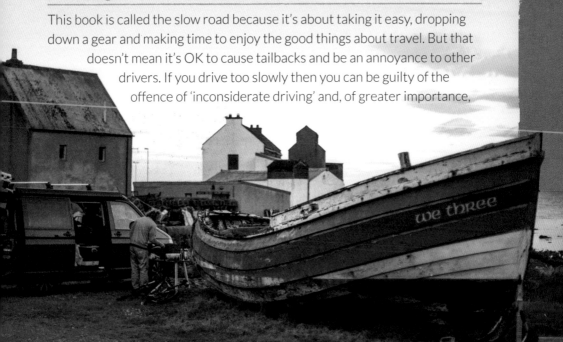

it can be just as dangerous as driving too quickly because it can cause impatient overtaking. So, while there is no minimum speed limit on most of Britain's roads, be mindful of how you appear to other drivers.

Head of the queue again? If you notice a build-up of a few cars behind you (do remember to look in your mirrors) then it's courteous to pull over and let them pass. Indicate when you see a lay-by or space and move over safely.

Single-track roads On single-track roads there are passing places that are often marked with a pole or diamond-shaped sign. They have two uses: first, to allow you to pass vehicles coming in the opposite direction; and second, to allow you to pull over so that cars behind may overtake you.

Reversing your unit If you are a bit rubbish at reversing or have no reversing camera and can't see out of the back of your vehicle then it is up to you to be vigilant on single-track roads. This means pulling in in good time to allow others to pass you rather than continuing, even when you see cars coming in the opposite direction. It is not acceptable to bully other drivers by insisting they reverse because you can't. If you are the only vehicle and you face two or more vehicles coming in the opposite direction then it is up to you to be able to reverse rather than causing a stand-off or blockage.

Buy local to support local jobs

Some parts of Scotland rely on tourism. Spending from tourism generates around £12 billion of income each year (from 2015 figures), with more than 215,000 jobs relying on it for their livelihoods.

What does this mean for you? Well, it's quite simple: the more you spend in local shops, with local businesses and local tourism providers, the more it benefits the local economy. Buying your groceries in Carlisle at the last supermarket before the border and then eking it out for the duration of your trip contributes nothing to Scotland. Indeed, buying from supermarkets generally benefits only the supermarkets and not the local economy.

So, if you can, spend wisely and don't be a skinflint! Make good buying choices, be generous at camping spots with honesty boxes and don't go to Scotland looking for a free ride. A pound spent in a locally owned and run shop, with a local guide or in a locally owned restaurant does more for Scotland that you might believe. Honesty boxes at campsites in the Outer Hebrides, for example, enable those camping spots to stay open and conservation work to continue.

Why say this? I like Scotland and I'd like to think that I help to keep it happy and healthy when I visit. I'd love it if we, as a collective, can help to keep it that way for others too. That's all.

Crime

Recent reports have stated that crime in Scotland has been falling, with the lowest crime rate overall since 1974. As one might expect, the lowest crime rates occur outside of the major cities, with fewer than 30 crimes per 1,000 people reported in council areas including Aberdeenshire, Western Isles, Argyll and Bute, Orkney Islands, Shetland Islands and the Scottish Borders.

Scotland is a relatively safe country for camper vanners and motorhomers. However, there are always risks and it's as well to make sure you are always vigilant. Keep doors locked at night and if you are away from your vehicle. Do not leave valuables in vision when you park up and don't flaunt your wealth. Also, don't leave items such as bikes, chairs and tables outside when you go off for the day. It is inviting theft! Basically, be sensible!

WHAT MAKES THE PERFECT TRAVELLING COMPANION?

On the journeys I have undertaken to write this book I have enjoyed varied company. The experience has been different with each person because each of them has brought a different quality to the trip, whether that's map reading, cooking, taking pictures, driving or making me laugh. Or all of these things at the same time. Mostly, it's about nothing more than having good companionship, because good companionship makes the motorway miles go quicker and mealtimes more enjoyable.

But companionship also brings something very special to a trip, and that, for me, is having someone to hold your hand, metaphorically or otherwise, and help you say yes to new experiences. It is having a sidekick, an ally, a playmate, a partner in crime and, most importantly, a friend to make new experiences easier to bear and to help you make the best of them. Even if you travel with a dog for company, they can still take you places or boost your confidence in unfamiliar surroundings. They can help you break the ice too. Moreover, dogs need to be walked and walking leads you places.

Travelling can be difficult if you don't have the confidence to walk into a bar alone, ask questions, get chatting to people or go somewhere that's out of your comfort zone. Sometimes you need someone to give you a prod and to say 'It's OK. I am with you. Let's do it.'

I have found, during the course of all my travels, that if you are able to appear to be happy, chirpy and having fun then people respond better. It can give you the confidence to strike up the kind of conversations that will yield results, such as a local's knowledge of a beautiful view or the best place to get a cream tea. Those are the conversations that make travel special. They are the map to the secret beach you have been dreaming of finding.

Driving is tiring, too, so it's always great to have someone to help with chores or who can jolly you along during difficult times, even if they don't take the wheel from you. Making a sarnie for lunch, opening a packet of sweets because you're driving, putting the kettle on or sorting out the bed can be a great help during, and at the end of, a long drive (do you hear me, kids?).

31

Travelling solo

I have done a few solo trips during the writing of this book. On these occasions I felt that it was something I needed to do. I needed the peace and solitude and to have some time alone. It was my decision.

However, some people have no choice but to travel alone. Despite being solo they go anyway rather than staying at home to fester. All credit to you if you do. It can be extremely rewarding but it can also be lonely. That's when you need to dig deep and be friendly and open hearted, even when you don't want to, because being shy or reticent or afraid can sometimes mean you miss out.

Yes, so sometimes it's easier to be a recluse in the van and keep yourself to yourself. On a trip to North Uist I was proud that I had 48 hours alone on an isolated beach, but after a while it was nice to have company. It's good to chat.

So, when you travel, take a minute to smile and say hello. It could make someone's day. It may even lead you down a road you never expected. At the very least you may end up having a cuppa with someone who knows stuff you don't. It's well worth making the effort.

Have you got the skills?

First, let's say that there is no such thing as perfection. So, by rights that means there may well be no perfect travelling companion. We all have our

foibles and annoyances, and living in a van can test the best of relationships. Here are a few of my personal requirements of a potential travelling mate:

- If I cook, they must like washing up.
- They must be self-starting, self-motivated and willing to work out the mechanics of the van in order to be able to put away the chairs by themselves without needing to be asked or shown how to do it.
- They must be able to read a map. This is mandatory. No excuses.
- They must have a similar taste in music – or at least an interesting taste in music – because 'musical differences' has split up many a promising young band. I do not want the same to happen to us.
- They must not fall asleep on the motorway either as a passenger or as the driver. If I am driving long stints then being awake as a passenger is vital for the well-being of the whole van, unless previously agreed.
- They must hand out sweets during difficult times. There is no known ill that a dip into the liquorice allsorts bag can't cure.
- They must like people. This means smiling, asking questions and being nice, even if others aren't.
- They must like going places they have never been before. This includes over barbed-wire fences, down little paths to the sea and along lanes with grass growing down the middle.
- They mustn't be afraid of cold water, spiders, pubs or long distances. Skinny dipping optional.

All good? You got the job.

WEST COAST

The west coast of Scotland is a wild place,
full of deep inlets, lochs and off the beaten track
places. It includes the wild and sparsely populated Mull
of Kintyre, the oasis at Applecross and the jumping off point
for many of the Hebrides, Oban. The coastline is convoluted and
difficult and the roads are often slow and marvellous, offering
views over the water to distant peninsulas, islands and
the promise of more to explore. It's perfect camper van
country and should not be missed – much like
the rest of Scotland.

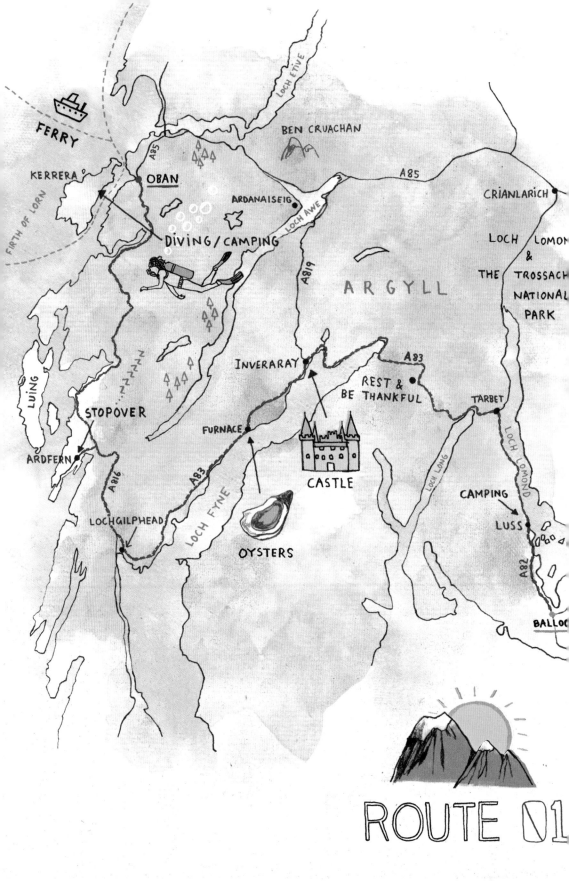

01

LOCH FYNE TO OBAN

THE SLOW ROAD TO OBAN

Oban is the jumping-off point for so many Scottish island adventures. It is the gateway to the Inner and Outer Hebrides, with CalMac ferries heading off to Barra, South Uist, Mull, Colonsay, Lismore and Coll from here, with connections to Tiree, the Uists, Harris, Lewis, Islay and Jura. It is the place to begin your island hopscotch without having to drive to the distant ports of Ullapool, Mallaig or Uig. It's also an inspiring destination in its own right, with all kinds of adventures available locally. Most people get there from Glasgow on the A85, but I prefer taking the slow road along the northern shore of Loch Fyne.

BEST FOR:
Getting a feel for Scotland

START:
Glasgow (M8)

END: **Oban**

MILEAGE:
125 miles (200 kilometres)

DAYS TO EXPLORE: **2**

OS LAND-RANGER MAP:
49, 55, 56

WEST COAST

I wake on the shores of Loch Lomond to a fine but cold autumn morning. There is no wind and the surface of the Loch is like glass, reflecting the surrounding mountains in its smooth, mirror finish. I open the blinds and look out at my first view of Scotland on this epic year of adventuring I have been on the verge of undertaking for the last few months. I am here, at last, in an incredible spot overlooking one of Scotland's most popular, and yet much maligned tourist hotspots.

There is litter at the side of the loch, so the first thing I do when I have dressed is to clear it up. It takes seconds but makes for a better view. 'If only,' I think to myself 'everybody did this. How nice it would be.' And how nice it would be for us – the motorhomers and camper vanners who love to be out in nature – to be welcomed at places like this. Instead, I am aware of the truth of things: Loch Lomond is under pressure from careless campers, littering and a lack of care, and that has resulted in a repealing of the sacred Land Reform Act for the area and the introduction of Camping Management Zones.

I arrived very late last night after a long drive from Cornwall, stopping for a few hours' sleep on a lochside road off the A82 near Luss. It's a good place to begin a Scottish adventure as it means I have bypassed Glasgow and southern Scotland and can now get on with the real business at hand: exploring the slow road. I pack up and drive on, confident that I have left my overnight stop nicer than it was when I arrived.

It's still early when I leave Loch Lomond at Tarbet to follow the A83 past the top of Loch Long and on towards Loch Fyne. This is the slow road and I take it easy, knowing I have all day before my ferry departs for Barra and the Outer Hebrides. I need to enjoy the drive for its own sake rather than rushing to my next stop.

I climb up to the Rest and Be Thankful, the highest point on this road, at 245m (803ft) above sea level, a famous landmark, and down Glen Kinglass towards Loch Fyne. Just after Clachan, at the uppermost reaches of Loch Fyne, I stop at the side of the road. The view, of the sun rising over the mountains, blows me away. It is my first 'wow' moment of the trip. The tide is in and the water still, pausing for a while before departing back out to sea. Mist hangs in the hills on the opposite bank over Cairndow, which looks beautiful but will have to wait for another day for me to explore. Steam rises gently from the water and all is still. The road, as if designed for pictures, curves around the loch in a series of elegant S-bends, while the foliage of oak, birch and beech, some of it turning for the autumn, hangs over the road in layers of vivid greens, stunning golds, deep reds and chocolate browns.

It's a picture-perfect scene. It's been perfect driving so far, with the appropriate number of 'wow's and gasps. But this takes the biscuit, for now, until I get to the River Oude. There I see layer upon layer of larches in their changing vestments reflected perfectly in the still water. I stop, as I do often, to take pictures that I hope will do justice to the scene in front of me. Snap! I couldn't hope for more. I finally begin to believe, that, after all the planning and negotiating to get this book made, taking the slow road is the only way to travel.

THE DRIVING

From Glasgow, the M8 heads west out of the city and then turns into the M898 and the A898 as it crosses the Clyde. Once on the north bank it's the A82 that will take you north past the west bank of Loch Lomond. This is when it starts to get good. The open country comes quickly after the tenements and high-rises of the big city. For anyone used to miles and miles of suburbs it's a blessed relief. You can be out in nature in minutes and enjoying a first taste of Scotland 'proper'. The western shores of Loch Lomond are open up to this point so the best views are of the eastern shore and the mountains behind. On a still day the reflections are beautiful.

About three-quarters of the way up Loch Lomond the A82 meets the A83 at Tarbet, which heads west for a few miles before skirting around the eastern end of Loch Long and heading

PLACES TO STAY

Luss Camping and Caravanning Club Site
Luss, Loch Lomond,
Alexandria, G83 8NT
web: www.campingand
caravanningclub.co.uk
tel: 01436 860 658

info: *This site consists of 90 pitches of lochside camping. I stayed here while writing 'The Camper Van Coast' and loved it. Perfect for the kids to explore and lovely views of the loch. Book early as it gets busy, and it is for members only.*

Ardfern Motorhome Park
Barrfada Farm, Ardfern,
Argyll, PA31 8QN
web: www.ardfernmotorhomepark.com
email: ardfernmotorhome
park@gmail.com
tel: 07808 276 944/01852 500 360

info: *I loved this place. Tucked away down a little offshoot, by the sea, away from the A816, it's got everything a motorhome stopover should have. It's cheap, too, and has a decent loo and nice, simple facilities. An aire in the Highlands. Go for it.*

Oban Camping And Caravan Park
Gallanachmore Farm,
Gallanach Road, Oban,
Argyll, PA34 4QH
web: http://obancaravan park.com
email: info@obancaravan park.com
tel: 01631 562 425

info: *Just 3 miles (5 kilometres) from Oban and yet a world away. With views over to the Isle of Kerrera, it's a beautiful and tranquil site. Perfect for over-nights on the way somewhere or even as a base for a holiday. But then, with the Western Isles just a boat ride away, why linger?*

up to the Rest and Be Thankful and then down to Loch Fyne. From then on until Lochgilphead it's a lochside saunter, with beautiful curves and even more beautiful views. At Lochgilphead the route takes a northerly turn towards Oban on the A816, skirting Loch Melfort and Loch Feochan before making the final descent into Oban. Views, as usual, abound.

Camping by Loch Lomond

In March 2017 Camping Management Zones were introduced in some areas of Loch Lomond during the summer season. Permits must be bought online in advance to stay at a number of designated hotspots. For more, see www.lochlomond-trossachs.org.

IN THE AREA

Loch Fyne Oysters The name has spread all over the world,
but this is the source, and what makes Loch Fyne famous before all else.
Aquaculture is big here and oysters have been farmed by the Loch Fyne
giants since 1978. So where better to sample Scotland's finest seafood
than at the side of the place where it all started? • **www.lochfyne.com**

Inveraray As you approach this planned Georgian town it appears to jut
out into Loch Fyne, with the small harbour wall projecting into the waters.
The Duke of Argyll has his pile here, a magnificent 18th-century castle with
Disney turrets and towers. It is the spiritual home of the Campbell clan, the
largest clan in the world. As befits a town with a Duke, there is also a jail in

Inveraray, no doubt for troublesome hoi polloi. It is considered one of the finest examples of a 19th-century prison and courthouse in Scotland. • **www.inveraray-castle.com** | • **www.inverarayjail.co.uk**

Puffin Dive Centre Forget Thailand or the Med: Scotland is the place to learn to dive! At the Puffin Dive Centre in Oban you can take your PADI Recreational Diver course as well as a whole lot of other qualifications, such as Drysuit Diver and Dive Master. You can also try out diving if you think it might be for you and aren't sure. I loved it, although what they say is true: if you get your buoyancy wrong in a drysuit you may well surface feet first. • **www.puffin.org.uk**

Nearest van hire

Atlas Motorhome and Campervan Hire, Glasgow
• www.atlashiredrive.co.uk

Four Seasons Campers, Loch Lomond
• www.fourseasonscampervanhire.com

Open Road Scotland, Paisley
• www.openroadscotland.com

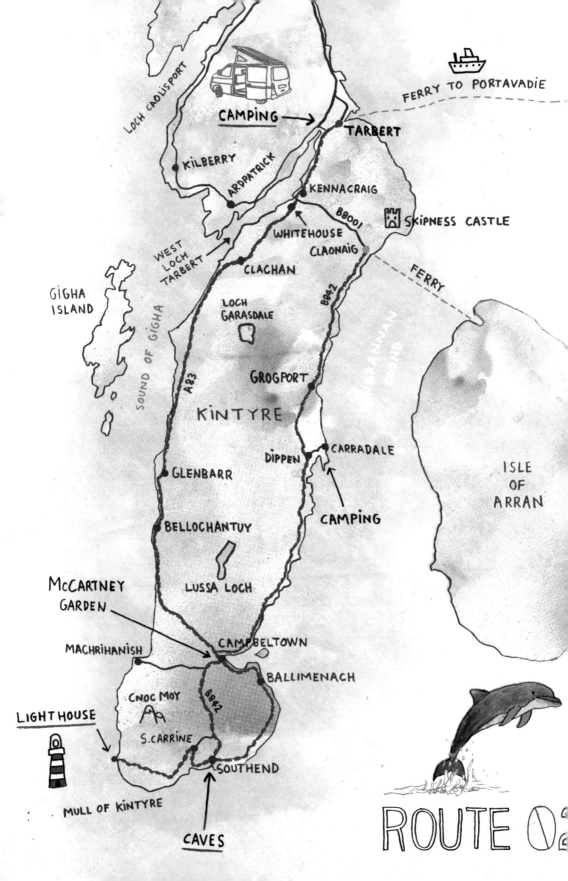

LOCH CAOLISPORT

CAMPING →

TARBERT

FERRY TO PORTAVADIE

KILBERRY

ARDPATRICK

KENNACRAIG

B8001

SKIPNESS CASTLE

WHITEHOUSE

CLAONAIG

WEST LOCH TARBERT

CLACHAN

FERRY

GIGHA ISLAND

SOUND OF GIGHA

LOCH GARASDALE

B842

KINTYRE

GROGPORT

A83

DIPPEN

CARRADALE

CAMPING

ISLE OF ARRAN

GLENBARR

BELLOCHANTUY

LUSSA LOCH

McCARTNEY GARDEN

MACHRIHANISH

CAMPBELTOWN

BALLIMENACH

B842

CNOC MOY

LIGHTHOUSE

S. CARRINE

SOUTHEND

MULL OF KINTYRE

CAVES

ROUTE

ROUND KINTYRE FROM CLAONAIG TO TARBERT

THE LIGHT AT THE END OF THE ROAD

From ferry to ferry, the Mull of Kintyre is a drive of great contrasts. It has a little of everything and is split straight down the middle. The east coast is dominated by views of Arran along the swooping, dipping, curving, often single-track road, while the west is more open and an easy cruise to Tarbert. Between the two lie the Mull itself and the steep and tricky trip to the lighthouse. It's worth every shake and rattle.

BEST FOR: Isolation, peace and quiet

START: Claonaig

END: Tarbert

MILEAGE: 100 miles (160 kilometres)

DAYS TO EXPLORE: 4

OS LAND-RANGER MAP: 68, 62

WEST COAST

47

If you are going to do something, you might as well do it properly. You might as well go the whole hog. There's no point in half-baked excursions or plans. That's what I think, anyway. And that's why we are rattling along the rough road at the end of the Mull of Kintyre, heading up, up and away from the beaches and perfect, Elysian landscapes of Southend, the little town at the tip of the flaccid phallus that is Kintyre. We could have called it a day at the beach, eaten our lunch and headed up the west coast of Kintyre, but we couldn't. A dotted yellow line on the OS map tempted us further on, so we are going to have a peek at the end of the world.

As we drive away from the valley floor and rise above Carskey Bay we stop to look behind us. We see the last house on this road and the clear blue waters of the Sound of Sanda. We get out of the van, climbing a steep bank to get a better view. Inland, the flat bottoms of the glens that almost meet at Southend deliver green pastures as far as the sea. Separating them, in the littoral zone, is nothing more than a slash of yellow sand, peppered with rocks and low cliffs.

Below us, even though the sky is grey, we can see dark shapes in the sea, as well as patches of sand, bordered by the dark browns and blacks of seaweed- and algae-covered rocks. It looks like a great place to snorkel or swim so I make a mental note that if I return I shall find the spot again. We look out to sea, for the telltale splashes of dolphins or porpoises. There? Was that something? The sea is choppy so every whitecap could be the flip of a tail.

We drive on, over cattle grids and streams that run across the steep and narrow road. There are few passing places and the steep drop-offs and hillsides would make it difficult were we to meet another vehicle. I'm not sure I like the idea of reversing here. However, we can't stop or turn around so we plough on.

As we rise we enter the mist. It leaves a fine layer of mizzle on the windscreen, making the visibility worse than it already is. Dark green plantations on the hillsides below us drift in and out of the clouds. We frighten a sheep that is grazing by the side of the track. Grass begins to grow in the middle, a sure sign that we are heading to a remote place.

I've been driving all day and my ribs are aching from being bent over the wheel to peer into the mist. For a moment I think about how far away we are from help, from a phone signal and from so-called 'civilisation'. I get a rush of adrenaline, the beginnings of a panic attack. We can't turn round, so I sit up straight, talk myself down and plough on.

I like going to the extremes. To have the opportunity to be superlative – to be different, taller, further, more distant – even if it's fleeting, fills me with a sense of achievement. I know I'll never be faster or stronger than most but I can, by my wanderings, be the furthest away or the most southerly, northerly or easterly. And yet sometimes that comes at a price. My

hypochondriac self is occasionally out of his comfort zone, even in Britain.

After 6 miles (10 kilometres) of driving uphill we start to drop and the road ends. There is a small car park leading to a track that leads off down the hill and into the mist, cracked tarmac meandering over the difficult terrain. It is steep and slippery but we walk it anyway as we know that, somewhere, at the end lies the Mull of Kintyre lighthouse. We walk for a few minutes and reach a promontory on the left, just before the road doubles back on itself down the hill. We brush past heather and jump over peaty puddles to stand and look out at what's below us, as much to get our bearings as to see any view.

We look. From deep within the mist we see the guiding light of the lighthouse. It protrudes from the drizzle, seemingly rising as the clouds retreat. The wind clears another patch of the sky and a break begins to form in the clouds to the west, enabling us to see out to sea for the first time. The water is silver, backlit by patches of bright sunshine, glowing beneath beams of radiating light. In the distance we see the coast of Northern Ireland some 12 miles (20 kilometres) away, dark against the late-afternoon sun. For a moment we understand the essence of this place. We see how close Ireland is to us, we see currents and eddies and a churning, turbulent sea. We see why the lighthouse is here.

Just as quickly the break in the clouds closes and we are back to mist and fog and mizzle. Visibility drops, wanderings over. But it was worth the climb and the walk, just to get a glimpse of the end of the world and the otherworld beyond. We turn and head back to the van.

THE DRIVING

It isn't easy to get to Kintyre. By the time you've arrived there you will have either driven along Loch Fyne or taken a ferry from the Cowal peninsula, or, as I did, island hopped on two ferries from Arran and the mainland. So by the time you arrive you should already have the feeling of remoteness. In spades.

Claonaig – where the CalMac ferry from Lochranza on the Isle of Arran deposits you on the Kintyre peninsula – isn't much at all. So don't rely on it for supplies or company. For that you'll have to head for Tarbert, at the narrow top of Kintyre, or Skipness, a little to the north-east of Claonaigh, where you can pick up essentials or stock up on local oysters, mussels and other earthly wonders at the Seafood Cabin.

However, if you want to take the long way round, you'll head south on the B842 at the junction with the B8001, a little way to the west of the ferry port. This is the start of the Mull of Kintyre loop. It's a small, winding road that stays high above the sea for much of its length, offering forestry to the right and views of Arran to the left. Often the road is single track with passing places so you may have to take it slower than usual. But is that a problem?

Arran, lying to the east, could be dappled in sunlight, the purples, grey and blacks of its mountains and slopes of scree contrasting with its green lowlands and brown upland hills.

At times the road dips down to the sea to sidle alongside beaches for a short while, perhaps over a river or, in the case of Grogport, to skirt around houses built into the craggy valley in a sharp hairpin.

After Grogport the road heads inland through plantations for a while, crossing a hill to enter Carradale and follow Carradale Water to the village of the same name. The valley offers a treeless welcome from the enclosure of surrounding plantations and leads you, eventually, to the rhododendron-lined lanes of Carradale and the only campsite on the eastern shore of Kintyre. This is a Caravan and Motorhome Club site that's run by a very jolly fellow who reminded me of the glass expert from *The Antiques Roadshow*. The site borders the beautiful, secluded beach, with direct access from the pitches.

Heading south from Carradale the road follows the same north–south route, kinking only to cross rivers as they tumble to the shore in tight-sided valleys, and then climb out of them again. It's a joy to drive this coast and there are lots of beaches at which to stop. Here and there you see magnificent houses, fly fishermen, standing stones, cottages on the shore and grassy picnic sites where you'd love to stop if only you didn't have to be

in Campbeltown by lunchtime. That's how it was for us. We dawdled as fast as we could, taking the slow road to enjoy views, but always eager to reach Southend before the end of the afternoon.

The approach to Campbeltown gives you fabulous views of The Doirlinn, a spit that connects Island Davaar to the mainland, before depositing you among suburbs of grand Georgian houses overlooking the loch. Then it's

straight into town without further ado, and suddenly you're on the harbourside.

Campbeltown is the largest settlement on Kintyre and looks a little jaded, though I found it to be a place of endless fascination. It has big supermarkets and out-of-town superstores but its character is in the way it clings to tradition. We found a butcher, a greengrocer and a fishmonger on Longrow in the centre of town. Surrounding it were all kinds of shops selling bric-a-brac, fishing tackle, clothing and home decor. A far cry from the sanitised city centres we accept too readily these days, it reminded me of another time, and of another place – my former home town of Bideford. It's being crucified by the big boys but fighting back with an independence of spirit that only isolation can bring.

The main road heads north-west from Campbeltown towards the west coast and the airport, but we weren't interested in that. We head out along the southern edge of the loch, on the unnamed coast road. As usual it's small and narrow and offers the best views. We crawl along the lochside for a few miles, looking at the seabirds drifting on the currents offshore, just above the high tide mark, until we reach Ballimenach. Then the road lurches upwards and takes to the hills again on its way to Southend. As usual the views are wonderful and the OS map reveals caves, tombs and megalithic sites galore. If only you had the time to explore them or to climb The Bastard, a hill of 188m (616ft) on the south-east coast. You do.

From The Bastard it's a stark change of landscape as you head to the tip of Kintyre. The hills, which were steep and fern-covered a few miles back, smooth out and roll like they would in Devon. This is drained land that is tended, worked and sanitised by agriculture. At the beach a caravan park

dominates the low cliff, obliterating any sense of the wildness of the place. It could be an oasis or a desert.

From Southend the road heads back up the valley to Machrihanish or up to the lighthouse in a gravity-defying cul-de-sac. It's worth the detour of course, but takes you nowhere. The journey begins its return trajectory on the B842 and then the A83, where it hits the west coast at the beautiful northern end of Machrihanish beach at Westport. There is surf here as there is a window to the Atlantic.

The A83 then makes a long 30-mile (50-kilometre) trundle up the west coast, skirting the strandline almost the entire way, often only a field's width from the beach. Here, along nearly the whole length, we saw wooden shacks and houses, caravans on the shore and unconventional, home-made homes. We assume it's because it's a good place to find another way, become lost or live out of the way of the rest of the world. If I wanted to hide I would consider here, too.

About two-thirds of the way up you leave the open sea and follow West Loch Tarbert to the narrow neck of Kintyre and the beautiful port of Tarbert. This is the place in which to stop and enjoy a pint, fill up on supplies and wait for the ferry to the amazing Cowal peninsula, or set off north for Lochgilphead and Loch Fyne.

PLACES TO STAY

Carradale Caravan and Motorhome Club Site
Carradale, Campbeltown, Argyll and Bute, PA28 6QG
email: info@carradalebay.com
tel: 01583 431 665

info: *I loved Carradale. It felt spacious and light, with big pitches and lovely views of the sea. Friendly owner too, who clearly loves camping. All in all, a favourite site.*

Muasdale Caravan and Touring Park
Muasdale, Tarbert, Argyll, PA29 6XD
web: www.muasdaleholidays.com
email: enquiries@muasdaleholidays.com
tel: 07473 869 983

info: *A Cool Camping favourite on Kintyre's western side, south of Tarbert. As with everything here, it's remote and with few trappings.*

Killegruer Caravan Site
Woodend, Glenbarr, Tarbert, Argyll, PA29 6XB
web: www.killegruercaravansite.com
email: anne.littleson@btinternet.com
tel: 01583 421 241

info: *No arcades, no bar, no restaurant, just great views, quiet and peace. Need anything else? Don't go to Kintyre.*

IN THE AREA

Keil Caves at Southend Heading west out of Southend the road hugs the coast as it rounds the point at Keil. There is a car park where it is possible to stop to see the seal colony on the rocks below the road, visit the caves (they aren't very big) or check out the old graveyard. There is also a curious deserted art-deco hotel here and what looks like the remains of an estate house and walled garden. Overall, a bit neglected but curious and beautiful nonetheless.

• www.undiscoveredscotland.co.uk/southend/footprintscaves/index.html

Mull of Kintyre Lighthouse A 6-mile (10-kilometre) track takes you out to the west of the Mull of Kintyre. It is steep in places and remote, but a relatively easy drive, all things considered. A breeze for a Cally, not so good for a big motorhome. The views over to Northern Ireland are stunning, when you get them, as are those coming back to Southend.

• www.nlb.org.uk/LighthouseLibrary/Lighthouse/Mull-of-Kintyre/

Linda McCartney Memorial Garden, Campbeltown We stumbled upon this little gem of an oasis while wandering the streets of Campbeltown. It is small and very pretty, with a centrepiece statue of Linda by British figurative artist Jane Robbins. • www.lindasgarden.co.uk

Tarbert Castle Essentially a ruin, but still a very nicely situated one. Tarbert is pretty enough, but from the castle it's even more so. A short climb from town and with great views. • www.tarbertcastle.info

Nearest van hire

Caledonian Campers and Conversions Ltd, Clydebank
• www.caledoniancampers.co.uk

Kombi Campers, Paisley
• www.kombicampers.co.uk

Open Road Scotland, Paisley
• www.openroadscotland.com

Rockin Vans, Kilmarnock
• www.rockinvans.co.uk

The Tartan Camper Company, Saltcoats
• www.thetartancamper.co.uk

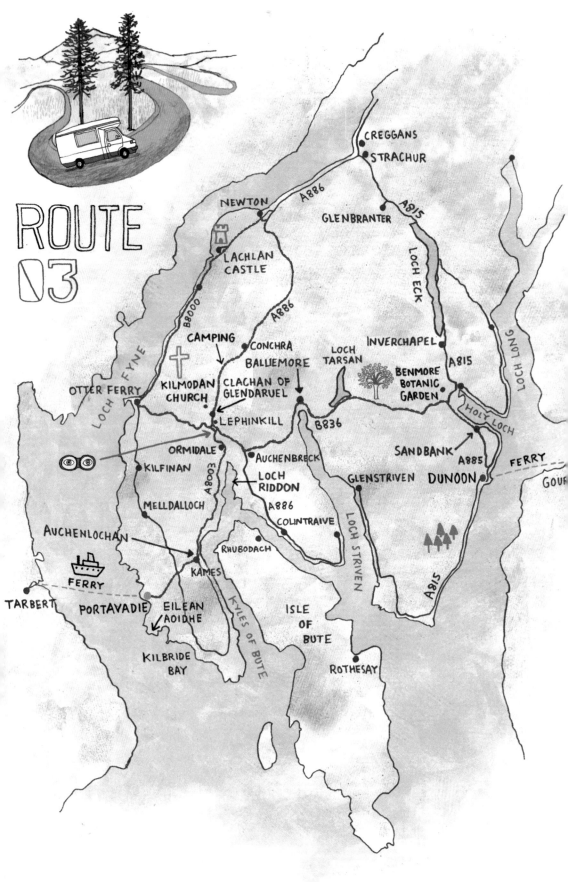

ROUTE 03

CREGGANS
STRACHUR

NEWTON

A886

GLENBRANTER

A815

LACHLAN CASTLE

B8000

A886

CAMPING

CONCHRA
BALLIEMORE

KILMODAN CHURCH

CLACHAN OF GLENDARUEL

LOCH FYNE

OTTER FERRY

LEPHINKILL

LOCH TARSAN

INVERCHAPEL

A815

BENMORE BOTANIC GARDEN

LOCH ECK

LOCH LONG

HOLY LOCH

ORMIDALE

B836

SANDBANK

AUCHENBRECK

KILFINAN

A8003

LOCH RIDDON

A886

MELLDALLOCH

COLINTRAIVE

GLENSTRIVEN

A885

DUNOON

FERRY

Gour

AUCHENLOCHAN

RHUBODACH

LOCH STRIVEN

A815

FERRY

KAMES

TARBERT

PORTAVADIE

EILEAN AOIDHE

KYLES OF BUTE

ISLE OF BUTE

KILBRIDE BAY

ROTHESAY

A CRUISE AROUND COWAL

A ROUTE WITH A VIEW

One of the finest views in Scotland can be found on this route from Portavadie, in a loop around the Cowal peninsula to Dunoon in the east that takes in forest, mountains and all that is great about the Highlands. Plus a ferry ride at either end. Big motorhomes might want to avoid the road to Otter Ferry, but it is perfectly possible to bypass it and still drive the southern shore of Loch Fyne.

BEST FOR:
Stunning views of Bute

START:
Portavadie

END: **Dunoon**

MILEAGE:
50 miles (80 kilometres)

DAYS TO EXPLORE: **2**

OS LAND-RANGER MAP:
62, 63, 55, 56

We wake up early, on the quayside in Tarbert, on the Kintyre peninsula, on a Monday morning. It's just before dawn, but as it's April it's not that early. The port faces east, towards the Cowal peninsula, so the early sunlight makes the water shine like silver. A sailing boat motors out of the harbour and into the loch, creating deep, dark ripples in the smooth surface. As it disappears to the south we see the Portavadie Ferry arrive. It's one of those tiny, flat-bottomed CalMac ferries that criss-cross the waters of western Scotland. We are the only tourists to board. The rest of the passengers are people going to work, no doubt saving a long drive up Loch Fyne. They all seem to know each other.

Our destination is Dunoon and the Greenock Ferry, which will take us on to Glasgow, but, as usual, we are in no hurry. Glasgow can wait. We are off to find a few of Cowal's tiny slow roads and search for a view over the Isle of Bute that we've been tipped off about. From the A8003, which runs from

Auchenlochan on the west side of the Kyles of Bute to Ormidale at the head of Loch Riddon, the views, we are told, are sensational.

But first we have to make our way from Portavadie across the peninsula. The road has no name but it's the main route from the port so we get overtaken at speed by rushing plumbers, electricians and fisheries vans on their way to work. We were first on the ferry so we're at the head of the queue but not going fast enough for the local traffic.

The road brings us to the shore of the Kyles of Bute at Kames, where it then follows the shoreline. We see elegant 1920s houses sitting on large plots overlooking the water, little jetties jutting out into the calm loch and sailing boats bobbing on their moorings, quietly, calmly waiting for wind. It's a beautiful place, the sort you could imagine yourself retiring to, if only you didn't mind being so far from so-called civilisation.

We join the A8003 as it rises above the village and takes us further north, running parallel to the shore, but at height above the water. A red squirrel darts across the road in front of us and climbs a tree, stopping momentarily on a gatepost before disappearing into the community forest.

As we continue the road stays high above the loch, offering tantalising glimpses of the Isle of Bute across the water. But the evergreens obscure the views, and anyway there is no place to stop that's safe. On the landward side the road rises steeply, with no verges to pull over on to, and on the seaward side a barrier stops us from stopping to peer through the conifers.

Eventually we find a small layby on the right-hand side, facing a rocky cliff. We see a break in the barrier and beyond it find a pathway that leads away into the scrub. We follow it, pushing aside the wet ground layer as we go, soaking our legs in the process. We duck beneath the barren branches of silver birches, through bracken, grasses and boulders. The path leads us away from the road, towards the edge of a steep drop and the view we've been searching for. Our height enables us to see over the conifers while the season makes seeing through the leafless birches possible too. I perch on a rock to get a little extra height to make even more of the view that lies in front of us.

To our left we see the bumpy terrain of the east side of Cowal. Plantations stand out dark green against the brown of died-back bracken, and wet roads, reflecting the brightness of the sky, run like silver threads through the early-spring landscape. Directly in front of us is the Isle of Bute, rounded and shapely, with low fields shining bright spring-green above the shore sitting in patches of sun. To our right, where we have just come from, is the steep east coast of Cowal, wooded and dark. Thin plumes of smoke rise up from a farmhouse way below us.

The water of the loch is flat and calm, like glass, with only the occasional patch of ripples where a current or eddy upsets the stillness. Light clouds, with the odd patch of weak winter blue, we can see in the expansive sky above us reflect in the surface. Where the water meets the shoreline we see a perfect mirror reflection of dark, tall pines.

I take photos to try and remember the view. They say a lot but they can't tell of the faint smell of wood smoke, the chilly breeze or the wet bracken soaking my trousers. Neither can they tell of the joy I feel at being here, on this slow road, taking my time with someone special to appreciate simple things. We drive, cook, eat, sleep and laugh because we have the time to do it. Nothing else matters.

I stand and stare for a moment more than is necessary, to allow the view to soak into my memory bank, so I can save it for another day. I want to be able to think back on this amazing drive through a quiet and isolated part of Scotland and remember the sharp, cold air on my skin, the smile on Liz's face and our breathlessness at finding this spot.

A few miles further on we arrive at a viewpoint, with map and legend pointing out all the landmarks in the distance. We stop briefly to appreciate it again. But really we'd prefer to keep hold of our little pathway through the bracken and gorse to the edge of Cowal. This was the view we chanced upon on our way to Dunoon.

You might not ever need to go this way. But do. It's worth every mile.

THE DRIVING

The round-Cowal drive I did will take you to parts of the peninsula you might not otherwise see. It cuts across its heart over a high pass with little room for manoeuvre if you meet another vehicle or if you drive something huge. The way the roads are in Cowal you could easily make a full figure-of-eight and see all of it while covering only a short piece of road twice. So it's a lovely, meandering place that's close to Glasgow and yet so very far away. Approaching from Portavadie, as we did, offers up a couple of possibilities. You can go up the west coast or cross the peninsula to Kames. You could also head south on a loop to Kilbride Bay or even take the track (walking) out to Eilean Aoidhe. We opted to make our loop via Kames, heading up the east side of the peninsula on the A8003, past the viewpoint at Craig Lodge and on to Glendaruel, before diverting and taking the steep road to Otter Ferry. The A8003 is a dream of a drive as it swoops and swerves high up along the side of the Kyles of Bute, offering tantalising glimpses of Bute all along its length until you reach the big viewpoint and get the full panorama. It's one of the finest I can think of.

At the hamlet of Lephinkill the road to Otter Ferry cuts back sharply and heads uphill steeply in a series of sharp bends. The first hairpin might make you wish you'd not come this way but it's the worst and steepest of them all. And besides, you won't find much space to turn around, even if you wanted to go back. You are committed to this road now. From a height above sea level of 12m (40ft) at the river, the road rises almost 250m (820ft) in about 1¼ miles (2 kilometres), so it's a steep and solid climb up into the forestry. Don't forget to look back at where you came from: it's a great view.

Once you reach the zenith, at just over 300m (985ft), you get fine views over Loch Fyne towards Lochgilphead before the roads drops sharply again and you enter a beautiful stretch of straight road that leads you to Otter Ferry, the site of an old passenger ferry to West Otter on the opposite shore.

Otter Ferry is home to The Oystercatcher, a pub in a very fine pub location overlooking Loch Fyne, at the end of a gravel spit that juts out into Loch Fyne for over a mile. It looks like a nice walk but don't be tempted: it's a tidal loch and it can race in here. You have been warned.

From Otter Ferry it's a magnificent, curvy, up-and-down ride along the southern shore of Loch Fyne, with plenty of opportunity to stop and stretch the legs at the water's edge. The road passes by forestry, farmland and deciduous forest, is walled for a lot of the way and is an absolute delight to drive. It's about 9 miles (15 kilometres) to Old Castle Lachlan fortress and

every one of them offers great views over Loch Fyne. At Castle Lachlan the road goes inland before arriving at Newton and the junction with the A886 at Leanach. This fast road will take you back down the centre of the peninsula, back to where you started, at Lephinkill. Pass the turn-off for the A8003 and then, after half a mile or so, take a left on the B836, a lovely, smooth road that makes a loop around the top of Loch Striven and then passes by the dam at Loch Tarsan. It's another great road that's lovely to drive – and it's been much improved, because of the amount of forestry work going on here. After climbing away from the loch the road follows the course of the Little Eachaig river towards Holy Loch (A815). We turned right to catch the ferry at Hunter's Quay, and drove straight into another world on the other side, hitting Greenock, Port Glasgow and a whole series of roundabouts on the banks of the Clyde.

With more time we'd have turned left on to the A815 and driven up the side of Loch Eck. But that'll have to wait for another day.

PLACES TO STAY

Glendaruel Caravan Park
Glendaruel, Argyll, PA22 3AB
web: www.glendaruel caravanpark.com
email: mail@ glendaruelcaravanpark.com
tel: 01369 820 267

info: *Cool Camping-recommended site with hard-standing touring pitches with electric hook-up, toilets, shower and laundry.*

IN THE AREA

Kilmodan Church and Standing Stones

A church with three entrances leading to three separate galleries so that – legend has it – local families could worship without having to speak to each other. The standing stones in the churchyard are an impressive collection of late-Medieval carved grave slabs and stones and a slab from 1636.

• www.kilmodan-colintraive.org.uk/history/kilmodan-church/

Benmore Botanic Garden Part of the route 5 but well worth a stop-off if you are in the area. Benmore has a magnificent avenue of sequoias as well as an incredible collection of plants from Bhutan, Tasmania and Chile, all set in a lovely mountain landscape. • www.rbge.org.uk/the-gardens/benmore

The Cowal Way This is a relatively new walking trail that covers 'Scotland in 57 miles' going from Portavadie to Loch Lomond. It is said to be one of Scotland's best Highland trails and is suitable for walking or riding. It is perfectly possible to walk some sections as the road, inevitably, meets the trail at plenty of points along the way, particularly at Kames and Portavadie, where detours will take you to Asgog Loch and ruins.

• www.cowalway.co.uk

Nearest van hire

Atlas Motorhome and Campervan Hire,
• www.atlashiredrive.co.uk

Caledonian Campers and Conversions Ltd, Clydebank
• www.caledoniancampers.co.uk

Kombi Campers, Paisley
• www.kombicampers.co.uk

Open Road Scotland, Paisley
• www.openroadscotland.com

The Tartan Camper Company, Saltcoats
• www.thetartancamper.co.uk

ULLAPOOL

GRUINARD BAY

LAIDE

BADCAUL

DUNDONNELL

A835

LOCH BROOM

LITTLE LOCH BROOM

COVE

AULTBEA

LOCH NA SEALBA

AN TEALLACH

AUCHIN

MELVAIG

LOCH EWE

TOURNAIG

INVEREWE GARDENS

POOLEWE

FIONN LOCH

CORRIESHALLOCH GOR
FALLS OF MEASACH

CAMPING

GAIRLOCH

CHARLESTOWN

LETTEREWE FOREST

LOCH GAIRLOCH

A832

SHIELDAIG

REDPOINT

SLATTADALE

TALLADALE

LOCH MAREE

LOCHAN FADA

SLIOCH

KINLOCHEWE

FIONN BHEINN

A83

FEARNMORE

LOCH TORRIDON

W E S T E R C R O S S

LIATHACH

APPLECROSS
SMOKE
HOUSE

SHIELDAIG

TORRIDON

ANNAT

CAMPING

COULIN FOREST

GARDEN

LOCH DAMH

LOCH LUNDIE

CRAIG

A890

ACHNASHELLACH FOREST

APPLECROSS

BEINN BHAN

A896

TORNAPRESS

BEALACH NA BÀ

ARDARROCH

A896

STRATHCARRON

LOCH KISHORN

LOCH CARRON

STROMEFERRY

KYLE OF LOCHALSH

ACHMORE

AUCHTERTYRE

A890

SKYE BRIDGE

EILEAN DONAN CASTLE

A87

LOCH ALSH

A87

LOCH DUICH

ROUTE 04

APPLECROSS OASIS

AN OASIS IN WESTER ROSS

When it comes to heading up to (or back from) the very north of Scotland you are faced with few choices. This route is the slow-road alternative to driving the Great Glen to Inverness and takes in one of Scotland's most famous passes as well as some truly spectacular scenery. The driving is exhilarating, too. There are hairpin beds, long straights, bumpy single tracks crossing remote glens and views aplenty. In short: the very best of Scotland.

BEST FOR:
Finding your little slice of heaven

START:
Ullapool

END: Kyle of Lochalsh

MILEAGE:
130 miles (210 kilometres)

DAYS TO EXPLORE: 4–5

OS LAND-RANGER MAP:
19, 20, 24, 25

WEST COAST

I sit on a bench in the garden, basking in the sunshine, wishing I had brought my sunglasses with me from the van. It's hot, around 24°C (64°F), and I am wearing shorts and a T-shirt. My bare feet feel the cool, damp grass in the shade beneath the picnic table. My shoulders are being well warmed by the sun.

I spread out maps on the table in front of me, with the intention of writing notes on the journey here. We came in on one of the only two roads that serve this area and will leave by the steeper of the two, Scotland's highest pass, the legendary Bealach na Bà, which reaches 626m (2,054ft) above sea level. At one time it was the only way in or out of this tiny place. It is often closed for long periods in winter. The drive up and down the other side is the stuff of legend, the road rising steeply to its apex directly from sea level, with twists and turns and hairpin bends near the top. It is one of the main reasons people drive this way.

In the meantime, and until it's time to hit the road again, I am waiting for my lunch, thinking about all the incredible views I have seen on the way here. I think of Torridon and the white sands at Gairloch and of the steep climb on to the Applecross peninsula. So much to take in. Distracted, I look around at the garden. It's a beautiful cottage garden with flowering plants and vegetables. It's also huge, at around an acre, with a surrounding wall that's at least 3m (10ft) tall. The wall, as I understand it, dates back as far as the nearby house, Applecross House, which was started in 1675. Inside the walls of the garden the air is still and warm. There is no breeze to cool the skin or bring a chill to the plants. But that's the point of this beautiful oasis. It is the walls that provide the microclimate that allows the plants to thrive.

There are bees and hoverflies flitting between the lavender, flowering shrubs and honeysuckle on a trellised pathway down the centre of the

garden. It's an idyllic scene and it's easy to forget that we are in the wild north-west of Scotland, among mountain passes, just a short drive from the treeline, surrounded by wild, open moorland and vast areas of not much at all. Heck, the road we came in by wasn't built until 1974 for crying out loud. This is historic isolation at its most extreme.

But isolation is what makes the area surrounding the walled garden, the Applecross Estate, so special and surprising. The geography of the Applecross River valley has kept outsiders out and warm air in. Fed by the sea, the winds warmed by the Gulf Stream and sheltered by the mountains on either side, it has long been a haven for trees and plants that belong further south, wildlife and people escaping 'modern' society. In 673 AD an Irish Christian, Maelrubha, founded a monastery here and called the area A'Chromraich, the sanctuary. Seeking it, then as now, is nothing new it seems.

I understand why. On the way in we passed lochs and peaks and drove through wide, wild river valleys, winding our way along the north of the peninsula. Passing the occasional village on rocky shores we felt we were getting further and further from civilisation the closer we got to Applecross. As we rounded the mountainside to see Applecross Bay for the first time we realised we had entered somewhere truly special. Like opening a door to a secret, perhaps forgotten, walled garden.

On the way we had also stopped at Inverewe Garden and admired the walled garden there. It was bursting with vegetables and beautiful flowers, planted in neat rows and enjoying the protection of its own microclimate. The estate garden at Inverewe, which was created in 1862 by Osgood Mackenzie, was planted with Scots pines, giving protection against the harsher weather outside and creating a microclimate within which his exotic species could survive.

At Applecross we saw people walking on the beach, kayaking on the water and walking with young kids and pushchairs around the estate. It was in complete contrast to the countryside we'd just passed through, where we'd have been surprised to see anyone walking, never mind walking with a pushchair. The main 'drag' and village centre, Shore Street, which is no more than a row of cottages and a pub, was busy with people enjoying seafood lunches in the July sunshine. On the opposite side of the road from the row of whitewashed cottages, where tiny gardens overlook the water and Skye beyond, people read newspapers in deckchairs while others sunbathed. Inspired, we decided to stop to get some food, so followed a sign down an avenue of elegant beeches leading to Applecross House. There we found the Potting Shed, the restaurant in the walled garden, an oasis within the sanctuary.

My lunch arrives before I can even look at any of the maps. I have to fold them quickly to make room for a salad of fresh greens. It's been grown in the garden itself and I am in heaven, with great food, sitting in the summer sunshine in a beautiful cottage garden in a sanctuary somewhere in the north of Scotland. It is just what I needed.

All we have to do now is get out of here. With Bealach na Bà and a lovely-looking dinner menu standing in our way it could take some effort.

THE DRIVING

Bealach na Bà is the pass that everyone comes to have a go at. Cyclists, motorcycles – and even the odd classic camper and motorhome – come here to climb steeply up to the top of the world. Whether it's for the views or for the challenge it's hard to tell. It may even be for the simple joy at finding the oasis of Applecross at the foot of the pass on the seaward side

However, this route is about more than just one of the highest passes in the UK or the sanctuary at Applecross. They might be highlights but there's more to it than that. Between Ullapool and Auchtertyre near the Kyle of

Lochalsh you can drive through some of the most spectacular scenery, along beautiful winding roads that climb away from small seaside towns isolated by steep sided U-shaped valleys, through glens of birch and pine where gushing rivers flow, across barren moorland and beside dark lochs.

This route forms part of the North Coast 500, a route that was set up by Visit Scotland to attract visitors to the north of Scotland. It's a route that skirts the coast and takes in Applecross. However, you don't have to do the whole

thing to enjoy this route, which would make a glorious swansong to a visit to the Hebrides if you are heading south or offer a spectacular alternative to crossing the great Glen on your way to Inverness and beyond. If you are heading up to Durness and Cape Wrath it is a fantastic 'what the hell, why not?' to complete along the way. It's one to tick off the list for sure, a feather in the motorhomer's cap.

The route begins (or ends) at Ullapool, the jumping-off point for the Outer Hebrides, and takes you as far south as Auchtertyre near the Kyle of Lochalsh and the Skye Bridge. Starting out from Ullapool you'll follow the A835 along the north side of Loch Broom to the turn-off with the A832 where you'll head off into the Dundonnell Forest. But first a stop at the spectacular Corrieshalloch Gorge and the 46m- (150ft-) high Falls of Measach to cross the Victorian suspension bridge and peek over the edge of the viewing platform.

From here the road follows the south side of Little Loch Broom, with a lovely section, from the head of the loch, along the side of the water. At Badcaul the road rises steeply, offering fabulous views back at the loch and the mountains behind and ending at a wild lookout offering spectacular vistas of just about everything. This is a great place to stop and was apparently the location for a feature film called *Shell* that was shot in 2011. It's a wild, barren spot but the views are incredible. It's easy to imagine it as a location.

The road then drops down to sea level at beautiful Gruinard Bay before rising steeply again to cross the peninsula and then drop down to sea level to skirt Loch Ewe at Aultbea. This is a gorgeous road with plenty of stops for views, especially by the fuel depot at Drumchork. Inverewe Garden is here too. It's a good opportunity to stock up on cake and biscuits as well as prepare yourself for sanctuary. The walled garden is lovely.

Gairloch is another lochside town offering great views and fantastic beaches and a very pretty harbour and inlet at Charlestown. Continuing onwards you follow the course of Loch Maree on a beautiful road (aren't they all?) with native Scots pine forest and falls near Slattadale. Across the loch the peaks of Letterewe Forest rise to around 900m (2,950ft), with Slioch reaching 980m (3,215ft).

At Kinlochewe you take a left turn on to the A896 along Glen Torridon. It's a single-track road with passing places that goes through a wide and empty glen. It's a stunning drive with peaks rising either side of the road and little forestry to spoil the views as the route follows the course of the river towards Torridon. The village itself is another tiny green oasis among the peaks and plantations of this vast and untamed land. From here it's only a few miles to Shieldaig and the junction with the road to Applecross. This is where it starts to get really wild.

From the lush of the lowlands around Torridon and the beautiful waters of Loch Torridon, where yachts bob in the shelter of the bay, it feels like things start to get serious from here. The single-track road with passing places rises up steeply after the turn-off, passing houses with lush gardens before coming out on to a wild clifftop with nothing but moor dotted with granite and views over the loch to tiny coves and inlets. You'll pass tiny communities at Kenmore, Arinacrinachd, Fearnbeg and Fernmore before you round the tip of the peninsula on to its western coast. There are glorious beaches along this stretch, with a stunning backdrop of the isles of Rona, Raasay and Skye looming further behind. Then you arrive at the sanctuary of the village at Applecross, a tiny dot on the map.

The road to Bealach na Bà heads straight up from here and just seems to keep going, past a sea of tiny cairns almost near the top, round a couple of serious bends before reaching its peak at 626m (2,050ft) and then heading back down to Tornapress in a series of hairpin bends. The descent is fantastic and just seems to keep going on and on, all the way down to sea level. I imagine going the other way might be less of a cruise, especially in something old. But lots come here to do just that. Stopping to take pictures at the top we were passed by a cyclist, a 1970s camper van and 1980s Type 25 chugging away at the incline. You meet the A896 again at Tornapress and it takes you all the way, easily and relatively quickly, to the A890 and the road back to the A87 at Auchtertyre.

PLACES TO STAY

Sands Caravan & Camping
Gairloch, Wester Ross, IV21 2DL
web: www.sandscaravanandcamping.co.uk
email: info@sandscaravanandcamping.co.uk
tel: 01445 712 152

info: *Pitches in the dunes near Gairloch, overlooking Skye. Amazing beaches nearby in this touring park in the wilderness of Wester Ross.*

Kinlochewe Caravan Club Site
Kinlochewe, Achnasheen, IV22 2PA
web: www.caravanclub.co.uk
tel: 01445 760 239

info: *Another oasis of Caravan and Motorhome calm in a wild, open landscape near Torridon.*

Applecross Campsite
Strathcarron, Ross-shire, IV54 8ND
web: http://applecross.uk.com/campsite/
email: enquiries@visitapplecross.com
tel: 01520 744 268

info: *A small, family-run site in the centre of Applecross. Busy, so book ahead in peak periods. Just a short walk from the walled garden.*

IN THE AREA

Inverewe Garden A lovely garden and estate, run by The National Trust for Scotland. A beautiful kitchen garden and a great house, with fabulously presented interpretation, particularly the comments about where all the birds have gone. • www.nts.org.uk/Visit/Inverewe

Potting Shed Café Lovely, friendly restaurant and café in a beautiful walled garden. Fresh produce, lovingly cooked. Must see.
• www.applecrossgarden.co.uk

Falls Of Measach A narrow, mile-long box canyon with bridge over and viewing platform to see the impressive 46-metre falls thundering into the narrow gorge. • www.nts.org.uk/Visit/Corrieshalloch-Gorge

Applecross Smokehouse
For home-smoked Scottish salmon and shellfish, direct from the smoke-house, on the road to Applecross.
• www.applecrosssmokehouse.co.uk

Nearest van hire

Western Isles Campers, Fort William
• www.westernislescampers.co.uk

ISLANDS

There is nothing like an island-hopping adventure by motorhome. Driving on to a CalMac ferry to take a trip out to one of Scotland's islands will make any visit feel like an expedition. You can start at the easier end of the scale with a jaunt to Arran or go further with an Island Hopscotch ticket to Barra, the Uists, Harris and Lewis. Whichever you choose it'll give your van or motorhome a chance to come into its own. Parking up at a remote, silver sanded beach, with nothing but you, the sea and the sky – and perhaps an otter, dolphin or golden eagle – for company is what it's all about for me.

Just go.

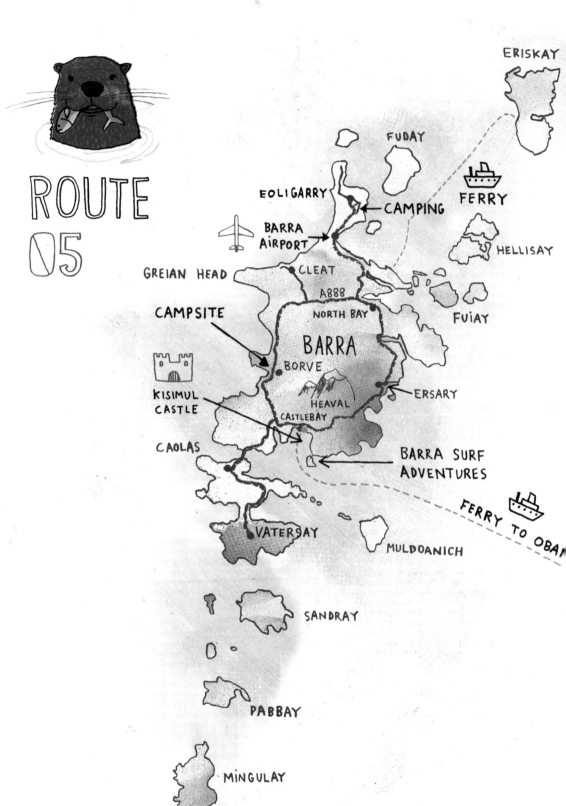

ROUTE 05

ERISKAY

FUDAY

EOLIGARRY

CAMPING

FERRY

BARRA
AIRPORT

HELLISAY

GREIAN HEAD

CLEAT

A888

NORTH BAY

FUIAY

CAMPSITE

BARRA

BORVE

KISIMUL
CASTLE

HEAVAL

ERSARY

CASTLEBAY

CAOLAS

BARRA SURF
ADVENTURES

FERRY
TO OBAN

VATERSAY

MULDOANICH

SANDRAY

PABBAY

MINGULAY

BARRA HEAD

A BUZZ AROUND BARRA

A LITTLE ISLAND WITH A BIG HEART

A ring-road road trip that's about as far from the M25 as you could ever hope to get. It's a slow road to get to the Isle of Barra in the Outer Hebrides, and not much of a drive when you get there, but every miles of it is a heart-bursting joy. There is no hope of getting lost on Barra. The A888 circumnavigates this tiny, 23 square mile (60 square kilometre) island and can be driven in a matter of hours, if you dawdle. But that's not the point. Barra is the ultimate slow-road adventure. So take it.

BEST FOR:
Island life

START/END:
Castlebay

MILEAGE:
23 miles (37 kilometres)

DAYS TO EXPLORE: **4**

OS LAND-RANGER MAP: 31

ISLANDS

I arrive at the ferry terminal early.

There's no one else around and I wonder if I have the day and time right. I check my ticket. No, I am in the right place, although it's about as un-terminal-like a place as I have ever been. There's a small, stone building, with a few chairs, a deserted counter and an out-of-order vending machine. It's parading as a passenger waiting area but I'm not tempted, even though the wind is cold outside and the view of the ferry, quietly sitting at anchor, is wonderful. Behind the terminal lie the mountains of Barra, while in front, across the water, lie the Uists and further island adventures. For now though, until the ferry takes me away, I am bound to this little island, Barra.

I walk back to the van, grab my camera and stride out on to a sweeping jetty made of large blocks of granite. I have a wide-angle lens fitted to the camera, and nothing else to hand, as I imagine I shall capture a pretty image of Barra's highest peak with the ferry in the foreground.

At the end of the jetty I look back towards the island I have just made my home for the last few days. It's a tiny place, with just one main road, the A888, a winding and swooping pathway that circumnavigates the whole island. From it run offshoots to the north and south, truncated asides to the narrative that is Barra's story that add colour and background to this little island with big adventures.

And, even though I am about to board a ferry to Eriskay and North and South Uist, my tales of Barra

are not over yet. I focus the camera, set the aperture to make the most of the dull October light and point it towards the white, black and red ferry. I squint and prepare to press the shutter. As I do I notice movement at the edge of my vision, in the water below me. I turn and see a splash. Something, about 3m (10ft) below where I am standing, has dived under the surface. I turn to look properly. A second passes and an otter resurfaces with a fish, which it eats as I stand and watch. It dives again and I wait. I focus the camera on the patch of water, but, with a 17mm lens, it looks like a vast stretch of sea. Bollocks! There's no point in trying to get the shot. It will be a pinprick in an ocean. So instead I stand and watch as the otter rises again and then twists and turns in the water, preening, playing. It can't have seen or smelled me, otherwise it would have been long gone. I watch and it plays. I have a phone so snap a couple of images, just to prove I saw it, then stand, quietly, to watch again. I think about running back to the van to get a telephoto lens, but I know it's pointless given the time it'll take, so I stand and stare, hardly able to breathe, knowing this is a rare encounter.

The otter swims between the rocks of the jetty to, I assume, a holt. I creep closer, to try, at least, to get near enough for a clear shot. I am about 2m (6½ft) away now and it sees me for a moment. It stops. I stop. For a moment we are

·still. Then it turns and disappears into a space between the rocks.

And that's that. My first otter encounter is done. Barra is done. I walk back to the ferry, to roll on and then roll off at another fabulous island in the North Atlantic. It's been immense, but tiny.

The journey to Barra, the most southerly of the Outer Hebrides, a few days previously, was equally special. I sat on deck for the first couple of hours looking at the colours change in the evening light. Dolphins swam by. Fishing boats made deep ripples in the glass-like water. I was ecstatic to be leaving the mainland and following my heart on the very first of my adventures for this book. I wanted to do things properly, to take a journey to the edges of Britain in a way that couldn't be done any faster.

I wanted to spend time with clear seas and clear skies to clear my thoughts in preparation for the times ahead. I had recently moved out of the family home and needed space and distraction from the drama unfolding in my personal life. Barra would provide a perfect backdrop: an interval before the final act.

I arrived on Barra in the dark, completely disorientated and not really knowing which way to head to find my campsite. I figured that I should drive west on the single-track road and see where it took me. Before too long I saw a sign to the site. Of course I did. This is a small island. The site was deserted. I parked up, plugged into the electricity, nabbed the Wi-Fi code from the shower block, cooked my dinner and hit the hay.

The next morning I woke to find myself in the most beautiful site, with the sea to one side and mountains to the other. Offshore, a submerged reef made the swell break in perfect, heavy tubes, left and right. Across the bay lay a cemetery, and behind that, a smattering of houses squatted on the flatlands between the spurs of the rocky hillsides. The location was nothing short of spectacular, possibly one of the nicest sites I'd ever been to.

Funded by grants from the EU to help bring tourism to Barra (so much for Brexit) the site is owned by local postie Donald, a lovely, chatty chap who came by to collect his fees and pass the time of day. It was incredibly cheap for two nights and the price included electricity – a bargain considering the toilets were immaculate, the shower hot and the Wi-Fi more than adequate (as long as you are parked up near the shower block!).

Below the site, basking on the rocks in the small bay, a colony of seals sat watching as I ate breakfast and planned my day. Barra seemed to me to be a place to explore slowly so I didn't decide much, except which way around it I'd go.

THE DRIVING

Barra is an island in the Outer Hebrides, so you can't drive around it without
getting there in the first place. Forgive me for stating what should be obvious,
but it's a five-hour ferry journey from Oban and just about an hour from
Eriskay. Oban is 500 miles (800 kilometres) from London, 650 miles (1,050
kilometres) from Penzance and 180 miles (290 kilometres) from the border
at Gretna Green. It's a long way. You'll need to board the CalMac ferry
from Oban to Castlebay if you aren't arriving from Eriskay and the Uists to
Ardmhor.

Once you board the ferry you have nothing to do but relax. Time on deck
will reveal stunning sights as the mainland, and your worries, slip away. You'll
pass the lighthouse at Eilean Musdile as you enter the Sound of Mull, guided

by porpoises and dolphins while the ripples from the ferry's bow wave track across the water. Arriving at Castlebay, for me, was a mystery, but a second look revealed a small village with a Co-op, adventure centre, school, hostel, pool, a couple of small pubs and a post office. It's the place to stock up at before heading off out of town, although if you forget something it's really not that much of a hassle to get back there.

The A888 circumnavigates the heart of the island, with offshoots heading to Vatersay in the south across a causeway and towards the airport and the beautiful Traigh Eais beach on its western flank. It is curvy and bumpy and swervy and narrow in places with little or no opportunity for overtaking. But that's island life. Get over yourself if you think it's a racetrack.

I set out to explore Barra from Borgh (Borve), the settlement behind the peninsula at Gob Bhuirgh. A series of sweeping bends took me past two beaches with offshore islands and then past the turn-off for Cleat, another wild and beautiful beach facing the Atlantic. From here the road winds east

past Loch an Duin and past the island's only forestry. There are few trees on Barra so it was a surprise to see trees at all in the steep valley that leads to the junction with the airport road.

Watching planes land on the beach isn't something you see every day so it's worth a look. I wasn't the only one. The small prop aircraft come in at different times each day according to the dropping tide and landed just as the water recedes across the sand flats. It's one of those island events, like the ferry arriving, that attract a few people, both locals and visitors, since it's a focal point of activities. But almost as soon as the planes take off again, back to Glasgow, the people disappear like will-o'-the-wisps. I stayed and walked across the machair and dunes to the beach, where the Atlantic surf was slamming on to white sand.

Along Barra's eastern shore the road changes, becoming narrower and more winding as it negotiates inlets and tiny bays before bringing me back to Castlebay and 'civilisation'. In Castlebay the road to Vatersay takes you across a causeway to the island, and along barren, open moorland. It is a beautiful place of dunes, rocks and deep-blue sea but seemed to me to be littered with broken cars and machinery, as if forgotten or neglected by its owners. The beaches on Vatersay, having said that, are astounding. So ignore the relics of past times and enjoy a lonely commune with wild nature in the middle of the North Atlantic.

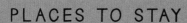

PLACES TO STAY

Borve Camping and Caravan Site

Mr Donald MacLean, 104a Borve, Isle of Barra, HS9 5XR

web: www.barracamping.com

email: donald@barra camping.co.uk

tel: 01871 810 878

info: *Seriously, one of the best-situated campsites I have ever had the pleasure of waking up in. Great views and nice, clean facilities. Nice owner. Dodgy Wi-Fi at the far end, but does that really matter when you can watch the local seals bask on the rocks below? From here it's possible to walk the western beaches or climb the island's tallest peak. I absolutely loved it.*

Croft No2 Campsite

Scurrival Point, 2 Eoligarry, Isle of Barra, HS9 5YD

web: www.barracamping.com

email: donald@barra camping.co.uk

tel: 0871 890 327

info: *Campsite at the northern end of the island with hook-up, water, loos, disposal points and beach access.*

Barra Holidays @Croft183

183 Bolnabodach, Isle of Barra, HS9 5UT

web: www.croft183.com

email: barraholidays @gmail.com

tel: 07908 267 265

info: *A small site on the east side of the island, with a few pitches for motorhomes and tents, as well as a self catering croft.*

A note about motorhomes on Barra

Barra is perfect for a motorhome trip. However, please note that the islanders have had to make polite requests for consideration when it comes to 'wild camping' as it's a small island and every visiting motorhome can have a big impact on it. Overnight parking facilities are provided at the ferry terminal, on Vatersay (Community Hall) and by various residents on the island, as well as in campsites. Please respect this and don't spoil it for others.

There is a chemical-waste facility at the ferry terminal at Eoligarry Jetty. See www.isleofbarra.com for more information.

IN THE AREA

Climbing Heaval   Barra is dominated by its tallest peak, Heaval (Heabhal), which stands at 384m (1,260ft) and overlooks Castlebay. It's a relatively easy walk up from the car park at Breibhig, but the path isn't always clear. Just walk upwards and don't fall off! There is a statue of the Virgin and Child, 'Our Lady of the Sea', which is worth seeing but the real attraction is the 360-degree views of the whole island at the summit. It's a great way of getting the feel for this tiny but beautiful island.

Surfing   Barra is off the map as far as surfing is concerned: there are only three surfers on the island and not much choice when it comes to beaches. However, those that exist are worth a look and there is almost always something to ride. There are also a few possibilities for reefs and points but it is largely unreportable so I won't say what these are. However, beach breaks at the airport and on Vatersay are worth a peep. I surfed with the locals – having bumped into them while searching for waves – and had a great time in beautiful clean waves in the cleanest water ever. Learn with Barra Surf Adventures. • www.barrasurfadventures.co.uk

Adventure centre   There is an adventure centre at Clearwater Paddling in Castlebay. They take out groups on sea kayaking trips as well as coasteering adventures. A great way to see the island's very best places.
• www.clearwaterpaddling.com

Nearest van hire

Harris Classic Campers, Seilebost
• www.harrisclassic campers.co.uk

**Western Isles Campers,
Fort William**
• www.westernisles campers.co.uk

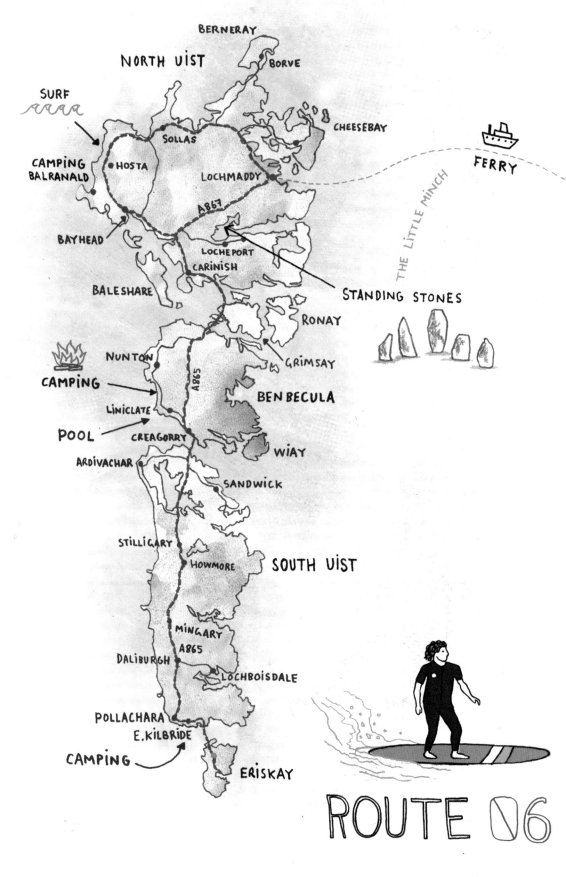

06

THE ISLANDS AND CAUSEWAYS

HEBRIDES HOPSCOTCH

For many, an island-hopping adventure is the ultimate in road tripping. Exploring remote corners and linking up ferries and causeways with remote beaches and wild open spaces is what camper vans and motorhomes were made for. And that makes a journey from tip to tip of North and South Uists among the very best adventures there is. So if you like nature, wild places, massive, open landscapes and the chance of seeing the starriest sky imaginable, this could be your best-ever slow-road trip (ever). And it's not just for the young or adventurous at heart: on my travels on North Uist I met a couple in their 80s in a VW T5. No excuses. Just go.

BEST FOR:
Island hopping by road

START:
Eriskay

END:
Lochmaddy

MILEAGE:
120 miles (193 kilometres)

DAYS TO EXPLORE: 6–7

OS LAND-RANGER MAP:
31, 22, 18

ISLANDS

There is good mobile reception and 4G internet on the beach at Hosta. I am glad about that, because it makes me feel less alone in this wilderness, this most remote of places on the north-western tip of North Uist. The surf is huge and clean and I am desperate to catch a few waves – to put a lifelong dream to bed – but it would be too reckless to enter the water alone. That's the rule of surfing, and the risk of travelling solo.

I wait for a text message from my 'wing girl' back in England, who has promised to watch over me from a distance. I look out to sea, from the comfort of the best seat in the house, inside the van, with the sliding door open so I can have a perfect view of this incredible stretch of coastline.

I have parked my camper van on the dunes at the north end of Hosta Beach. A little track through the machair brought me here, a little beyond a parking and picnic area, to a flat-enough space to make sleeping a possibility. Someone has been here before me and created a circle of scallop shells on the grass, a reminder that others come here too, but maybe not that often. To the north the dunes drop off sharply to a rivulet that empties peaty water into the surf. It meanders down the beach, past pinky-grey granite boulders, lazily making its way to the high-tide mark and out into the ocean.

To the south, the bay curves towards me, backed by high dunes until it reaches the rocks at the far end, about 100 metres (yards) away. From there, the low

cliff continues north-westwards to a low point with a grassy top. I can see a footpath around the headland leading to the next bay to the south and remind myself to check it out as a potential fishing spot. I know I'll catch nothing, but it's a good way to pass an hour or two on this slow-road journey from Eriskay, through South Uist, over the causeway to Benbecula and on to North Uist.

Hosta is the last stop on this adventure to the Outer Hebrides. I have driven north from the ferry port on Eriskay, on an Island Hopscotch ticket that has taken me to Barra and will deposit me on Skye in a few days' time. Time on the Uists has been peaceful, beautiful, driving mile after mile of undulating tarmac veering around lochs and bogs, over causeways between islands, but always heading north, and always with mountains to my right and vast, white sand beaches and islets to my left. I have seen a lot of peaty standing water and crofts, squatting against the elements, as I have covered the miles. I have stopped on beaches with banks of kelp on the high-tide mark and low, grassy splash zones where I have parked for the night under clear and dark skies. I have seen standing stones, megalithic tombs and the ruins of once-illegal side schools. I've walked dark and muddied drovers' roads into the wild centre of this incredible island chain.

It's October and the weather is warm and sunny. The tourist season is over and the islands have been getting back to work. Back to the onset of winter. Back to the business of being out in the North Atlantic. Back to being the Hebrides.

Looking now, from the comfort of the van, I see a splash out to sea, a few hundred metres offshore. It's hard to tell what it is from here but it looks like a common dolphin is cruising. A flock of funny-flying puffins flap past, their wings beating fast and furiously as they cross the bay. I find my binoculars to get a better view but they have gone by the time I focus. Instead, I lock on to a series of jagged shapes in the far distance, jutting out of the horizon. I realise that it's St Kilda, some 40 miles (64 kilometres) offshore. It is the last outpost of the British Isles, the furthest point upon which you can be declared on UK soil, if you want to make the day trip. I'm OK here, to be honest, I think to myself. This is remote enough.

And it is remote. I haven't seen another soul since I arrived here four hours ago and I won't for another 20 hours, although I have had some contact with the outside world, thanks to the phone mast on the hill behind the beach. My phone beeps. It is my wing girl, ready to watch over me from a distance. If I don't text back in two hours' time she'll call the coastguard and tell them I was last heard of at Hosta, preparing to go surfing.

I suit up, wax up and hit the water, hopefully not St Kilda bound.

THE DRIVING

Driving across South Uist felt, at times, like driving on a strip of tarmac matting laid on top of a bog. Or on a boardwalk across shifting sands, with dips and banks. The road undulated and twisted, threatening to change its course at any moment.

Sometimes, passing lochs and inlets and watery bogs, it was hard to know where the land stopped and the water began. The causeways that link up the five Islands in this chain – Eriskay, South Uist, Benbecula, Grimsay and North Uist – blur the lines between island hopping and driving but make a single trip possible, and for that we're grateful. It's about 60 miles (97 kilometres) from Eriskay to Berneray so it's no distance at all, but it'll take a lot longer than you might imagine, because you just can't rush.

I arrived on Eriskay from Barra. The road here is unnamed and tiny and passes a few houses and the village stores, where it's possible to stock up on just about everything you can get on the mainland, or in any standard village shop. Eriskay is so tiny that a couple of minutes of driving brought me to the first of the causeways. I stopped here to take pictures of the water and the beach. Even though the sky was dark the sea looked impossibly blue. As I looked back towards Barra a porpoise cruised the waters between the two islands, its black dorsal fin cutting the water in dazzling white splashes.

Once on South Uist the road gets a name, the B888, and takes you to the main road, the A865, which begins in Lochboisdale, a small port with hostel, bar and cafe. If you skip Barra and come on the CalMac from Oban you'll arrive here.

The A865 is the main artery for the island chain, separating the mountainous east coast from the low, wet western coast. So, as you drive south to north you keep the peaks to your right. Offshoots from this road will take you either to tiny communities around craggy rocks and inlets or out on to the flat beaches of the west. Passing crofts always brought the same peaty smell of fires burning day in, day out in blackened hearths, an enduring memory of communities on the edge. It's a homely, distinctive smell that, if I were to smell it now, would transport me straight back there.

Heading north still the road leads you over the long causeway to Benbecula, where it continues ever northwards. The B892 will take you around the western coast, past the school and sports centre, and out on to some great beaches before heading back towards the A865 and the causeway to North Uist via Grimsay.

Once you arrive on North Uist the A865 continues north until you arrive at a junction and a decision must be made. Do you go left or right? Does it matter? Not much. It's the same road really, it's just that

PLACES TO STAY

Balranald Hebridean Holidays
Hougharry, North Uist,
Outer Hebrides, HS6 5DL
web: www.balranaldhebridean
holidays.com
email: info@
balranaldhebrideanholidays.com
tel: 01876 510 304 or
07748 267 996

info: *A lovely little site with two hardstanding pitches with electric. It's just about 20 metres (yards) from a gorgeous, west-facing white-sand beach. Perfect for watching the sun go down.*

Moorcroft Holidays
17 Carinish, North Uist,
Outer Hebrides, HS6 5HN
web: www.moorcroftholidays.co.uk
email: morrisons17@hotmail.com
tel: 01876 580 305

info: *Family-run site on a working croft on the southern coast of North Uist and overlooking Benbecula.*

it forms a heart-shaped loop around North Uist's boggy and mountainous centre. Head left and you come to the peninsulas at Balranald and the beach at Hosta. Thereafter the road continues north, with an aside to the Isle of Berneray after the estuarine sands, dunes and machair that surround the islet of Vallay. Continue on and you'll reach Lochmaddy, the port on North Uist's eastern side. Like all Hebridean ports it's tiny, with a few houses and a shop, school and outdoor centre. It's also home to the Taigh Chearsabhagh Museum & Arts Centre. Find art exhibitions, a museum and home-made cake here.

If completing the loop back to the junction of the A865 and the A867 from Lochmaddy you'll pass the magnificent chambered tomb at Barpa Langass and the short walk to Pobull Fhinn, the lovely stone circle that overlooks Loch Langass.

General dos and don'ts

The Uists make good motorhoming country. However, as with all places where free camping is a reason for going, it shouldn't be a reason for upsetting anyone. That means staying out of sight of houses, or, if it looks like the land belongs to someone, asking permission. Also, of course, it's important to respect the machair and dunes and to never leave litter or empty loos anywhere other than waste-emptying points.

There are loos and showers and a chemical-waste disposal point at the ferry terminals at Eriskay, Lochboisdale and Ardmaree on Berneray. Public loos at Berneray harbour also have showers. There are recycling points all over the Uists.

IN THE AREA

Pobull Fhinn The translation of this into English from Gaelic is 'Finn's People', and the story goes that the stones in this small circle were named after legendary Gaelic hero and hunter warrior Fionn Mac Cumhail (Finn MacCool). It's a lovely circle with magnificent views over Loch Langass and is apparently one of the most photographed spots on North Uist. I loved it, although it was just me and an otter there at the time.
• www.ancient-scotland.co.uk/site/128

Barpa Langass A partially collapsed, Neolithic chambered tomb with a passage grave that's located on the A867 just outside Lochmaddy. It is still possible to enter the tomb but I didn't. Would you? If not, you can still peer into the darkness and see the pillars and lintels that have held up the mound for thousands of years. A lovely, lonely site. • www.isle-of-north-uist.co.uk/what-to-do/barpa-langass

Nearest van hire

Harris Classic Campers, Seilebost
• www.harrisclassic campers.co.uk

Western Isles Campers, Fort William
• www.westernisles campers.co.uk

Hebridean Smokehouse If it's possible to smoke it, this is where to try it. It's on the road to Lochmaddy from Hosta, just south of Balranald. The peat-smoked salmon is fabulous, as is the smoked salmon pâté. Lots of great stuff to try and a chance to see the smokehouse in action.
• www.hebrideansmokehouse.com

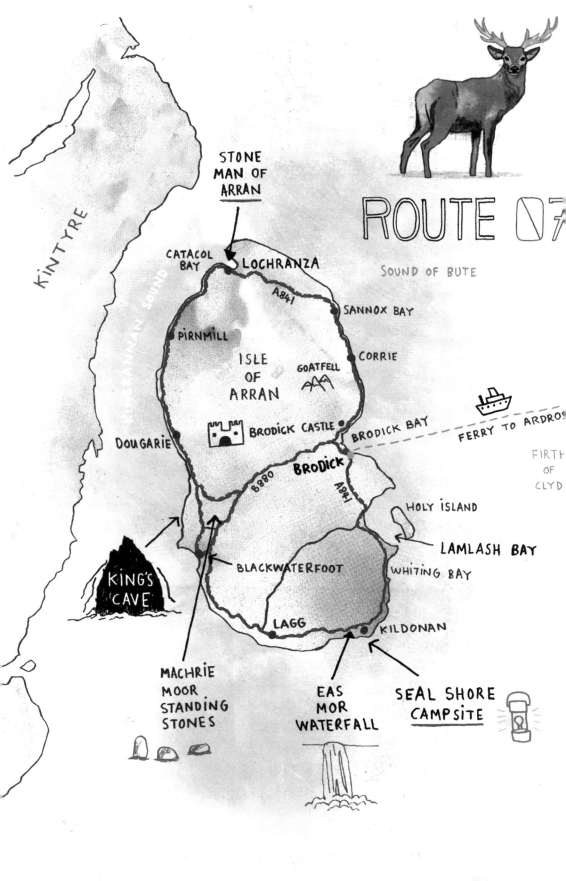

KINTYRE

STONE MAN OF ARRAN

ROUTE 07

SOUND OF BUTE

CATACOL BAY

LOCHRANZA

KILBRANNAN SOUND

A841

SANNOX BAY

PIRNMILL

ISLE OF ARRAN

GOATFELL

CORRIE

DOUGARIE

BRODICK CASTLE

BRODICK BAY

FERRY TO ARDROS

FIRTH OF CLYD

B880

BRODICK

A841

HOLY ISLAND

LAMLASH BAY

WHITING BAY

BLACKWATERFOOT

KING'S CAVE

LAGG

KILDONAN

SEAL SHORE CAMPSITE

MACHRIE MOOR STANDING STONES

EAS MOR WATERFALL

SCOTLAND FOR BEGINNERS

WHERE THE REAL WORLD MEETS FAIRYLAND

Arran is an island adventure that anyone can have. It's got all the bits and pieces you could ever want from a trip to Scotland, and it's right there, just a short ferry ride away from Ardrossan, ready for you to explore. In just a few short miles you'll see a little of everything Scotland has in spades: history, landscape, ancient sites, beautiful waters, mountains and myths.

BEST FOR:
Seeing Scotland 'in miniature'

START/END:
Brodick

MILEAGE:
50 miles (80 kilometres)

DAYS TO EXPLORE: **4–5**

OS LAND-RANGER MAP: **69**

ISLANDS

113

Maggie, my daughter, and I are driving up the west coast of Arran. We've had a remarkable time on this little island so far, exploring it for a few days, enjoying the views and enjoying our amazing luck in experiencing good weather. Maggie says it's her new favourite place ever.

We have walked to the King's Cave and discovered a field of tiny cairns below basalt cliffs, we have been startled by a stag standing off against us in the pub garden at Catacol (the barman wasn't startled at all), we have free camped out of sight of any lights or houses on the wild west coast and we've snorkelled among the rocks in cold, clear water. It's been perfect, and full of surprises.

But the best is yet to come. As we round the last bend before Lochranza on the A841, the tiny main road that circumnavigates the island, skirting around the west coast just above the shoreline, we get our first view of the bay and the opposite bank of the loch to the north. And we also see something that simply can't be ignored but definitely doesn't belong in this most bucolic of landscapes. It's an enormous boat, like a Sunseeker on a crash course of powerful steroids, a superyacht. It's sleek and vast, with five decks, a helicopter on a helipad at the back and launches hanging off the side.

We stop, laughing that it's like the secret lair of a Bond villain, unable to work out just how big it is. Then, as if by magic, to give it some scale, the CalMac car ferry to the Mull of Kintyre pulls out from the jetty. The superyacht is at least four times the size of the ferry. We decide it's definitely a Bond villain. Sure enough, when we turn up at the pier head a few minutes later we see a launch with dark-uniformed and scary-looking henchmen packing away cases of whisky before speeding off to the boat-landing platform at the back of the mothership.

We decide to walk out to the point to the north of the village and see if we can find the Fairy Dell, a small white cottage on the edge of the sea, a place where, it is rumoured, you can find the gateway to the land of the fairies. It's a warm day and the sky is blue, with a few wispy clouds. It's spring, so we pass foxgloves and wild flowers in brilliant bloom along the way. In front of the picture-perfect whitewashed cottage the meadow is filled with buttercups, daisies and the wind-blown seed heads of meadow grasses. Maggie builds a small cairn on the beach to mark her arrival at this beautiful spot. We look out at the Mull of Kintyre, and the Isle of Bute to the north-east and explore a gorge that follows a stream up from the shoreline. There we find a tiny bench, 'a wee resting place for the faeries', with a plaque devoted to Bill Stark 'at his favourite place'. Is this the gateway? What did Bill see here? We will never know.

It is a peaceful place and yet, still, the superyacht manages to dominate. We hear the helicopter buzz overhead a few times on the walk, shattering

the peace of the sunny afternoon. We walk away from the cottage, up the glen and over a hillock to a small lane that passes a cottage doubling as a craft shop. Inside we discover hundreds of hand-painted stones and a little workshop. It is, of course, the Stone Man of Arran, local craftsman and painter of stones for the tourism industry. He tells us that the superyacht belongs to Roman Abramovich. It is the *MV Eclipse*, the second-largest yacht on the planet, with two helicopter pads, two pools and three launch boats. Apparently they have been loading up whisky and buzzing about the island for days, intimidating all the locals and upsetting the red deer. So this is where the oligarchs have their holidays! We are in good, if not interesting at least, company.

Before we go we choose some stones for the folks back home and, after seeing a couple of guitars lying about, ask if Stone Man has a spare string

for ours since we broke one a few days ago. He obliges and we trot off down the hill and back to our van along a shady lane where the grass is growing in the middle and the vivid, spring-fresh leaves on the trees make the sunlight dance on our faces.

Later, I take a picture of Maggie at our camping spot. She sits strumming her guitar in the back of the van while it is parked on the seashore, just above the high-tide mark. In the foreground we see gorse and rapeseed, green and yellow, a splash of colour. Behind her is a green hillside, and behind that, the glimpse of a mountain disappearing behind a cloud. Across the water the darkened shapes of distant lands hint at further adventures.

It sums up camper vanning and motorhoming for me. Maggie is concentrating, at peace, in a landscape, with no agenda other than to make nice sounds. The superyacht is far away and nothing else matters. Not Abramovich, not helicopters, not school or homework or even the future. It's just about the moment. And that is it.

When we get home we send the Stone Man a new guitar string, hoping we'll be back one day to thank him personally.

THE DRIVING

Like all islands, Arran's driving is limited to the few roads it has. But what roads exist there are worth driving, if only to give you a first taste of a first-rate island adventure. In a few short hours you will drive through all kinds of landscapes, from mountains to empty hinterland via jolly seafronts and high cliff routes.

The ferry from the mainland arrives at Brodick, Arran's capital and main settlement. This is the place to buy outdoor gear, supplies at the Co-operative or books and postcards to keep you amused on long nights. The seafront has lots of seafronty things, such as jolly flowerbeds and crazy golf and families enjoying strolls. Just out of town, to the west there is a castle and country park as well as a heritage museum.

From the ferry terminal you can go left or right around the island. So let's imagine we have turned to the left, on the A841, towards the south and Lamlash Bay. The road rises out of Brodick and passes through coniferous plantations before offering up the first views as you descend through Blairmore Glen to Lamlash, a lovely little beach town with cafes and coffee shops, an outdoor centre and, offshore, the enigmatic Holy Island. Next stop, Whiting Bay is another beachside settlement with elegant houses with great views that will

make you question your own existence. Could you live here? I could.

From Whiting Bay things get good. The coast changes and for the next few miles the road sits at the top of the steep slopes leading down to the sea. It passes the gorge at Eas Mor Waterfall with a whipped-back turn over a little bridge before offering you the opportunity to head down the hill to Seal Shore Campsite. Well worth it, if you can get in. After that you stay high, along a series of straights and bends at river valleys, almost always with fine sea views, until you finally hit sea level at Blackwaterfoot, where I recommend you get out and stretch the legs with a walk to the King's Cave.

You hit the wild west after Machrie Bay Golf Course, where one of the island's central roads – the B880 – will lead you back to Brodick, if you let it, across the boggy, forested hinterland and ending in stunning views of Brodick Bay on the descent. Otherwise it's carrying on to Lochranza along the coast. I love this part of the journey because it skirts the shore, almost along the entire length of the island, offering places to halt and enjoy the beach. There are stops and villages at Pirnmill and Catacol where you can visit the local shop or hotel for supplies or refreshments.

At Lochranza the road changes again and travels up the loch before passing high over the mountainous north of the island, to about 200m (650ft) up a steep-sided and open valley with views of the mountains of Goatfell to the south. As you descend to the east coast, and drop below the treeline the road becomes more enclosed until you arrive at Sannox Bay and begin the delightfully twisty, seashore-skirting meander back to Brodick via the lovely little beachside hamlet at Corrie.

PLACES TO STAY

**Seal Shore Camping
and Touring Site**
Kildonan, Isle of Arran, KA27 8SE
web: www.campingarran.com
email: enquiries@campingarran.com
tel: 01770 820 320

info: *Amazing site right on the shore. It's small so book ahead to avoid disappointment. Snorkelling and fresh fish in season. Nice hotel bar next door. Book it!*

**Lochranza Caravan
and Camping Site**
Lochranza, Isle of Arran, KA27 8HL
web: www.arran-campsite.com
email: info@arran-campsite.com
tel: 01770 830 273

info: *Nice, open site that's handy for the north, for walks to Fairy Dell and the distillery.*

**Bridgend Campsite
and Cottage**
Bridgend Cottage, Shiskine,
Isle of Arran, KA27 8EN
web: www.bridgend
holidays shiskine.co.uk
email: christine@bridgend
holidays shiskine.co.uk
tel: 01770 860 597

info: *A small certificated site in the centre of Arran. Few pitches. Book ahead!*

How to camp on Arran

Each time I have been to Arran I have free camped on the western shore. However, the last time I went I got into a conversation with a campsite owner who informed me that 'the people of Arran are sick of wild campers in motorhomes'. His reasons? Blocking views, leaving mess, parking inappropriately where they shouldn't. I have to say that I never experienced any of this animosity, but I would warn anyone who thinks Arran is a free-for-all to be wary and act accordingly, please. There aren't a lot of spots where you can tuck away out of sight and there are fewer places to charge or empty tanks. Most of the public toilets have closed, too, thanks to council cuts, and campsite owners won't let you service your motorhomes.

So, my advice? Book into a campsite, charge your tanks and then do a mix of wild and site camping, but only if you find a spot that's away from anywhere, and where you won't upset the neighbours. It is their island, after all.

IN THE AREA

King's Cave A hidey-hole in the cliffs near Blackwaterfoot where Robert the Bruce is said to have had his epiphany relating to spiders and never giving up the struggle. You can make it a short walk from a car park on the main road or walk from Blackwaterfoot and enjoy the full effect of the glorious location. Along the way you'll see the field of minicairns and get to see the basalt cliffs of The Doon. Great adventure or short stroll. You choose.
• www.visitarran.com/what-to-see-do/arran-attractions/kings-cave

Goatfell I am ashamed to say this is unfinished business, due to my being in the company of anti-walkers on my trips. It is said to be well worth the climb for the views of the island. At just 874m (2,870ft) it's mini, but still too mighty for my lot. Next time.
• www.nts.org.uk/Visit/Goat-Fell/

Fairy Dell Lovely walk to a funny old cottage with whitewashed walls in a magical meadow by the sea. Said to be the place where fairyland meets the real world. The rivulet that tinkles down to the shore up a mini gorge is certainly a little otherworldly. No fairy sightings for me, but we live in hope.
• www.walkhighlands.co.uk/arran/fairy-dell.shtml

Isle of Arran Distillery tours If you like whisky, like Roman Abramovich, you'll like any kind of distillery tour. But this one is a good 'un as it's situated in a lovely spot just outside of Lochranza. Learn, taste, tour. What's not to love?
• www.arranwhisky.com

Eas Mor Waterfall I'm not sure what was going on here when I last visited (spring 2017) but it seems they are in the middle of a facelift. The falls are managed by a green trust that looks after them and provides educational resources, so there's every reason to go along and support them. And the falls are great too!
• www.easmor-ecology.com

Nearest van hire

BC Motorhomes, Ayr
• www.bcmotorhomes.co.uk

The Tartan Camper Company, Saltcoats
• www.thetartancamper.co.uk

Rockin Vans, Kilmarnock
• www.rockinvans.co.uk

Bonny Scotland Campers, Kilmarnock
• www.bonnyscotland-campers.co.uk

Stone circles at Machrie Moor A series of stone circles about half a mile from the main road. Well worth the yompette over the moor to see this group of lovely stones in a very wild landscape. Boggy but brilliant. Take boots.
• www.undiscoveredscotland.co.uk/arran/machriemoor/index.html

SCOTLAND FOR BEGINNERS

ISLANDS

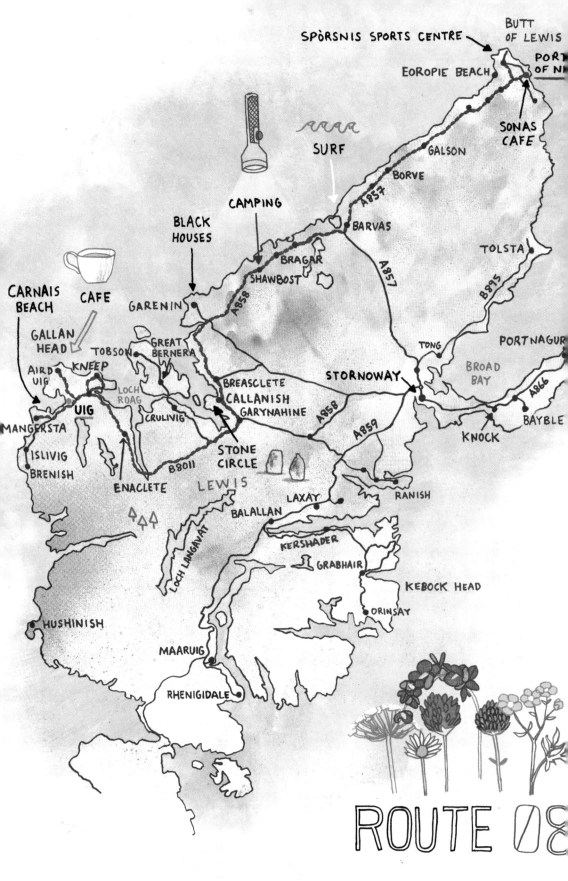

ROUTE 08

NORTH LEWIS

THE CAFES ON THE EDGE

North Lewis, from Uig to Port of Ness, offers a vast range of fabulous landscapes, including acres of machair, sublime beaches, great swathes of undulating, endless bog as well as mountainous and high terrain. This route takes you from Gallan Head in West Lewis to the most north-westerly point of the British Isles at the Butt of Lewis and includes a blackhouse village and some of the best standing stone circles outside of Stonehenge.

BEST FOR: Machair, standing stones and beaches

START: Uig

END: Port of Ness

MILEAGE: 60 miles (97 kilometres)

DAYS TO EXPLORE: 4–5

OS LAND-RANGER MAP: 13, 8

ISLANDS

125

We're exploring West Lewis, searching for somewhere to surf and stock up on supplies for the next few days. Last night we camped wild on the beach at Cliff, another incredible stretch of sand, backed by multicoloured machair grassland containing orchids, yellow rattle, purple clover and wild carrot. Together with a blue sky reflecting in a clear blue sea, the white of the sand and the rainbow riot of the grass and flower-topped coastal meadow it's a picture-perfect spot, and it was hard to leave.

We arrive at Uig and follow signs for the road out to Gallan Head and the promise of a slice of cake and a cup of tea at The Edge Cafe. Below us, to the left, the vast white sands of Traige Uige curve away from us, shielded by offshore islands and jutting promontories. Houses dot the landscape in

a loose settlement, with a school, a garage and community shop the largest buildings we can see. We pass the school and the coastguard and fire station on the narrow single-track road and follow it to Aird Uig, a tiny village overlooking a small rocky bay. There is no sign of the cafe so we pass through the village, on to rougher roads. We pass what looks like a flat-roofed and dilapidated hotel, looking sad,

despite a stunning location and the bright and sunny day. The road weaves between a collection of half-broken, cheaply made prefabs. It looks like a forgotten place. The buildings, low, square boxes with crumbling brick towers for water tanks appear to be severely neglected, until we look more closely. Some of them are in mid-repair, or half covered by hit-and-miss cedar cladding. Some are painted in jolly colours, while others have neat gardens. It feels like a melancholy place trying hard, forgotten, like a disused army base or long-forgotten Cold War relic, built cheaply by government.

We pass through the encampment and on to Gallan Head, where we stop at a pebble-dashed bungalow by a farm gate that leads to another collection of depressing, army-green painted buildings. But here, at the bungalow, it seems things are happening. Kids are playing outside while their mums chat. A hand-painted sign says 'welcome' and the door to the house is open, so we tentatively walk in, saying hello to a woman who is wandering out. She says hi and then disappears off, leaving us in a large room with a big table and a menu on the wall. Another table, full of mismatched and antique crockery, separates us from the kitchen. A woman works away quietly preparing food, seemingly oblivious to our presence, even when we pop our heads around the kitchen door. I'm not sure what we expect but this clearly isn't a run-of-the-mill cafe so we look around, read the menu and gaze out of the window, not wanting to disturb the cook. Despite feeling unsure of what to do we continue as we always do – we inspect the pictures on the wall, talk about the views from the window, laugh, enjoy ourselves. We are open-minded and open-hearted and it always seems to bring out the best in people. A smile and a laugh is the best way of raising a smile if a smile is there to be raised.

We begin to chat with the cook, Fiona. She's from Strandhill in Sligo on the west coast of Ireland. It's a place I know well so we have common ground, opening up the opportunity for more light-hearted conversation. We learn that Aird Uig is a wild place where the wind often reaches 150mph (240kph), the stars shine bright and the aurora borealis is easy to see when it's on. We are enthralled. But what of the wrecked buildings?

The area, Fiona tells us, is an old MOD and RAF base. It was first commissioned in the Second World War as a place to watch for shipping in the Western Approaches. It then continued to be used as a listening station until 2010. It wasn't until January 2016 that it fell into the hands of the community when the MOD announced it would sell the land on the open market and the

Gallan Head Community Trust bought it to ensure its future for the benefit of the local community. The buildings we passed outside the village were sold in the 1980s and some are still in the process of being upgraded and rebuilt. The cafe, which Fiona runs as a hub for the community, as well as a way of bringing income into the trust, marks the beginning of the trust's land. They have plans for a whale watching station or dark sky park and we love it, particularly the idea of a community working together to fill the gaps where a government has left a mess or a hole or is sidestepping its responsibility to the community it owes a favour to. It's not the first time we've seen this in the Outer Hebrides and it seems to be the way things are going. It's a brilliantly indignant fingers-up to authority for forgetting about the outposts. Communities taking care of themselves, making it happen.

I feel completely different about this place now I have had the chance to find out about it. I feel lucky to have found this cafe, and had the chance to talk to Fiona. As we leave I feel we have seen a community flexing its muscles, in flux, on the edge of the world but also on the edge of great and positive change.

Fiona gives us recommendations for places to surf, beaches to visit and things to see. We follow her instructions to the letter and find a small, sheltered beach at Carnais. It is completely deserted and the water is clear, the sea blue and the sun shines. We snorkel around the cliffs on the western side, seeing shoals of sand eels and jellyfish, pairs of fighting velvet swimming crabs and the odd wrasse among the seaweed. It's a magical place and the sun warms us after our snorkel. We strip off our wetsuits and skinny dip in

the cold, clear water, laughing at our good fortune in finding the cafe at the edge. Life doesn't get any better than this. We pinch ourselves that we are in the Outer Hebrides when it could be anywhere.

We leave Uig with a smile on our faces and head north-east towards the Port of Ness (Port Nis), one of the furthest places we will get to during the writing of this book. We visit the Callanish (Calanais) Stones, Dalmore (Dhail Mhor), the blackhouse village at Gearrannan and finally, the epic beach at Eoropie, one of my favourite spots in the UK. The waves look fantastic.

But before we stop to surf or camp we have one thing to do: cycle to the edge of the UK at the Butt of Lewis. We set out from Port of Ness, parking near to Cafe Sonas, the cafe overlooking the lovely harbour. The cycling on the deserted roads is good and we return an hour or so later, sitting on the harbour wall in the sunshine to enjoy a homespun lunch from leftovers in the van.

Later we go into the community cafe at Port of Ness for a cuppa. We are greeted with smiles, a loving pride and a strong sense of community. The lady in the gift shop tells us the best things to see while we are on the island. Have we seen the stones? Have we walked in the forest? Have we been up to the lighthouse? She gathers us and her other customers in a joyful conversation so we feel as if we are old friends. We learn about a couple who are on the last mile of an island-hopping cycle. We meet a couple buying postcards. It's joyous to be here. We order cake and coffee and sit down. The crockery is mismatched, but who cares about that? It's not slick or corporate in any way, and that's the way we like it. We are happy in happy places.

THE DRIVING

Of all the routes I have driven in Scotland, this one stands out as being one of the most varied and interesting. Much of the driving in West Lewis is on narrow single-track roads but this changes once you reach North Lewis. The A858, which winds its way up the spine of Lewis, is comparatively wide and fast and a pleasure to drive.

Starting out from Uig there are a number of options, depending on how much you want to explore. The road to the west, a narrow tarmac road with passing places, heads out to Mangersta and beyond. Mangersta is a small community with interesting eco houses and eccentric places to stay. There are camping pods and shepherds huts here as well as a gorgeous cove, a set of spectacular sea stacks and a stone-built bothy dedicated to a Scottish aid worker. However, a word of warning! Don't be tempted to drive all the way to the beach at Mangersta unless you have a 4 x 4 camper: you might not make it back out.

Between Mangersta and Uig you'll find Carnais beach at the end of a track opposite the Uig distillery with parking for just a couple of vehicles. Walk over the machair and around the farms to a beautiful sandy cove with few visitors.

At Uig the road has a name, the B8011, even though you'd be hard pressed to tell the difference. It crosses the peninsula from east to west along a steep-sided gorge that follows a stream to the sea at Miavaig. At the junction here you have another choice, to head on towards North Lewis or follow the signs for the scenic drive to Cliff, Reef and Kneep. It's worth it. You can wild camp on the machair at Cliff for a fiver (in the honesty box) but there are no facilities. It a great place to wake. Further round this little tour of the tiny island you'll find the lovely sheltered beach at Kneep behind the machair. Thereafter it's a winding, undulating route through Reef, past tiny houses with tamed gardens, bungalows with billowing washing lines and a beautifully made monument to the Reef Raiders, a group of local protesters who fought for the right to recroft the area in the early 20th century, before the loop arrives back at Miavaig and the B8011. Well worth the detour.

The road then heads south, rounding Loch Roag before heading north-west over typical Lewis countryside. It's rocky, wet and devoid of forest but no less beautiful. Much of Lewis is open, undulating peat bog, so this will be your last chance to enjoy some craggy rocks and peaks before the peaks peter out beyond Callanish. Before you reach the A858 you'll have the chance to visit Great Bernera on the A8059, if you have the time.

At the junction with the A858 the landscape makes a shift towards a flatter profile that is typical of Lewis. The road is better and the going is good. Pass the stones at Callanish (but don't forget to stop) and on to Barvas. Along this stretch you'll pass numerous turns to the north, which inevitably lead to tiny beaches or communities. It's a busier landscape than Harris or West Lewis, with more houses and bigger villages, but still no major infrastructure, pubs or restaurants. There are galleries and potteries but not a great deal else, so plan your meals and stops if you want to eat out. The beaches at Dalmore and Dalbeg offer surf, with Dalmore being a popular overnight spot for surfers.

Barvas is another surf spot, with a super long right-hand point that's accessible across the machair down a bumpy track. In summer the meadow is spectacular, with a carpet of wild flowers stretching out into the distance. Barvas is the point at which you can take a turn off to cross the bog to Stornoway, but don't go just yet. While the countryside is undulating and devoid of any mountains or peaks, the end of the road, at Port of Ness, the Butt Of Lewis and Eoropie, is worth a visit, if only to say you've been to the wildest part of Britain. And even then, it's not, and is rather a beautiful little port with whitewashed cottages, pebble-dashed bungalows and plenty of sun and wind.

There is a fantastic play park at Eoropie, as well as a sports centre with showers and toilets – and even a motorhome service point – that are open until late in the evenings. The lighthouse at the Butt of Lewis is well worth a cycle or drive out from Port of Ness. It's the very last outpost and is tall and fine, towering over dizzying cliffs and spongy, peaty grassland. From here it's non-stop across thousands of miles of ocean until Greenland or the eastern seaboard of Canada. That's a dizzying thought in itself.

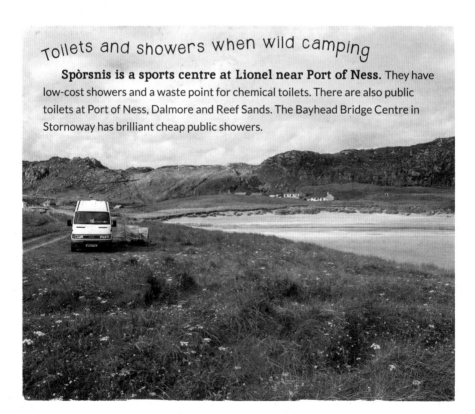

Toilets and showers when wild camping

Spòrsnis is a sports centre at Lionel near Port of Ness. They have low-cost showers and a waste point for chemical toilets. There are also public toilets at Port of Ness, Dalmore and Reef Sands. The Bayhead Bridge Centre in Stornoway has brilliant cheap public showers.

PLACES TO STAY

Wild camping spots Lewis is a great place to take a motor-home or camper van. However, as always, there are issues with wild camping at some places. Moreover, there are *always* issues with wild camping if people leave a mess or don't clear up after others. Some places tolerate wild camping and ask for donations to help with upkeep of the precious machair, which I think is fair enough. In other places they request you keep to tracks and don't go off-piste. That machair is vulnerable and people driving over it can damage it.

Cliff Beach, Cliff *A wild-camping spot on the machair at which we pay £5 in the honesty box for the privilege of staying in a beautiful and wild spot and that goes towards the upkeep of the beach. Please don't abuse it: pay your money and tread lightly! There are toilets and reasonably priced showers at Kneep Campsite, approximately a mile away.*

Dalmore *A wild spot with a toilet and tap and two graveyards. There are a few level 'pitches' near the beach but the car park is very slopey, so take chocks. I wish there was an honesty box here for the upkeep of the loos but there isn't, so please, treat it with respect.*

Kneep Campsite
Kneep, Isle of Lewis, HS2 9HS
web: www.visitouterhebrides.co.uk/accommodation/
traigh-na-beirigh-kneep-campsite-p557511
tel: 01851 672 265

info: *Toilets and showers. Camping right on the beach.*

Uig Sands Ardroil Beach
6 Ardroil, Timsgearraidh, Isle of Lewis, HS2 9EU
web: www.visitouterhebrides.co.uk/accommodation/
ardroil-sands-campsite-p541251
tel: 01851 672 248

info: *A simple site right on the machair next to Uig Sands. Lovely.*

Eilean Fraoich Campsite
77A North Shawbost, Isle of Lewis, HS2 9BQ
web: www.eileanfraoich.co.uk
tel: 01851 710 504

info: *A neat and tidy site on the wilder side of Lewis. Handy for Callanaish and the north coast.*

IN THE AREA

Callanish Stone Circles There are three stone circles at Callanish, and all are free to visit. The biggest of the three, which rivals anything further south (except maybe Stonehenge), is set out in a cruciform, with a central stone that is almost 5m (16ft) high. It's an impressive site and you'd be a fool to visit Lewis and not see it, whether you feel the magic of such a sacred and ancient site or not. There are also two other stone circles nearby, and although not as big, the stones are just as friendly. • www.callanishvisitorcentre.co.uk

Commun Eachdraidh Nis A community centre with café, museum, shop and archive for locals and visitors. A very friendly and welcoming place that serves a great carrot cake with decent icing and not that fluffy stuff. Highly recommended. • www.eachdraidhnis.org

Gearrannan blackhouse village A traditional blackhouse village that's also holiday accommodation but that can be visited during the day. There are also ruins of blackhouses and a nice view of the sea. • www.gearrannan.com

Nearest van hire

Happy Highland Campers, Inverness
• www.happyhighland campers.co.uk

Harris Classic Campers, Seilebost
• www.harrisclassic campers.co.uk

OutThere Campervans Scotland, Inverness
• www.outthere campers.co.uk

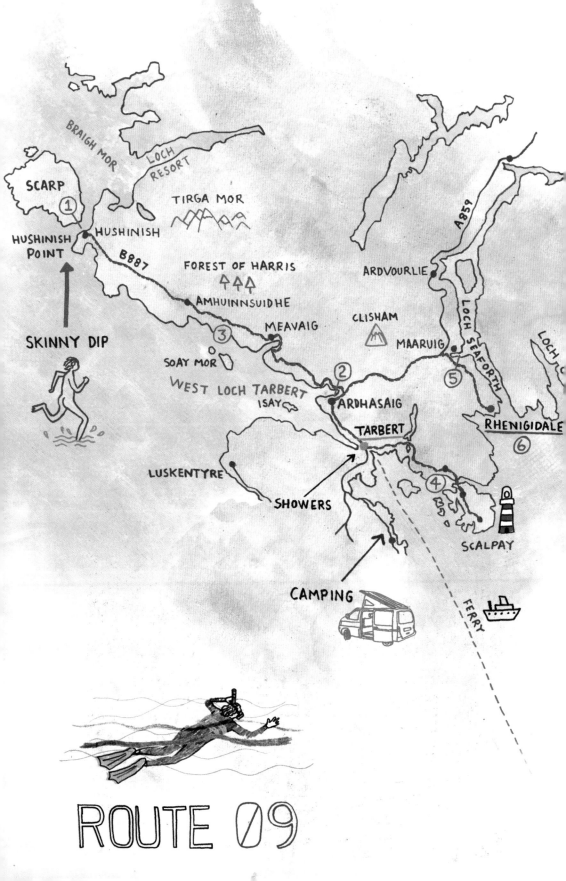

SCARP

①

HUSHINISH
POINT

SKINNY DIP

BRAIGH MOR

LOCH RESORT

TIRGA MOR

HUSHINISH

B887

FOREST OF HARRIS

AMHUINNSUIDHE

③

SOAY MOR

MEAVAIG

WEST LOCH TARBERT

ISAY

②

ARDHASAIG

TARBERT

LUSKENTYRE

SHOWERS

CLISHAM

MAARUIG

A859

ARDVOURLIE

LOCH SEAFORTH

LOCH

⑤

RHENIGIDALE

⑥

④

SCALPAY

CAMPING

FERRY

ROUTE 09

09

HARRIS SNORKEL

SNORKELS AND SKINNIES

This route is based on an initiative by the Scottish Wildlife Trust to encourage more people to explore the beauty of Scotland's living seas. Accordingly, they have identified six sites across the centre of Harris that are east and west of the narrow strip of land that probably should mark a geographical boundary between Harris and Lewis, but doesn't. Even if you don't snorkel, this route will take you to one of Harris's finest beaches and give you an opportunity to stay overlooking a fantastic and unspoiled beach.

BEST FOR:
Underwater landscapes, machair and winding roads

START: Tarbert

END:
Rhenigidale

MILEAGE: 30 miles (48 kilometres)

DAYS TO EXPLORE: 2

OS LAND-RANGER MAP: 13, 14

ISLANDS

139

We leave Tarbert, heading north to look for places to snorkel that we have marked on our OS map using the leaflet about the North Harris Snorkel Trail. We drive on the A859 as far as the junction with the B887 and turn off past a neat row of cottages with fantastic views up the loch. It's a tiny road that follows the north side of West Loch Tarbert and weaves its way around the loch's steep sides and inlets. We drive slowly, stopping to allow others to pass, to take photographs or simply to take it all in. It's a sunny day and Harris has never looked better to me, with a clear blue sky showing no sign of clouding over for the foreseeable future. It's hot too, at around 24°C (75°F), a temperature we'd never have expected, so we drive with the windows down to feel the sun on our arms and the wind in our hair. It's a joyful drive, with plenty of 'wow's along the way.

After driving for the best part of an hour we crest a final hill before the descent into Hushinish, the hamlet at the end of the road. We stop at the apex to admire the view. Immediately we can see why this is a popular place on the tourist trail. To the left of us a bay of white sand curves away from the road. Beyond that lie a series of smaller bays, punctuated by dark outcrops of rocks and seaweed. At the back of the beach we see that the machair, Scotland's rare coastal grassland, makes a narrow isthmus between the mainland and the headland. The machair, we see from the dots of

flowers, is in full summer bloom. A couple of motorhomes have grabbed
the top spot overlooking the beach, despite the onshore wind. Behind the
machair, looking like a rocky blimp lingering hopefully in the bay to the north,
is Scarp, one of the smaller isles in this island chain. To the left, the grey and
green headland marks the end of the point. Rusty-roofed and pebble-dashed
houses dot the coastline. A Highland cow, its wild woolly coat blowing in
the breeze, stares at me as I climb out of the van to take pictures. A sheep
meanders across the road, pausing only to look at me. It's about as Hebridean
as it gets. I snap a few pictures and return to the van.

We drive to the beach and then across a sandy track over the machair to
the tiny beach on the leeward side of the isthmus. There are a few camper
vans here, enjoying the shelter. People have set up tables and chairs and a
couple dig holes in the sand for their toddler down on the beach. We park up
in a likely spot for an overnight stay, kit up for snorkelling and head down to
the beach. The section we have chosen is marked as being 'advanced' on the

Wildlife Trust spot list as it's rocky with patches of white sand between. I am looking forward to getting into the water since it'll be the first time on my adventures in Scotland that I have a chance to see the underwater landscape as well as the landscape above the surface.

As we wade into the water, wobbling as we put on our fins, we pass the green and red seaweeds, stepping over dulse and carrageen before entering the mid-tidal zone where the water is deeper. Wracks, their fronds buoyed by plump circular bladders, swish in the lapping swell. As we put our heads into the water to look at the landscape for the first time we find the lower reaches of the tides. We kick out into the bay. This is where the kelps grow. Long strands of sugar kelp compete with wide, comb-like hands of oarweed and the long, paper-thin leaves of dabberlocks. The kelps look very different below the water than it does when stranded on big spring tides or when washed up in rotting piles. It's elegant and graceful when it's in its element, blowing backwards and forwards with the swell. Hiding between the weed, in the crevices between the rocks, are shy wrasse. If we lie still on the surface they become accustomed to our presence and grow bold, only to dart into the weed again if we move a little. Occasionally we see angry velvet swimmer crabs in the sandy patches between rocks, their red eyes and waving claws up for it if we dare to approach too near.

The visibility in the water is excellent, probably around 10m (33ft), and enables us to see any life before we get too close to scare it away. A shoal of juvenile fish, or perhaps sand eels, murmurate in the water like a flock of winter starlings in front of us. As we approach they scatter, separating and dispersing before coming back together as one when out of our range. We lie face down on the water, supported by our wetsuits. As we breathe through our snorkels we can hear our lungs pull clean, fresh air into our chests. The more I relax, the more my breathing slows to a steady, slow rhythm.

It's an exhilarating and yet languid drift across a different landscape, and, surprisingly, it's not that cold. I am wearing a 4mm wetsuit with a hood and I can manage 60 minutes in the water. Considering we are at lat 58°N, it's warm. The sun on my back helps, and the fact that we are out of the wind makes for a really lovely hour in the water.

We set up ready for the night and decide to take a walk around the headland to the beaches on the other side of the isthmus. It's 8pm but it feels more like five in the afternoon. That's because it won't get dark until past

10pm, owing to the time of the year and the fact that we are so far north. We traverse the cliff, and hop over the boggy machair, leaping from lichen-covered granite boulder to boulder to avoid dark, peaty pools.

We hop fences and wade through fields of fluffy cotton grass and orange bog asphodel, arriving at a tiny cove at the far end of Hushinish's main beach. It's about 20 metres (yards) wide, with rocks at either side. Multicoloured granite pebbles, worn smooth by centuries of wave action, separate the machair from the white sand. We take off our boots to walk on the beach, the first people to make footprints on this stretch since the last tide. It's so fine that it feels silky between my toes as I walk.

I wander to the edge of the water and paddle. The water is so clear that I can see my feet. I can see worm casts in the sand below the surface, as well as bits of seaweed and shells. Further out to sea the water is stunning azure, reflecting the blue sky and making it look, for want of a better phrase, Caribbean. And yet we are so very far from the tropics.

Even so, the water is inviting. I have no towel or costume with me, so if I want to swim I shall have to skinny dip. What the hell. I put it to Liz. There is no one about, so why not? We strip quickly and run at full speed into the water, as if going any slower would allow us to change our minds halfway. We run into the water and almost fall in, porpoising into deeper water. It's cold, but without the tentative inching reserved for colder seas, we catch our breath quickly and begin to stroke out into the bay. Treading water 20 metres (yards) offshore we can still see our feet below us when we peer into the water because it is so clear. We laugh as we swim slowly back to shore. I never thought I'd be doing this in Scotland. We are like children, giggling at our own naughtiness and laughing at our good fortune to find a little stretch of deserted sand and exercise our right to the ultimate in Scottish freedom.

We dress slowly, allowing the warm breeze to dry us. My skin prickles as the fabric of my T-shirt slides over the goosebumps on my arms, but I don't feel cold in the least. In fact, I feel the opposite. My heart is racing and I feel warm and alive. For once I have done more than just look at the Scottish landscape. I have dived in, head and heart first, and I feel on top of the world.

THE DRIVING

Driving on Harris is exhilarating, and also slow on the lesser roads, of which there aren't many. In fact, apart from stretches of the A859, it's all pretty much the same. Expect single-track roads with passing places. That said, the passing spaces are always marked with a white sign, which means you can make judgements as to when to pull over and when to carry on if you see another car approaching. Or you could simply play chicken.

The snorkel trail has a beginning and end at Tarbert – its central point – and spreads out east and west from there. To the west there are two spots along the B887, a fantastic road that dips and weaves along the north side of West Loch Tarbert. There are spectacular views all along the length of the road towards Taransay and South Harris and even a massively incongruous but quite pretty castle about halfway along the 9-mile (15-kilometre) stretch at Loch Leosavay. Along this stretch there is also an old whaling station that is largely derelict, except for the brick chimney. It's possible to stop and wander around and walking on the slipway where the whales were butchered and subsequently processed is quite moving. When I was there a German whale enthusiast was snorkelling for artefacts in the loch.

To the east you'll find one spot on the unnamed road to the island of Scalpay, another snorkelling spot recommended by the Scottish Wildlife Trust. Leaving Tarbert isn't particularly attractive since you have to go past the public recycling depot (good opportunity to do yours) and out of Tarbert's 'suburbs'. However, once you round Urgha Bay and rise to the top of the hill you'll be among the pretty views again. From the top, which is about 50m (165ft) above the sea, you will find some fantastic views. It's also one of the few places on Harris with a half-decent phone signal (network depending) as there is a mast high on the hill. The snorkelling spot, which involves a walk down a hill by a stunning house, is wild and remote and promises a lot of good stuff – reef, cliff and sandy patches – in a small area. While you are going that way it's worth a crawl along the road to the Scalpay Bridge and over to the Isle of Scalpay.

Once back in Tarbert you'll need to head back out of town again on the A859 and to the right-hand turn for the unnamed single-track road that ends at Rhenigidale, the final destination. Along the way you'll stop at Loch Maaruig, which has a different kind of habitat from the other sites. As usual the going is island-like, with narrow roads and passing spaces. And, of course, wonderful views. Enjoy.

PLACES TO STAY

Horgabost Camping And Wild Camping

Horgabost, Isle of Harris, Outer Hebrides, HS3 3HR
web: www.westharristrust.org/camping-2/camping
tel: 01859 550 386

info: *A brilliantly located site overlooking the beach at Horgabost. Popular but still lovely.*

Hushinish

At the time of writing the local community were in the process of building a new visitor centre at Hushinish, which will have toilets and five designated motorhome spaces. This is to encourage campers to avoid damaging the machair and to aid tourism. They have had overcrowding issues with motorhomes so please go carefully and respectfully, don't drive over the machair and don't leave a mess.

Toilets and showers

Harris Tourist Information, Tarbert has a public shower that can be used by motorhomers.

Isle of Harris Sports Centre at Tarbert also has a shower that can be used by motorhomers.

IN THE AREA

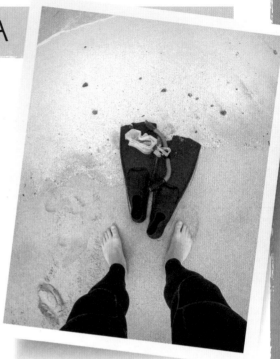

Scottish Wildlife Trust Snorkel Trails Officially organised and researched, these six trails (see map on page 138) give advice and safe places to snorkel for novices and 'advanced' snorkellers. Often their location coincides with the presence of a car parking space or two as Harris has very limited off-road parking, mainly because of the narrow roads and difficult terrain. Even so, the six locations will give you a great start in exploring Harris's underwater life, and the water is amazingly clear, too!

- https://www.scottishwildlife trust.org.uk/things-to-do/ snorkel-trails/

Nearest van hire

Harris Classic Campers, Seilebost
- www.harrisclassiccampers.co.uk

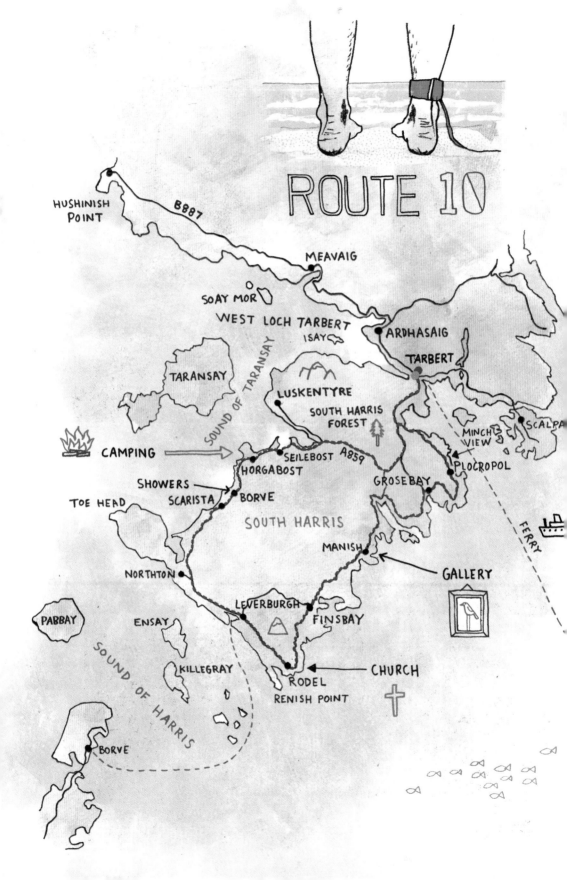

ROUTE 10

HUSHINISH POINT

B887

MEAVAIG

SOAY MOR

WEST LOCH TARBERT

ISAY

ARDHASAIG

TARBERT

TARANSAY

SOUND OF TARANSAY

LUSKENTYRE

SOUTH HARRIS FOREST

MINCH VIEW

SCALPA

CAMPING

SEILEBOST

A859

HORGABOST

PLOCROPOL

SHOWERS

GROSEBAY

TOE HEAD

SCARISTA

BORVE

SOUTH HARRIS

MANISH

FERRY

GALLERY

NORTHTON

PABBAY

ENSAY

LEVERBURGH

FINSBAY

SOUND OF HARRIS

KILLEGRAY

RODEL

CHURCH

RENISH POINT

BORVE

TARBERT TO TARBERT

SEEING THE BIGGER PICTURE

South Harris hasn't got many roads, but those that exist allow you to more or less circumnavigate the whole of this part of the island, give or take a few diversions. Each side of the island has its own atmosphere and charm and you can appreciate it only by doing the round tour, as many do. To the west you'll find all the big-hitting white-sand beaches, while the east offers inlets and winding, soaring roads over barren moor and bog, with views of Skye and the Minches.

BEST FOR:
The world's best beaches, wild lowland moonscapes

START/END:
Tarbert

MILEAGE:
50 miles (80 kilometres)

DAYS TO
EXPLORE: **2–3**

OS LAND-
RANGER
MAP: **14, 18**

ISLANDS

151

Arriving on an island is always a thrill. Whatever the weather, I love to stand on deck and take in as much as I can. If I have done my homework then I'll have an idea of what is what and where I need to be heading, but there is only so much you can glean from a map. You don't get the smell of the land or the smiles on people's faces as they prepare to come home, perhaps for the first time in a while, or the apprehension and excitement as passengers ready themselves to see somewhere new for the first time. Even when it's in the UK, going somewhere different will always give you a culture shock of some kind. It might be something simple, like the way people greet you or the fact that you can't shop on a Sunday, but it can still take some kind of adjustment, and the experience is enriched for it.

I drive off the ferry at Tarbert slowly. We are one of the last vehicles to disembark and I don't want to follow everyone else blindly or drift with the traffic. I have been here before, but my attitude is different to how it was at the last visit. I have a plan and I am determined to make the most of every second on this magical island. I came in less happy times, when camping was a struggle and opportunities went sailing by for one reason or another. I left from Tarbert the last time I came to the Hebrides, some five years ago, having not seen much of West Harris, deeply regretting having to leave so soon. Things have changed for the better since, so this is my big return, when I need to make things right for myself.

The port is tiny, and Tarbert is even smaller. We park up in the town's main car park and have a wander. It has a couple of hotels, a few small supermarkets, a hardware store that sells absolutely everything (or so it seems, on the surface). However, it soon becomes clear that you might need to bring most of your camping kit with you, apart from your food supplies: there isn't much here so don't count on getting it when you arrive. It's part of the charm. We saddle up and head out of town to look for a place to park up for the night.

We drive south, on the island's west coast road, the A859. Almost immediately we leave the buildings behind and enter a rough, tough landscape of Lewisian gneiss, sparkling lochs and dark, peaty bogs. Cotton grass and bog beans wave in the breeze as we sweep around long bends on the single-track road. It's stark, perhaps a little forbidding and barren in many ways, but Liz is thrilled to be here. Instead of a 'lunar' landscape she sees detail in the flora that's in full, energetic bloom in the summer sunshine. Every time I get out of the van to take pictures she kneels down in the grass to investigate something new, conjuring up the Latin names like mantras.

Progress is slow. We are looking at too much detail. We fuss over and get excited about the little things, determined to take it all in with one great big breath.

But then we approach the estuary at Luskentyre and we suddenly see the big picture. In fact it's about as big a picture as we have ever seen. We follow the main road along the south side of the river, slack-jawed and in silence. I stop at Seilebost so we can take it all in. Before us is a version of

heaven, as many would see it. The sun is out and we are looking at a wide estuary of white sand. The water is shallow and blue. A family of four, with dad towing one of the kids in a dinghy, wade out to an island in the middle of the estuary. The water is about knee deep. Also wading, sea birds search in the sand for titbits while overhead birds of prey swirl on the thermals. Behind the sands lie the dunes and the machair, Scotland's colourful grasslands. Behind that, and at the edges of the beach, are glacier-rounded clumps of cool-grey Lewisian gneiss. Offshore the surf tumbles through the haze on to a silver sandbar. Save for the family and a few walkers it's deserted. This is what we came here for. This is West Harris, famous for its beaches and wild Hebridean landscapes. It could be the Caribbean, for all the colours in the water, as many would have said, but it isn't, because it's remote and to the far north and we are very, very lucky to have caught it on a good day.

We drive on, eager to find a spot at which to camp and surf. We pass the beaches at Horgabost and Borve (Na Buirgh) and round a bend to Scarista, a long sweep of white sand backed by the mountains of Toe Head. The surf looks good, with whale tails of spray arcing off the back of the sets as they roll in and break with a distant crack.

We find a gateway and follow it on to a parking spot by the beach, strolling over crunching sand to check the waves. When I see the surf I am apprehensive about jumping straight into the water. It's looking good, but unfamiliar. And there's nowhere to stop between here and Canada! As we

debate getting into our wetsuits and paddling out, a Dutch couple arrive and pull boards out of their car. We get chatting. They know the place well and have been coming back for years to this spot to surf. They camp and surf here often. The sea, they say, is kind, although the waves are good. It's all we need to hear and in moments we are suiting up in the sunshine. It's a big moment for me. I needed to come back here to put the ghosts of past visits to bed. I needed to surf this island to make me feel new again.

We walk over the dunes, breaking the crust of the silky white sand. Apart from the Dutch couple in the sea we are the only ones on the beach. I bend down to tie my surfboard leash to my ankle, looking up at the waves. I squint at the sparkling water. After a year of turmoil I am about to enter the ocean and come out of the other side. I straighten up, pick up my board and walk into the cool, clear, churning and cleansing water of the North Atlantic.

THE DRIVING

The only way of getting to know South Harris is to go and see it. And that means driving around it, taking a big loop around its perimeter from Tarbert and ending up back in Tarbert again. Once you have driven the loop, stopped a few times and taken it all in you can begin to meander a little. Just remember to take your time. You can't rush this slow road, no matter how good the surf or how much you can't leave the mainland ways behind.

The A859 is the main road on Harris. In fact, for a long time it was the only road, simply because of the geography. The west coast is sandy, with wide estuaries allowing for easy access from Tarbert to Rodel (Roghadal) at the very southern tip. Inland from the west it's mountainous, and there are few roads to speak of, but at least it's a solid, tangible landscape with a beginning and an end. It's a forgiving landscape and it's easy to see why it's so popular with tourists searching for solitude or wide, empty beaches. As soon as you hit the west coast, at Seilebost and the estuary at Luskentyre (Losgaintir) it's all 'wow's until you reach the end of the road. Even there, at the former historic capital of Harris, Rodel, it's seemingly benign, with a beautiful 16th-century gneiss church presiding over a lovely loch. With dappled light hitting the field and illuminating the church it could easily be somewhere in the Lake District, or even, dare I say, the Cotswolds. The village is deceptively bucolic and most definitely pastoral, on the surface at least.

However, to know West Harris is not to know South Harris. The east side of the island is a complete contrast to the west side. Of course it can be approached from either end, from Rodel or from Tarbert, but I tackled it from the north, taking the first turn off the A859, which is signposted to 'The Golden Road'. There is little information about why it's called that, but a little digging reveals that it was so called because of the apparent cost of building it.

The Golden Road, a road without a number, is just a small section of the road between Tarbert and Rodel, running from Ceann Dibig on the A859 and Grosebay (Greosabhagh), although the term is often used to describe the entire length of the winding, narrow, twisting and turning route.

The Golden Road, as I understand it, started off as a track in 1897, used primarily by children to get to school, and didn't become the route it is today until 1947, because of local politics, cost and, possibly of most relevance, the difficulty in mapping a solid route through the landscape. Once you turn off and start to drive the road you'll see why the locals used to get around by boat most of the time. It's extremely tricky terrain, filled with lochs and bogs, peaks, inlets and steep cliffs. There is none of the gently undulating estuarine sands of the west. Instead it's rocky, tough and seemingly barren (unless you take a botanist with you). That said, it's a great drive, if a little slow, with fantastic views, tiny ports and moments of rugged, sublime beauty. Along the length you'll encounter wild moors contrasting with calm, lily-filled lochs and occasionally the tamed gardens of islanders eager to create an oasis among the chaos of Scotland's rockiest low-level scenery.

There are ways of cutting short the journey by looping back to the A859 at Grosebay and Aird Mighe but I'd recommend going the whole way otherwise you'll miss the great views and those moments of absolute beauty that you'll find along the way.

Strung along this coast there are weavers, artists and plenty of small-scale cottage industries. The Mission House Studio is one such place. Outside, this retains its sombre looks as a former chapel but inside it has been transformed into a beautiful, open art space with fabulous work from the resident ceramicist and photographer. I can see why artists would want to set up shop here. It's inspiring, wild and untamed for the most part. Summer trade along the route, with little else to stop for, I assume, is good. At least it was when I visited. Having said that, I doubt we should ever underestimate the life of artists brave enough to live at the edge. Your support, I am sure, would be appreciated.

There are a couple of campsites along the route but not many places to pull off the main road and stop, simply because of the terrain. Campsites are at Fleadabay and Minch View. There is also a seal-spotting stop at Aird Mighe, with a handy telescope on a mound for easier observation (at a cost).

This part of the route is to savour, for it soon ends. Stop where you can and take pictures because you'll miss it when you hit the west coast and enjoy the easy life among the dunes. Admire the scenery, visit the weavers and artists who eke out a living here and enjoy this most wild of places that, until less than 75 years ago, didn't have a proper road. Take it slow. Enjoy the route.

PLACES TO STAY

West Harris Trust Camping Spots The West
Harris Trust was set up in 2010 to revitalise the villages along the
west coast of Harris. This has led to a positive attitude towards
motorhomers looking for places to wild camp. It's a great thing for
the community to do and we all applaud it. However, let's not forget
that staying here is a privilege not a right by keeping it clean and tidy
and ensuring we leave it well and make donations when asked for.
Camping spots are at:

- Seilebost School (nightly fee including hook-up)
- Talla na Mara (nightly fee including hook-up)
- Seilebost and Luskentyre (£5 donation)

web: www.westharristrust.org/camping-2/camping

Toilets and showers
Harris Tourist Information,
Tarbert has a public shower that
can be used by motorhomers.

Isle of Harris Sports Centre
at Tarbert also has a shower that
can be used by motorhomers.

There are showers at
Talla na Mara (see page 163).

Horgabost Camping
Horgabost, Isle of Harris,
HS3 3HR
web: www.westharristrust.org/
camping-2/camping
tel: 01859 550 386

info: *Insanely brilliant location
right on the machair. As a result
it's busy, but hey, that beach!*

IN THE AREA

Isle of Harris Distillers Right by the port in Tarbert, the Isle of Harris Distillers have a different view of how things should be done. They have created a 'social distillery' as part of their contribution to the island, helping to galvanise the community. There is a canteen, shop and, of course, you can go on a tour. • www.harrisdistillery.com

Harris Tweed Isle of Harris shop Warehouse and shop of tweedy delights, all hand woven in the Outer Hebrides. Great for picking up that jacket or a peaked cap, or just about anything you can think of. However, if you want sharp style, maybe best to buy a few yards of fabric and have it made up when you get home. • www.harristweedisleofharris.co.uk

Talla na Mara A fantastic Community Enterprise Centre owned and managed by the residents of West Harris. Facilities include campervan hook-ups, showers (pay by donation), chemi-loo disposal, a gallery, artists' studios and craft workshops, a performance space for film, theatre and live music events, office spaces and a restaurant. • westharristrust.org/talla-na-mara

The Mission House Lovely gallery featuring the work of photographer Beka Globe and ceramic artist Nickolai Globe. • http://missionhousestudio.co.uk

St Clement's Church, Rodel
16th-century Lewisian gneiss church that's 'the finest medieval building in the Hebrides'. Looked after by Historic Scotland.
• www.historicenvironment.scot/visit-a-place/places/st-clements-church

Nearest van hire

Harris Classic Campers, Seilebost
• www.harrisclassiccampers.co.uk

**Western Isles Campers,
Fort William**
• www.westernislescampers.co.uk

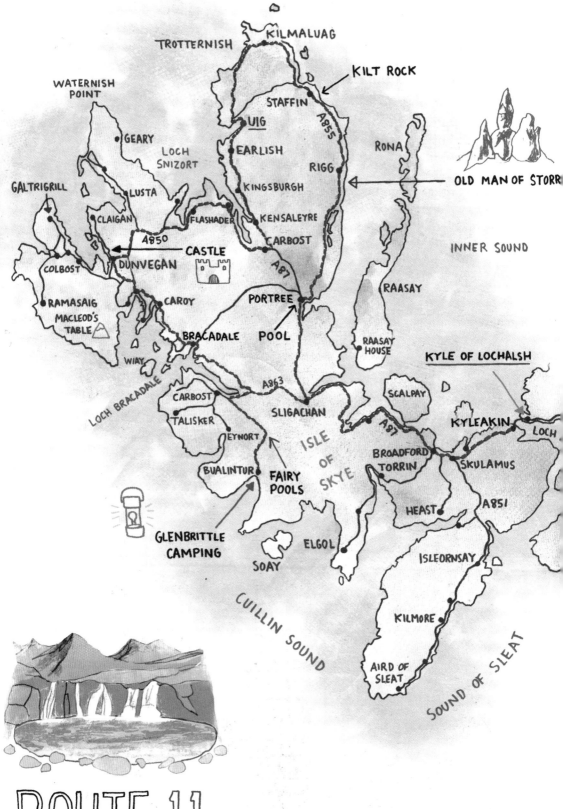

KILMALUAG

TROTTERNISH

WATERNISH POINT

KILT ROCK

STAFFIN

A855

UIG

GEARY

LOCH SNIZORT

EARLISH

RONA

GALTRIGRILL

LUSTA

RIGG

KINGSBURGH

OLD MAN OF STORR

CLAIGAN

FLASHADER

KENSALEYRE

INNER SOUND

A850

CARBOST

COLBOST

CASTLE

DUNVEGAN

A87

RAASAY

RAMASAIG
MACLEOD'S TABLE

CAROY

PORTREE

RAASAY HOUSE

POOL

KYLE OF LOCHALSH

WIAY

BRACADALE

LOCH BRACADALE

A863

SCALPAY

CARBOST

SLIGACHAN

A87

KYLEAKIN

LOCH

TALISKER

ISLE OF SKYE

BROADFORD

SKULAMUS

EYNORT

FAIRY POOLS

TORRIN

BUALINTUR

HEAST

A851

GLENBRITTLE CAMPING

ELGOL

ISLEORNSAY

SOAY

CUILLIN SOUND

KILMORE

AIRD OF SLEAT

SOUND OF SLEAT

ROUTE 11

RETURN TO SKYE

LOOKING TO THE SKY ON SKYE

A figure-of-eight around Skye taking in the best of the natural wonders and some of the best views. Swim in Fairy Pools, climb the Old Man of Storr and explore wild beaches, vertical cliffs, open moorland and high mountains on this magical, popular island. It's easy to get to, which means it's popular in summer and attracts large numbers of visitors eager to discover the very best in island life. Skye has it all, and more. With luck you'll have more success seeing the Northern Lights than I did. Keep an eye out for clear skies.

BEST FOR:
Natural wonders

START: Kyle of Lochalsh

END: Kyle of Lochalsh/Uig

MILEAGE:
220 miles (355 kilometres)

DAYS TO EXPLORE: 4–5

OS LAND-RANGER MAP:
23, 32

ISLANDS

165

It's a nasty, late-October night, so I have retreated to the Merchant Bar in Portree. I find a seat in the corner and take out my notebook to write up the last few days of exploring. I order a pint of golden ale and look around the bar. It's cosy and warm. A few of the tables are occupied by American, European and Japanese tourists. I feel a small wave of culture shock as I listen for accents and languages. I haven't been in a pub for a while, never mind enjoyed the company of fellow tourists – because I have just arrived on a boat from a very quiet and uncrowded North Uist. It occurs to me that the Outer Hebrides, although just an hour or so away by ferry, may be just a step too far for your average tourist. If you need to see all of Scotland in a week it's too distant, too remote, too difficult and not varied enough to warrant taking the time. Skye, on the other hand, offers it all: culture, natural wonders, amazing scenery and nice, cosy pubs.

Now that the weather has broken and a dreary drizzle has set in from the west, I am glad I went the extra mile to get a few days of glorious sunshine and solitude. I needed the remoteness. But now things have changed. Skye is different, it seems. Connected to the mainland by the magnificent arched Skye Bridge across the Kyle of Lochalsh, it's a relatively easy ride to get here.

I sip my pint and look out of the window at the wet road leading to the harbour that's being lashed by waves of windy mizzle. I can see glimpses of the port through the swishing branches of the sycamores that line the way down the hill to the quayside, although I can't see the van. It is parked next to the water, just yards from the working fishing boats, bars and chip shops. I couldn't find anywhere better for an overnight in the darkness and all the campsites are closed at this time of the year, so it's a last-resort overnighter that I am actually really enjoying.

I get a text. It's a bit of a surprise because I've been without a decent signal for days. And it's even more of a surprise to get a text from Liz, at home in Bude. She tells me there is a red alert for the Northern Lights, something we have talked about previously. Ever hopeful, she is currently standing on the cliffs above Wrangles Rocks searching the northern sky. In her text she wonders if I am still in Scotland and can I see the aurora? Surely I would be able to with an alert like that? She's right. A red alert is about as good as it gets when it comes to the aurora borealis so it's exciting to be in the right place at the right time. Disappointingly, however, there's no point in me going outside. I know there's no chance of seeing this magical phenomenon because of the street lights and the cloud cover. I sip my pint and reply: no chance, but Scotland is lovely, I could disappear here.

We'd miss you, she replies.

The next day I drive around the north-western tip of Skye. I hike up to the Old Man of Storr in the rain, I take photographs, say hello to groups of Japanese and American tourists, stop at Staffin to admire the view, jolly myself along with jelly babies and chat on the radio. I have been in the van for ten days and the presence of other people in the pub last night – and my texts from home – reminds me that, actually, despite the twisted romantic notions of being alone on an island, it's time to go back to Bude. I take the A87 from Uig through the big beautiful heart of Skye and on to the bridge over the Kyle of Lochalsh. The clouds clear for a few moments as I approach Loch Sligachan, giving me a momentary glimpse of the thin blue skies behind, but it's gone too soon.

Eight months later, I am lying in the van at Glenbrittle Campsite, on the west coast, waiting, half asleep, for the alarm to go off. Liz is asleep beside me. As it's July it got dark only about two hours ago, at around 10.30pm.

We are exhausted from the drive and from exploring the western half of the island but we are determined to put this aurora thing to bed once and for all. We have a clear sky, for the first time in a while, and our phones have been pinging with amber alerts, while we've had signal. So things are good, but not 100 per cent perfect. Even so, I agree to get up at 2am, well before the dawn, to search the northern sky.

I love being so far north at this time of the year. The days are incredibly long with just under 18 hours of daylight to look forward to and plenty more half-light to eke out the best of the summertime. On Harris we got up early to surf before the rest of the world was awake and stayed up late watching the sun's glow on the horizon. Between dawn and dusk we explored, not fearing the oncoming of night like we do at home in Cornwall, where we have around four hours of daylight less each day.

Of course it isn't the most conducive time to search for the aurora borealis because what we need for that is night, a dark sky and no light pollution. It's the main reason most people go searching in the winter. The more darkness you experience, the more chance you have of catching it – if there is any geomagnetic activity! However, if you want dark skies and no light pollution, Glen Brittle couldn't be better. It's a long drive from the A863 at Drynoch over wild, treeless moorland, past the Fairy Pools and down to the beach at Loch Brittle. There are no streetlights and no lights from any dwellings to interfere with the night sky.

Finally the alarm buzzes. Liz stirs. We dress quickly and quietly and open the van door, walking the few yards on to the sand. We turn and look back to the north, hopeful, ever hopeful that something will show for us. I set up the camera to take a 30-second exposure, taking care to get the settings right. The Northern Lights can sometimes be seen by a camera when it is invisible to the naked eye so this is a safeguard in case we miss it. I click the shutter and wait. The image shows the dark mountains, stars, a few wispy clouds and a faint glow of light beyond the horizon that's probably nothing more than the last light of the sun or the first light of the dawn. It's difficult to tell, since at this time of the year the sun sets in the north-west and rises in the north-east.

It's hard not to be disappointed, but we still count our lucky stars. The last time Liz was on Skye was more than 30 years ago. The last time I was here I was alone. It's a still, dark night and we are the only ones awake. For all we know we could be the only ones on Skye tonight. It's a beautiful feeling. And while we haven't yet put the aurora borealis to bed we have every reason to visit and try again.

THE DRIVING

Skye is an easy place to get to compared with many of the Scottish islands, thanks to the Skye Bridge. In fact, you might as well consider it to be part of the mainland, despite what the letters I will receive will tell me.

Yet in spite of its proximity it's still a wild and beautiful place, with lots to see and do and plenty of great – and some not so great – roads to drive. Climbers come here to take on 12 of the toughest of Scotland's Munros while sea kayakers love the relatively calm inshore waters and inaccessible bays and inlets.

For drivers and motorhomers it's a way to get to somewhere else, but also a destination in itself. The main road, the A87, runs between the Skye Bridge and Uig, the jumping-off point for North Uist and Harris, via Portree. It also forms part of a figure-of-eight loop that takes in the north-east and north-west peninsulas of the island, with a diversion to Glen Brittle to see the Fairy Pools.

From the Skye Bridge the A87 heads first west and then north-west around Broadford Bay and Loch Ainort. It then skirts around the Cuillins, offering magnificent scenery and views, especially at Sligachan where the loch head meets the foothills at the Sligachan Hotel and Campsite. There is a bar here that has more than 400 Scottish malt whiskies and that is a multiple winner of Whisky Bar of The Year. At Sligachan you can choose to take the A863 up on to the moorland towards Drynoch to begin the left-hand loop. It's a good, two-lane road that winds up into the northern reaches of the Cuillins before the turn-off for the B8009 to Carbost – where you'll find the Talisker distillery – and Portnalong, and after a couple of miles, the Fairy Pools and Glen Brittle.

The road to Glen Brittle isn't easy, partly because of the single track, but mostly because of the number of cars on the road. The Fairy Pools are incredibly popular so expect lots of hire cars not really understanding the nature of the passing places, coupled with some terrible parking at the side of the road. However, it's a great drive after the pools into a magnificent glen and then down to the loch and the campsite. Sadly it's also a cul-de-sac so you'll have to navigate your way back up and out again before continuing on the A863 along Skye's west coast to Dunvegan where you pick up the A850 to Borve. As always it's a beautiful road that's a laid-back and easy drive with no need to rush. We stopped at Bracadale to watch a bird of prey flying overhead and the shadows of the clouds race across the loch and fields opposite.

The A850 joins the A87 again after Portree, so if you don't want to miss some fantastic sections of the route, the best advice would be to continue past the A863 turn-off and save it for later by travelling along the A87 through Glen Varagill towards Portree and then taking the A855 along the east coast into Trotternish. This is where the roads start to get a little more interesting with a fabulous view of the Old Man of Storr as you approach Loch Leathan. The views over to Raasay are incredible, especially from the Old Man, and the path on the way up. It's a steep climb but if the clouds part it's magnificent. Expect tourists in inappropriate footwear.

A little further along the road you'll come to Kilt Rock and Mealt Falls, a basalt cliff that, rather handily, looks like a kilt and its matching waterfall that tumbles into the sea. There is a viewing point. You can't miss it since there will, inevitably, be busloads of tourists stopping too.

At Staffin the road reverts to the beloved single track with passing places. The car park for walks into the Quiraing, one of Scotland's most beautiful landscapes, is here. On the north side of the peninsula the road cuts across the tip and then returns to the coast at Duntulm where a wild rocky beach leads to tall vertical cliffs and hillsides of scree. It's pretty wild along this section, with the road following the contours of the hillsides as they slope off into the sea below, eventually leading you past hamlets and houses with magnificent views before taking you steeply into Uig via a sharp hairpin bend. Uig is a great place to stop for supplies of beer from the Isle of Skye Brewing Company or cake from the cafe next door. Maps and fishing tackle are available at the garage as well as last-minute gas and camping stuff for the Hebrides.

From Uig it's a busy (especially if the ferry has disembarked) but easy drive up the hill and out of town (great views), along the west coast of the Trotternish peninsula and along the side of the wonderfully named Loch Snizort and back to Portree.

PLACES TO STAY

Glenbrittle Campsite and Café
Glenbrittle, Isle of Skye, IV47 8TA
web: www.dunvegancastle.com/your-visit/
glenbrittle-campsite-cafe/glenbrittle-campsite
email: glenbrittle@dunvegancastle.com
tel: 01478 640 404

info: *Perfect base for exploring the Cuillin Mountains and right on the beach. A wild camping experience, in the wilds, but with facilities and a coffee machine.*

Sligachan Hotel
Sligachan, Isle of Skye, IV47 8SW
web: www.sligachan.co.uk/camping
email: reservations@sligachan.co.uk
tel: 01478 650 204

info: *A beautiful site adjacent to the A87 main road and run by the Sliagach Hotel.*

Kinloch Campsite
Dunvegan, Isle of Skye, IV55 8WQ
web: www.kinloch-campsite.co.uk
email: info@kinloch-campsite.co.uk
tel: 01470 521 531/07732 897 511

info: *A waterside site near Dunvegan Castle, one of Skye's most popular attractions.*

Torvaig Campsite
Portree, Isle of Skye, IV51 9HU
web: www.portreecampsite.co.uk
tel: 01478 611 849

info: *Close to Portree, Skye's main town.*

IN THE AREA

Fairy Pools A series of 'magical' pools in Glen Brittle with natural arches, big jumps and world-famous wild swimming. Busy but worth the walk. Bring swimmers.

Dunvegan Castle The heart of the MacLeod Estate, a fairy tale castle with five separate buildings offering a timeline of the estate's history, starting in the 1200s. You can also see the Fairy Flag, a 4th-century artefact either from the faeries or from the Crusades...
• www.dunvegancastle.com

Dinosaur prints on Staffin Beach You better believe it. A few million years ago a family of dinosaurs walked on Staffin beach. Go find.

Kilt Rock Sea cliffs in north-east Trotternish. Vertical columns of basalt form the pleats. Handy for tourism, but also very pretty.

Nearest van hire

Western Isles Campers, Fort William
• www.westernislescampers.co.uk

Happy Highland Campers, Inverness
• www.happyhighland campers.co.uk

Old Man of Storr The most popular natural wonder on Skye, the Old Man is a pinnacle of rock, and the highest point on the Trotternish Ridge. There is a well-made path from a car park to the pinnacle, from which the views are astounding. Everyone goes, so you must too.

SOUTH AND CENTRAL SCOTLAND

Don't set your sights on Scotland and drive past the Scottish Borders, Dumfries and Galloway or the Trossachs without stopping for a look. You might miss something spectacular. The hills might not be as high or the lochs so deep but there is plenty to keep you interested. There are also lots of fantastic slow road alternatives to the motorway if you are heading north and plenty of scope for fabulous coastal driving if you arrive from Ireland. And if you like cycling there is some of the best mountain biking in the world.

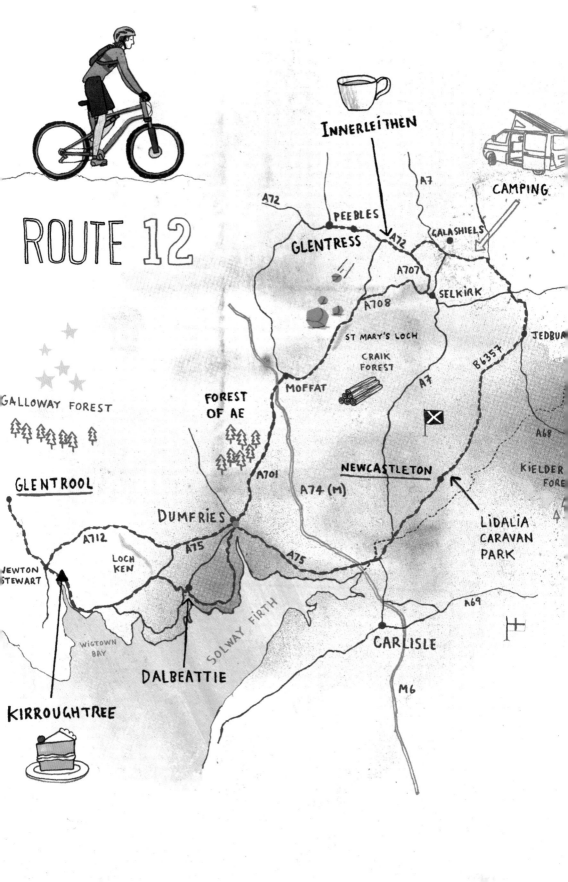

ROUTE 12

INNERLEITHEN

CAMPING

A72

A7

PEEBLES

GLENTRESS

GALASHIELS

A72

A707

SELKIRK

A708

JEDBUR

ST MARY'S LOCH

CRAIK FOREST

B6357

GALLOWAY FOREST

FOREST OF AE

MOFFAT

A7

GLENTROOL

A701

NEWCASTLETON

KIELDER FORE

A74 (M)

A68

DUMFRIES

LIDALIA CARAVAN PARK

A712

LOCH KEN

A75

A75

NEWTON STEWART

A69

WIGTOWN BAY

SOLWAY FIRTH

CARLISLE

DALBEATTIE

M6

KIRROUGHTREE

THE 7STANES FIGURE-OF-EIGHT

DOWNHILL ALL THE WAY

Best for bikers, walkers and families looking for adventure, this fantastic, 250-mile (400-kilometre)-long, figure-of-eight route in southern scotland takes in the 7stanes cycle routes.

All seven of the 7stanes are located on Forestry Commission land and offer 'world-class' mountain-biking trails, ranging from easy family-friendly green routes through the forest to bum-busting black runs down terrifyingly steep and tricky, specially made paths. There's something for every kind of rider, even ones like me who rarely place backside on saddle, and certainly *never in anger*.

BEST FOR:
Mountain biking and exploring Scotland's forestry

START/END:
Dumfries

MILEAGE:
250 miles (400 kilometres)

DAYS TO EXPLORE: 4–5 **(with two rides a day)**

OS LAND-RANGER MAP:
77, 78, 83, 84, 79, 73

I am ten years old again.

I haven't felt like I was ten years old in a long time. I won't say how long, but suffice to say it feels so good to live briefly, in the moment, with abandon, like I did when I was a child, tearing it up in the woods on a dodgy second-hand bike. All that matters is the air in my lungs, the branches touching my bare legs and the feeling of the cold January air on my face as I hurtle downhill. I am on the verge of being out of control and I absolutely love it.

When I was ten I spent many evenings in my local woods, on my bike, riding around the 'dips' – a series of huge Second World War bomb craters. In those dips my friends and I pioneered a series of jumps and berms that we rode again and again and again. It was a perfect time. No matter my mum was working or my dad was somewhere in Africa selling lorries to dictators. No matter the school bullies.
No matter anything.

That's how I feel now, on this cold and misty hillside in Scotland. I am in the Borders, near Newcastleton, on my first mountain-biking adventure on the 7stanes, a series of world-class mountain-bike routes. The light is fading fast, even though it's only about 4pm. Liz and I had been lost, but not any more. We have just located the way out of the wilderness to the north of Kielder Forest, a vast, forestry-run plantation, smattered with unsigned tracks and logging roads. We had missed a waymarker and

cycled a few miles too many up a steep track, but now we are haring down the right track towards our campsite, the pub and warmth. Nothing else matters except reaching the bottom. I am cautious but this soon changes. We hit a section of sharp turns and berms, mini jumps and S-bends. My confidence – and recklessness – grows. I pedal faster, ease off the brakes, and soon I am ten again.

It's a great reintroduction to cycling and I am grateful for the push that Liz has given me to link up each of the 7stanes in a big figure-of-eight loop. It's a perfect route, a slow road with even slower interludes of pedal-powered travel that takes in glens, lochs, open parkland and rolling hills typical of the Southern Uplands. It takes us four days to drive the route and cycle five of the seven routes. Some we cut short because of the fading light, others we do twice, just for the hell of it, because we can.

Our favourite of the 7stanes, at Kirroughtree, has a cafe, bike shop, jet wash for cleaning bikes and hot showers for cleaning ourselves. The Blue Route follows a winding course through the woods and down a series of long wooden boardwalks over a boggy forest floor, ending in an exciting final section with big banked curves and jumps. Of all the routes we cycle it is the one that makes me feel more like the boy I used to be.

The single-tracked routes, at most of the 7stanes centres, are purpose built, with little sections of tree roots, manicured stone or larger drops, and

jumps that are designed to test your skills. There are fast downhills and winding uphills, sections of forestry track with stunning views and lovely reveals, as well as cruises for kids or people who don't want to hare about like ten-year-olds. And if you don't like the riding you can always push up the steepest sections, just to see the views.

I defy anyone active to fail to get something out of the 7stanes. Even if it's a slice of cake in the cafe afterwards.

THE DRIVING

The 7stanes can be linked up with a figure-of-eight route centred on Dumfries, about 12.5 miles (20km) from junction 17 of the A74 (M) at Lockerbie. That makes it an easy foray into Scotland for those travelling north from England. The A74 bisects the eastern loop twice, which means it's possible to start at a number of points along its length.

I travelled from England, at the routes' southernmost point – junction 22 of the A74 (M) – where the A6071 passes through Hobbit-like countryside before joining up with the A7 and then veering off along the border on the B6357 and the beautiful Liddesdale.

First stop is Newcastleton, a smart, 19th-century 'new town' of ordered streets and laid-out squares, where the Lidalia Caravan and Motorhome Club site offers a perfectly located overnight that's right on the trailhead for the two 7stanes runs. You can pitch up and kit up on site as it's only around 100m (yards) from the start.

From Newcastleton the route continues along the border on the B6357 towards Jedburgh and then follows the spectacular A68 and A6091 to Melrose. It's a winding affair that wends its way along Liddle Water through

dark forestry plantations and, occasionally, out into the light above the treeline. At Saughtree the landscape opens up as you begin to descend towards the A68, revealing the low hills of the Cheviot Hills and the occasional distant peak. This isn't the Highlands by any means, but it's a wild and empty landscape dotted with fields, dark patches of forestry and open moorland.

The A68 offers long vistas and castle views as it weaves through Jedburgh on the way to Galalshiels and the Tweed Valley on the A6091 and A72. Here you encounter the trails at Glentress and Innerleithen. Of the two, Glentress has the better facilities, with a cafe and bike shop, while Innerleithen offers a series of serious red and orange extreme downhill trails in a quiet corner of the Tweed Valley. All you can hear is the rush of adrenaline. At Glentress it's the sound of cake being ridden off.

The road from Glentress offers the most spectacular drive of all. Follow the A72, then A701 to Selkirk. The A708 leaves Selkirk and then sets off upstream along the Yarrow Water to St Mary's Loch and a spectacular pass through the Moffat Water Valley. It's one of those roads that gives moments of utter joy as you pass through boulder-strewn, steep-sided valleys with tumbling falls adjoining every few metres. We stop, take a few pictures, find snow and chuck a few snowballs before climbing quickly back into the van. The wind is cold on our faces, making our ruddied cheeks ache as we grin with the wildness of it all. This is what the slow road is all about for me: taking the

chance to stop, take stock and admire the journey and the places it takes you.

After the A708 hits Moffat and the A74(M) the route heads west towards the Forest of Ae on the A701. The next 7stanes stop is at Ae itself, and offers a cafe and shop, along with a mixture of trails for riders of all abilities. One of the extreme routes, 'The Shredder', sounds ominous. We don't ride it, instead continuing on to Dalbeattie, number five on our list of seven. Once through Dumfries, the route follows the Nith estuary on the A710 around the coast to the west, offering views over the Solway Firth to Cumbria, and then joins the A75. It looks simple but, just as we get used to an estuarine landscape, the road rises up to pass through a granite boulder field, by a loch or through parkland before skirting a headland and revealing a golden-sanded beach. Every bend in the road brings new riches.

Kirroughtree, our penultimate 7stanes stop-off, offers a fantastic downhill finish to the red, black and blue runs, followed by a hot shower, a jet wash to clean off the bikes and a slice of cake with a cup of tea in the cafe. From Kirroughtree, follow the A75 up the eastern shore of Wigtown Bay

and through Newton Stewart, following the River Cree into the Galloway Forest Park to Glentrool. This is where you pick up the 'Big Country Route', a 36-mile (58-kilometre) epic cycle across the open spaces of Galloway's Dark Sky Park. For the ride back home, and the A74(M), follow the A712 through the park to New Galloway and then on to Dumfries.

PLACES TO STAY

Lidalia Touring Caravan Site
Old Station Road, Moss Road,
Newcastleton, Scottish Borders,
TD9 0RU
web: www.lidalia.co.uk
email: eddie@lidalia.co.uk
tel: 01387 375 587

info: *A small, friendly site with great showers just a minute's cycle from the 7stanes route at Newcastleton. Even in January it was busy with motorhomers and caravanners, so perhaps book a little early. Just be careful how you reverse on to your pitch: we took off the corner of the grass. Sorry, Eddie.*

**Melrose Gibson Park
Caravan Club Site**
High Street, Melrose, Scottish
Borders, TD6 9RY
web: www.caravanclub.co.uk
tel: 01896 822 969

info: *A well-manicured, friendly, 58-pitch club site with smart uniforms and smart loos. Also close to town, restaurants, shops and rugby club. A great stop at which to refresh and fuel up for the next adventure. A short drive from Innerleithen and Glentress 7stanes centres.*

**Garlieston Lodge
Caravan Park**
Burnside Lane, Garlieston,
Wigtownshire, DG8 8BP
web: www.garliestonlodge.co.uk
email: rusty@garliestonlodge.co.uk
tel: 01988 600 641

info: *Adults-only Camping and Caravanning Club CL site with five pitches for caravans and motorhomes and a further three for tents set around a small fishing lake. Traffic-light system for the single loo and shower so you won't stand outside for ages!'*

IN THE AREA

Dark Sky Park The Galloway Forest Park is Britain's first Dark Sky Park. There is very little light pollution in the centre of the park so the chances of seeing the starriest of skies is high. If you get a clear night. However, of course, this being Scotland, you may well find it's not. Even so, to be among such space is very special. Visit the Bruce's Stone in Glen Trool where it is said that Bruce commanded an ambush on English troops in the narrow glen. The Scots dislodged boulders on the slopes above the path and sent them down the steep-sided valley to rout the English force.

Southern Scotland's highest peak, the Merrick (843m or 2,764ft) can be scaled from here. • http://scotland.forestry.gov.uk/forest-parks/galloway-forest-park

Jedburgh It's right on the border so it's seen a lot of action. Mary, Queen of Scots stayed here in 1566, at Mary, Queen of Scots House, although it wasn't called that at the time. The house, which is open to the public, tells the story of the Queen's tragic life, and contains a death mask taken after her execution. Also on offer here is Jedburgh Abbey, one of the finest Norman buildings in Scotland, now ruined but open to the public; and Jedburgh Castle, home of the notorious Jedburgh Jail.
• www.jedburgh.org.uk

An alternative route

From Glentress it's possible to follow the River Tweed to its source. It's a winding, wooded affair that cruises easily out of the treeline and into open moorland around a series of sweeping bends. Beyond the source the road offers incredible views south over Moffat and the steep-sided valley that contains the source of the River Annan. It's a true moment of revelation. Pull over and enjoy the UK at its finest.

Nearest van hire

Classic Camper Holidays, Hawick
• www.classic-camper-holidays.co.uk

Adventure Wagons, Dalkeith
• www.adventure wagons.com

Lowland Motorhome Hire, Newtongrange
• www.lowlandmotor homehire.co.uk

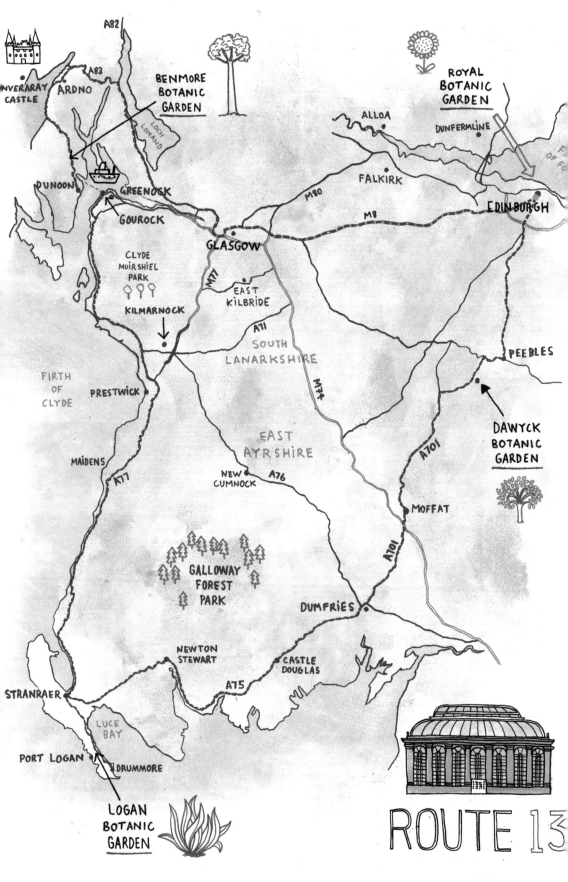

INVERARAY CASTLE
A82
A83
ARDNO
BENMORE BOTANIC GARDEN
LOCH LOMAND
ROYAL BOTANIC GARDEN
ALLOA
DUNFERMLINE
DUNOON
GREENOCK
GOUROCK
FALKIRK
M80
M8
EDINBURGH
F. OF FO
CLYDE MUIRSHIEL PARK
GLASGOW
KILMARNOCK
M77
EAST KILBRIDE
A71
SOUTH LANARKSHIRE
PEEBLES
DAWYCK BOTANIC GARDEN
FIRTH OF CLYDE
PRESTWICK
M74
MAIDENS
A77
EAST AYRSHIRE
NEW CUMNOCK
A76
A701
MOFFAT
A701
GALLOWAY FOREST PARK
DUMFRIES
STRANRAER
NEWTON STEWART
CASTLE DOUGLAS
A75
LUCE BAY
PORT LOGAN
DRUMMORE
LOGAN BOTANIC GARDEN

ROUTE 13

THE BONNIE BOTANY TOUR

FROM GARDEN TO GARDEN LIKE A BEE SEEKING POLLEN

A gigantic 380-mile (610-kilometre) loop around the four gardens of the Royal Botanic Garden Edinburgh. Add in a ferry trip and a cruise up the Firth of Clyde, plus a trip into the Trossachs, and you've got a southern trail to rival the North Coast 500. Wake up to coastal views near Stranraer, drive mountain passes, navigate glens, skirt lochs and strain your neck at the grandeur of 50 gigantic sequoias. Epic!

BEST FOR:
Scotland's best botanic gardens

START/END:
Edinburgh

MILEAGE:
380 miles (610 kilometres)

DAYS TO EXPLORE: 7–8 (to include garden visits)

OS LAND-RANGER MAP:
82, 83, 76, 70, 63, 66, 73, 72, 78

Liz is a botanist. She's a gardener too, speaking to plants by their Latin names, explaining to me with scary binomial accuracy how and why their names reveal their genus and species. At times she forgets the name of some shrub or tree momentarily and searches in her cerebral reserves for reasons to classify the greenery she sees before her. And there it is: genus and species, in a neat and orderly scientific row in her mind. She quotes Fibonacci and the mathematical sequence of seeds in a flower head, striding around the garden like a bee seeking pollen, testing me on genera and challenging me to look at the shape of the flowers, the similarities with other plants, and how many other bits and pieces of botanical anatomy it's got.

I'm lost. I'm enthralled. Liz is in seventh heaven.

Looking up at the 50 sequoias that tower above me, stretching off into the distance along a verdant avenue carpeted with vibrant, early spring grass, I suddenly glimpse the beauty of this place. I see a history of the earth rising up from the elephantine trunks of those giant redwoods. Liz is looking at something at the opposite side of the avenue – while I take myself back to the days when the gardens we are walking through were designed. It must have been the ultimate in exoticism to be able to plant an avenue of 50 Sierra redwoods in your 120-acre back garden. Travel was the internet of its time, so places such as Benmore Botanic Garden near Dunoon were the windows on to the world. With plants brought back from faraway lands you could see, smell and touch the other side better than any painting, writing

or photograph. This is where you'd come to learn about what lay beyond. You could look at those huge trees and imagine yourself there, in majestic forests among the beasts you'd seen stuffed in a museum or snarling at you from a zoological park. Frightening. Literally, awesome. Nowadays we'd log on to a live stream to interact with the people posing in front of the camera. You could see and hear them. But to touch, smell and taste the air?

Somehow, I think, the fragrant bark of the redwood is far, far better.

The Bonnie Botany Tour, imagined by the Royal Botanic Garden in Edinburgh, takes in four of their gardens, near Stranraer, in Edinburgh, near Peebles and near Dunoon, with options for more along the way, if you need more oxygen than the average motorhomer. It is their answer to the North Coast 500 for horticulturalists and green-fingered campers, taking in some of Scotland's best bits as well as some unexpected vistas.

I'm here for the driving, of course, so I can't linger too long over the laburnum, and soon we are away, to Hunter's Quay to catch the ferry to

Greenock on our way to snag the mothership of the gardens we've visited so far, the magnificent Royal Botanic Garden of Edinburgh. We are off-piste, of course, and heading straight there when we should be going south to Stranraer in a big loop, but we've done this the wrong way around. We started out at the M74 just across the border because we travelled from England and it seemed logical to go clockwise. The official route would have had us start in Edinburgh, hiring a motorhome in the city and heading north-west to Stirling and Callander, through the magnificent Trossachs National Park, skirting the top end of Loch Lomond before heading west to the southern shores of Loch Fyne along the A83 at Tarbet. But we're powered by our own steam so we have no need to divert away from our plans.

Until now we've been in the wilds, staying in uncrowded sites or on lonely beaches with no company save for the wind. On this leg though, we realise it's Good Friday, which for many is the start of the camping season. We're too early to stay outside the Royal Botanic Garden as the route is too new and things haven't been sorted yet for motorhomers to overnight in the car park outside the gates. Besides, our fresh tank is empty, the liquefied petroleum gas (LPG) tank is empty and the waste needs sorting out, desperately. We require a site for the night or environmental

disaster looms. Calls are made to all the sites we can find that are in or near Edinburgh, but everything is full, except the site at Musselburgh on the banks of the Firth of Forth.

The drive from Glasgow to Edinburgh is uneventful, save for phone calls. The signal is good, which is a relief, at least. Along the banks of the Clyde there are too many roundabouts and out-of-town shopping centres where we guess once there were shipbuilders, so we pass the time talking about where we have been so far and the countryside we've seen.

The garden at Logan near Drummore on the Mull of Galloway is our first stop. Here, spring comes early, encouraged by the Gulf Stream and the mild maritime climate. It's Scotland's most exotic garden and, even in early April, is awash with colour provided by rhododendrons, magnolias and camellias. For me though, it is the giant tree ferns, gunnera and Cornish palms that steal the show. I am shallow like that because I want drama and the ancient ferns provide it.

The second garden, Benmore at Dunoon, in Argyll and Bute, gives me all I could possibly wish for, and more, in the way of drama. There is nothing subtle about the avenue of 50 giant redwoods that provide the glorious fanfare to your arrival in the grounds. And it goes on from there, with zoned areas giving glimpses into other worlds visited by the explorers and botanists of the day. The garden has more than 300 species of rhododendron, a mighty collection of magnolias and areas devoted to the plants of Bhutan, Chile, Japan and Tasmania.

The third garden, at Edinburgh, is, of course, the highlight. Even someone like me, who has been hardened to garden visits by years of traipsing behind horticulturalist grandparents, can appreciate the magnificent beauty of the 70 acres of immaculate planting and the 11 glasshouses chock-full of orchids, ferns, rain forest riches and tropical wetland plants. With Liz as my guide, I see things I'd never have seen without her aimless and excited wanderings leading me into vegetable gardens, through tropical glasshouses, through the formal gardens and around the boulder-strewn rock garden.

Finally, a stop at what the botanic gardens describe as one of the world's finest arboreta, at Dawyck, where Douglas firs grow side by side with ancient larches, maples, copper beeches and azaleas. For me, a few more trees and a slice of cake and Wi-Fi. For Liz, another world of random wanderings among the trees: she, still in seventh heaven, me, relaxed and happy, ready for the final drive.

Perfect.

THE DRIVING

The Royal Botanic Garden at Edinburgh is the start and finish of this epic drive around Scotland, especially if you are flying in and want to hire a camper or motorhome. As cities go, Edinburgh is one of the finest, with wide streets and a cosmopolitan feel. Stay as long as you like but take the M8 towards Glasgow when it's time to make your escape. It's not wildly exciting for the first section, but once you cross the Clyde on the Erskine Bridge and follow the A82 up the western bank of Loch Lomond it starts to get interesting. As with Route 4, take the A83 at Tarbet up to the Rest and Be Thankful before hitting the southern shores of Loch Fyne on the A815. You'll enjoy fine views of Inveraray Castle opposite as you drive right along the lochside to Strachur, where the A815 turns southwards towards Benmore Garden along the shores of Loch Eck. You'll know when you have reached Benmore as you'll notice the trees get larger here...

From Benmore, travel south on the A815 into Dunoon to take the Western Ferries' crossing to Gourock. Now you're on the coast you'll skirt the shores of the Firth of Clyde until you reach your next stop at Logan Botanic Garden. Follow the A770 south and then join the A78 towards Ayr via Largs and West Kilbride and then turn inland at Ardrossan. At Turnberry the road hugs the coast again, along a stretch of road that's at once beautiful and a bit grubby, busy but isolated.

Continue travelling south on the A77 to Stranraer and take the A716 along the coast on to The Rhinns of Galloway towards Logan Botanic Garden. This is a great part of the drive and includes some lovely stretches of unspoiled costal road, with views over the bay to the Galloway hills.

On leaving Logan Botanic Garden travel north to the A75, which takes you all the way to Dumfries. At Dumfries take the A701 to junction 15 of the M74 where you cross the motorway (don't go on to it) and pass through Moffat before continuing on the A701 to the source of the River Tweed. This will bring you neatly to Dawyck Botanic Garden. From here it's a relatively easy roll back into Edinburgh on the A703. And you're done.

PLACES TO STAY

New England Bay Caravan Club Site
Port Logan, Stranraer, Dumfries and Galloway, DG9 9NX
web: www.caravanclub.co.uk
tel: 01776 860 275

info: *Situated right on the water overlooking Luce Bay and the Mull of Galloway, a Caravan and Motorhome Club site with excellent facilities, direct access to the beach and big, private pitches.*

Edinburgh Caravan Club Site
35–37 Marine Drive, Edinburgh, EH4 5EN
web: www.caravanclub.co.uk
tel: 0131 312 6874

info: *Vast and orderly. Handy for Edinburgh and VERY friendly staff.*

Drummohr Holiday Park
Levenhall, Musselburgh, East Lothian, EH21 8JS
web: www.drummohr.org
email: admin@drummohr.org
tel: 0131 665 6867

info: *Mixed-use holiday park close to Edinburgh and close to the coast on the eastern side of the city. Camping for caravans, campers, motorhomes and also glamping pods and lodges to rent.*

IN THE AREA

The champions of trees at Ardkinglas The European silver fir at Ardkinglas Woodland Garden, situated on the north end of Loch Fyne, is the so-called 'mightiest conifer in Europe' with a girth of more than 10m (33ft). It's not alone in being among the tallest or broadest examples in the British Isles (which is how a Champion Tree is defined), since there are others at Ardkinglas: the Patagonian cypress (*Fitzroya cupressoides*), Hinoki cypress (*Chamaecyparis obtusa*), Western red cedar (*Thuja plicata*) and the unusual mountain hemlock (*Tsuga mertensiana* subsp. *mertensiana* var. *jeffreyi*) are also on the Tree Register of the British Isles. It's got a lot to do with the climate apparently, with wet weather and shelter meeting sandy loamy soil for perfect growing conditions.

▪ www.ardkinglas.com

Culzean Castle and Country Park The National Trust for Scotland's second-most popular visitor attraction sits on a clifftop overlooking the Firth of Clyde, with views of the Isle of Arran. The estate includes 40 buildings and follies, parkland, formal gardens, cliffs and beaches as well as a scarily complete collection of arms and armoury.

▪ www.nts.org.uk/visit/culzean-castle-and-country-park

Royal Botanic Garden Edinburgh The mothership of Scotland's gardens. Right in the centre of the city, it comprises more than 70 acres of beautifully landscaped and zoned grounds. Home to the largest collection of wild-origin Chinese plants outside China, more than 5,000 alpine plants in the rockery and a magnificent (that's the only word possible here) 100-year-old beech hedge guarding a 165-year-old herbaceous border. Also here you'll find the Victorian Temperate Glasshouse, the tallest of its kind in Britain.

▪ www.rbge.org.uk

Benmore Botanic Garden A mountainous setting provides the backdrop for this lovely 'alpine' garden that was started in 1863 with the planting of an avenue of giant redwoods. Using the terrain the garden include areas devoted to the plants of Bhutan, Chile, Japan and Tasmania.

▪ www.rbge.org.uk/the-gardens/benmore

Dawyck Botanic Garden One of the world's finest arboreta, with an Azalea Terrace offering outstanding colour in late spring. Plenty of beautiful trees including Douglas fir, castor aralia, larch and beech. Lots of man-made interest too, including Italian stonework and a series of ornamental urns.
  • www.rbge.org.uk/the-gardens/dawyck

Logan Botanic Garden

A garden that benefits from the Gulf Stream, Logan is famed for its tender plants, walled garden, fish pond and amazing collection of ferns. Its tree ferns are particularly magnificent, unfurling in spring in vivid greens and browns. • www.rbge.org.uk/the-gardens/logan

Nearest van hire

Lowland Motorhome Hire, Newtongrange
• www.lowlandmotorhomehire.co.uk

Roseisle Luxury Campervans, Whitecraig
• www.roseislemotorhomehire.com

Adventure Wagons, Dalkeith
• www.adventurewagons.com

Motorhome Hire Scotland, Dechmont
• www.motorhomehire-scotland.co.uk

Bunk Campers, Broxburn
• www.bunkcampers.com

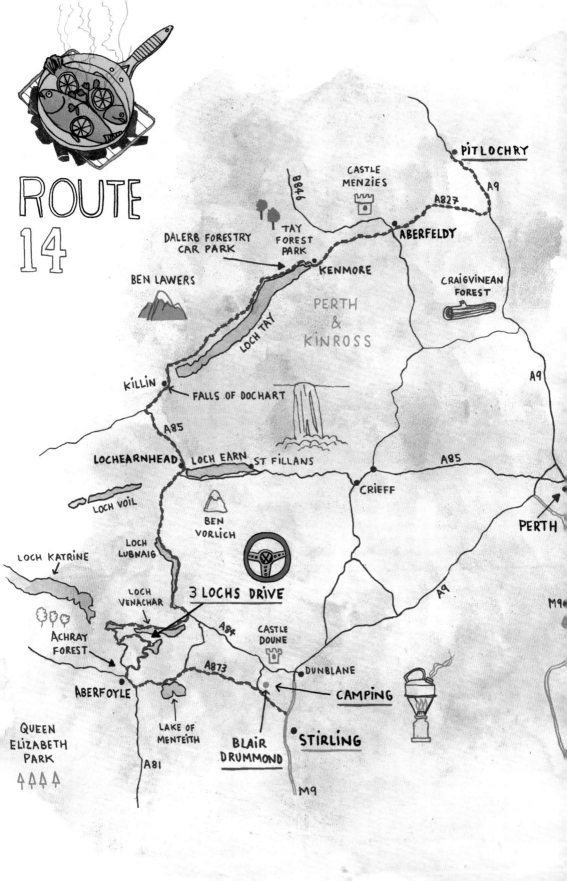

ROUTE 14

PITLOCHRY

CASTLE MENZIES

B846

A827

A9

ABERFELDY

DALERB FORESTRY CAR PARK

TAY FOREST PARK

KENMORE

CRAIGVINEAN FOREST

BEN LAWERS

PERTH & KINROSS

LOCH TAY

A9

KILLIN

FALLS OF DOCHART

A85

LOCHEARNHEAD

LOCH EARN

ST FILLANS

A85

CRIEFF

PERTH

LOCH VOIL

BEN VORLICH

LOCH LUBNAIG

LOCH KATRINE

3 LOCHS DRIVE

LOCH VENACHAR

A9

M9

ACHRAY FOREST

A84

CASTLE DOUNE

ABERFOYLE

A873

DUNBLANE

CAMPING

QUEEN ELIZABETH PARK

LAKE OF MENTEITH

BLAIR DRUMMOND

STIRLING

A81

M9

STIRLING TO PITLOCHRY VIA THE TROSSACHS

A KICK UP THE TROSSACHS

Comprising around 100 miles (160 kilometres) of beautiful roads, climbing high into The Trossachs National Park and skirting some of its loveliest spots and lochs, this is a true slow road. It makes a right meal of getting from Stirling to Pitlochry in a hurry, and even takes time out to pootle about on 7 miles (11 kilometres) of forestry track. You couldn't hurry if you tried.

BEST FOR:
Lochs, walking, fishing

START: Stirling

END: Pitlochry

MILEAGE:
100 miles (160 kilometres)

DAYS TO EXPLORE: 4

OS LAND-RANGER MAP:
57, 51, 52

SOUTH AND CENTRAL SCOTLAND

As I climb out of Aberfoyle, 'the gateway to the Highlands', I keep an eye out for red squirrels. You never know around these parts, as this is one of their last strongholds against the larger and more aggressive greys. Ever more reason to take it easy on the road.

I have left the Scottish Wool Centre behind me and I am now rising rapidly, above the valley floor, in a series of smooth hairpins that ascend steadily through Achray Forest. I pass the Go Ape centre and continue into the hills, with Loch Katrine and Brig o' Turk in my sights. I reach the top of the climb and the road plateaus in a lovely open valley with gently sloping sides. There are pools of standing water, trickling streams and spring flowers on the verges. Pinks and yellows under a deep-blue sky. The road turns to the right, heading uphill slightly towards the highest point of the Duke's Pass. It's a good place to stop and take stock so I pull into a gravel road on the right-hand side. I notice a signpost to the Three Lochs Drive.

It sounds good so I take the turn-off and follow the forestry track uphill and into the scrub of a managed forest. Patches of weather-bleached tree stumps poke out from a carpet of bright green, spring-fresh bracken.

The road is good, better than you'd expect a forestry track to be, with few potholes. Like much of Scotland's forestry it's well managed. Signs declaring the area as a camping permit zone remind me that new measures to control wild camping have been introduced. They have had problems here in the past, I know, and the new scheme enables anyone to buy a daily permit to wild camp. The idea is simple but effective. If they have your details and car registration they can find you if you leave a mess.

I stop at a glade by a loch. The sunlight beams through the leaves of the larch and birch, playing on the grass and the water. I take pictures of a glade where there is a fire pit and picnic bench. It's perfect, like a scene from a painting. Then I have a recollection, suddenly, that I have been here before. I try to place it, but can't, and neither can I let it go. There is a familiarity about the loch and the trees and the road that I cannot recall.

I carry on driving, around the loch, enjoying the views and the ride. Then I realise that I do know this place. It reminds me of the loch where I filmed a scene for *One Man and His Camper Van*, more than seven years ago. I had followed a ghillie here, down the track, to a place at the side of the loch where we went tube fishing. It was a first for me. I had no idea what I was doing and no idea where I was going, totally at the mercy of my guides. At the lochside I had to put on waders and flippers then sit in a rubber ring, kicking my way out on to the water, presumably to avoid frightening the fish. Once I got out there I realised that I hadn't a clue how to cast a fly. Every time a fish rose and rippled the water close to me I'd whip my rod across the sky, snagging trees, myself and anything nearby, except the fish. Even so, while I never caught anything on the fly I did catch a tiddler on a spinner once the ghillie realised I might be better off with a technique I knew. Desperately afraid of losing my catch I beached it by the side of the loch. I remember well how we got ravaged by midges as I cooked the trout in oatmeal. It is a great memory of an interesting time. But how naïve I was to believe that TV producers might be interested in anything other than their own survival.

I drive onwards. I am almost sure it is the place, but so far I haven't found the exact spot where I landed and cooked my first and only wild brown trout. I follow the road, down the side of the loch. And then, across the water,

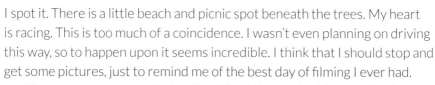

I spot it. There is a little beach and picnic spot beneath the trees. My heart is racing. This is too much of a coincidence. I wasn't even planning on driving this way, so to happen upon it seems incredible. I think that I should stop and get some pictures, just to remind me of the best day of filming I ever had.

There are two cars parked at the side of the road, with a couple of tents and a couple of men fishing. I grab my camera from the van, rehearsing what I'll say to excuse myself from intruding on their afternoon by the lochside.

I wander through the trees. It is an idyllic scene. There are young birch in the clearing, a picnic bench and a fire pit. The grass is impossibly green and the water of the loch a peaty, yellowy brown. I call to the guys fishing to say hello and apologise for disturbing their peace. They turn and face me.

'I recognise you,' says one of them, 'It's funny we should see you here. This is where you caught that trout.'

It's too weird to be true but I go with it. I rarely get recognised anywhere. But here, in the wilder corners of the Trossachs, it seems improbable. We chat. Ali and Duncan are from Glasgow. They are enjoying a few days away, wild camping in their favourite spot. They tell me the National Park is better since the permit system was introduced. It's cleaner, more respected, better overall. This is good news. When I came here before I remember seeing beer cans, bottles and toilet debris everywhere. Today, there is nothing – no mess, just camping things waiting to be cleared up. And it will be, because the rangers have Ali and Duncan's details. They like it like that. Me too.

I promise Ali and Duncan that I'll remember them in this book. For a chance meeting, in the middle of nowhere, at a spot where I had one of the best days of my life, seven years ago, almost to the day.

So here's to Ali and Duncan and a chance meeting on the slow road.

THE DRIVING

You could go to Pitlochry, Highland Perthshire's largest town, on the A9 from Stirling or the M90 via Perth, or you could veer way off course and head into the Trossachs National Park on the A84 from Stirling. I started out from Blair Drummond, at the Caravan and Motorhome Club site, heading west on the A873 towards Aberfoyle. This is a road of transition, taking you from the rolling flats of the Lowlands, across the Highland Boundary fault at Aberfoyle and up into the Highlands. Europe's largest raised peat bog occupies part of the Forth Valley to the left, along with agricultural land and, on the opposite side of the valley, managed forest on the slopes of the Gargunnock Hills.

At Blairhoyle take the left turn towards Aberfoyle on the A81. You'll pass the Lake of Menteith, Scotland's only 'lake' and an important trout fishery, on the left-hand side. Moss-covered stone walls line the road while copper beeches, chestnuts and beeches dot the roadsides and side roads, contrasting beautifully with the dense, ordered monoculture of the managed forests in the hills above.

At Aberfoyle the route takes a sharp right-hand turn on to the A82, the Duke's Pass. It's a winding, steep drive with hairpins and steep sections, with a gradient as steep as 10 per cent. Once at the top you hit the plateau before encountering the right-hand turn for the Three Lochs Drive. It's worth the detour for the scenery and the picnic options. Once regaining the tarmac, the road drops down to Loch Achray, offering a left-hand turn to Loch Katrine. Take it. It might be a tourist honeypot and you may wonder how coaches get down the narrow winding road and you may find yourself in the company of visitors from abroad, but it's worth it. Katrine is a truly beautiful spot and is often described as the centrepiece of the Trossachs.

Back at the A821 the road follows the north bank of Loch Achray before following the Black Water through the village of Brig o' Turk to Loch Venachar and, eventually, the A84 west of Callander. Heading west still you'll climb the impressive Pass of Leny and the Falls of Leny. It's one of those long, slow chugs so no need to rush. At the top you can look back at the valley or truck on past Loch Lubnaig and on to the lovely village of Lochearnhead at the head of Loch Earn. At the junction with the A85 turn left, staying on the A85 through Glenogle and down towards Lix. Turn right on to the A827 to Killin. The road crosses the impressive Falls of Dochart at Killin Bridge and then continues on past Loch Tay, high above the water on the north bank until it drops into Kenmore, the village at the head of the loch. It's a pretty spot with a bridge crossing the Tay and a beach.

There aren't many places to stop on the A827, apart from the Dalerb Forestry car park and picnic spot, where there are picnic tables, BBQ areas, toilets and lots of ducks. There is also a bronze of the ultra-rare capercaillie bird in the car park (this is one of their final strongholds) and incredible views across the loch.

From Loch Tay it's a straightforward cruise in to the A9 at Ballinluig and, regretfully, dual carriageway in to Pitlochry.

PLACES TO STAY

Blair Drummond Caravan Park
Blair Drummond, by Stirling, FK9 4UP
web: http://blairdrummond
caravanpark.co.uk
email: office@
blairdrummondcaravanpark.co.uk
tel: 01786 841 208

info: *A walled Caravan and Motorhome Club site in lovely surroundings near Blair Drummond Safari Park. No animal noises reported.*

Loch Katrine Aire
Trossachs Pier, Loch Katrine,
by Callander, FK17 8HZ
web: www.lochkatrine.com/aire
email: enquiries@lochkatrine.com
tel: 01877 376 317

info: *A new aire in the car park at Loch Katrine with toilet, showers, chemical-waste disposal point, electrical hook-up, recycling and visitor Wi-Fi.*

Aberfeldy Caravan Park
Dunkeld Road, Aberfeldy, PH15 2AQ
web: www.aberfeldycaravanpark.co.uk
email: info@aberfeldycaravanpark.co.uk
tel: 01887 822 103

info: *A large, well laid-out touring park wedged between the Tay and the A827 near Aberfeldy.*

Maragowan Caravan Club Site
Aberfeldy Road, Killin,
FK21 8TN
web: www.caravanclub.co.uk
tel: 01567 820 245

info: *Brilliantly situated site on the banks of River Lochay, a little downstream from Killin on the A827.*

IN THE AREA

Scottish Wool Centre, Aberfoyle In the season they have sheepdog duck-gathering trials (or something) to entertain the tourists before they go inside and munch on healthy local food and snap up bargain tartans, fridge magnets and other assorted Scottish frippery. If you want a wool blanket or tweed cap, this is the place. Aberfoyle is the popular 'gateway to the Trossachs' and, as such, is the place to get your tourist tat. However, it's also very pretty and worth a stop, if only to get some rugs or scarves or to look out for red squirrels.

Doon Hill, Aberfoyle Why do people love to jam pennies into old bits of wood? For good luck? Or just because someone else did? Anyway, whatever your motivation, you'll find a carved wooden something to stick your ha'penneth in on a walk up Doon Hill to the fairy tree, an old pine that is said to contain the imprisoned spirit of Reverend Kirk.

• www.walkhighlands.co.uk/lochlomond/doon-hill.shtml

Loch Katrine Loch Katrine, despite being a tourism honeypot, is a fantastic place. Most of the tourists take a trip on the steamship *Sir Walter Scott* to see this most scenic of Scotland's lochs but I jumped on my bike – and promptly broke my chain. Thankfully, the local hire shop had a spare one (they also hire bikes) so I was able to do a few miles on the traffic-free lochside road.

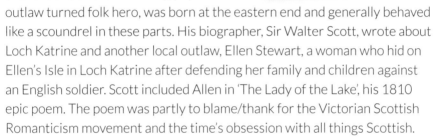

Loch Katrine is also a place of legend and lore and all that. Rob Roy, popular outlaw turned folk hero, was born at the eastern end and generally behaved like a scoundrel in these parts. His biographer, Sir Walter Scott, wrote about Loch Katrine and another local outlaw, Ellen Stewart, a woman who hid on Ellen's Isle in Loch Katrine after defending her family and children against an English soldier. Scott included Allen in 'The Lady of the Lake', his 1810 epic poem. The poem was partly to blame/thank for the Victorian Scottish Romanticism movement and the time's obsession with all things Scottish.

• www.lochkatrine.com

The Three Lochs Drive A stunning 7½-mile (12-kilometre) drive on forestry tracks that follows a one-way route and starts and ends on the A821. The route passes Loch Drunkie and returns to the road just before Loch Achray. It's all within the Queen Elizabeth Forest Park. There is a toll to go along the road, payable by a machine at the start of the drive.

Nearest van hire

Big Tree Campervans, Bankfoot
• www.bigtreecampervans.com

Four Seasons Campers, Loch Lomond
• www.fourseasonscamper vanhire.com

Motorhome Adventure Scotland, Kinross
• www.motorhomeadventure scotland.co.uk

The Lodge Forest Visitor Centre This features a cafe and information centre, with plenty of walks in the Queen Elizabeth Forest Park, plus a Go Ape course with a 426m- (1,400ft-) long zip wire.

• http://goape.co.uk/days-out/ aberfoyle

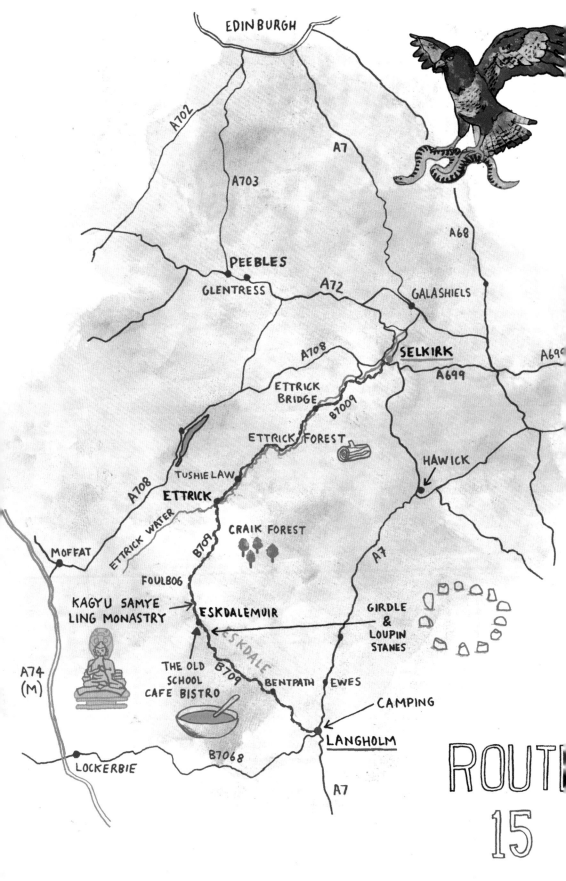

EDINBURGH

A702

A703

A7

A68

PEEBLES

GLENTRESS

A72

GALASHIELS

A708

SELKIRK

A699

A690

ETTRICK
BRIDGE

B7009

ETTRICK FOREST

HAWICK

TUSHIE LAW

A708

ETTRICK

ETTRICK WATER

A708

MOFFAT

CRAIK FOREST

B709

A7

FOULBOG

KAGYU SAMYE
LING MONASTRY

ESKDALEMUIR

GIRDLE
&
LOUPIN
STANES

A74
(M)

ESKDALE

THE OLD
SCHOOL
CAFE BISTRO

B709

BENTPATH

EWES

CAMPING

LOCKERBIE

B7068

LANGHOLM

A7

ROUTE

15

SELKIRK TO LANGHOLM

THE HIDDEN VALLEY

A true slow-road paradise in a hidden corner of Scotland, with lots to see and plenty of great driving to boot. Dawdle to your heart's content in a hidden valley, stop at standing stones and take time to appreciate nature, Buddhism and beauty by the camper van-ful.

BEST FOR:
Standing stones, secret valleys, unexpected passes

START: **Selkirk**

END:
Langholm

MILEAGE:
40 miles (64 kilometres)

DAYS TO
EXPLORE: 2

OS LAND-
RANGER MAP:
73, 79

SOUTH AND CENTRAL SCOTLAND

Andy and I are on our way home, back to England. We have eaten haggis and drunk whisky in Edinburgh's old town, driven along the coast at Montrose, eaten smokies straight out of the smoker on the beach in Arbroath and driven an old VW Type 2 Westfalia around Royal Deeside. It's been another wonderful slow-road adventure, but now we need to get ourselves back to the M6. In how we do it we have a choice. We can head back towards Glasgow on the M8 and then join the M74, surely the quickest route, or we can go across country. We decide to take it easy – we have a long day ahead of us anyway – and explore a little more.

We head south on the A703 to Peebles and then on to the A72, which follows the beautiful Tweed Valley south-east towards Selkirk. At Selkirk we take a turn towards St Mary's Loch and find ourselves on the B7039 then the B7009, crossing a bridge over Ettrick Water and heading south-east towards Ettrickbridge. It's a tiny road that winds its way up Ettrick Water to the pass at Foulbog along a beautiful valley.

We arrive at an old private bridge, leading to a brick-built lodge. We stop to take photographs of the bridge, the hand-painted sign and the setting. It's lovely, a great driving road with low hedges and a mixture of plantations, open fields and hillsides. We drive away from the bridge slowly, looking across the fields towards the river. I notice something rising up, out of the field, a rabble of a bird, chaotic in flight, close enough to make out the shape of its feathers but flying too quickly to identify.

'Look! What is that?' I ask Andy.

'What?' he replies.

'There.' I point out of the window at the huge bird that is flying alongside us, about 6m (20ft) away. 'It looks like an eagle. What kind of an eagle is that?'

Andy looks. 'Christ. It's huge!'

He goes to grab the camera that is resting between our seats. I stop the van to look. I notice the bird has something in one of its talons. Something long and dark. It looks like a branch, except it's moving. Maybe it's an eel or, worse still, a snake.

Andy has his camera almost ready and opens the window to get a shot. The bird (I am convinced it's an eagle by this time) moves ahead of us, although it is still flying alongside, in the field. As I start up to give chase the bird flies across the road in front of us, about 4.5m (15ft) away, directly

above the windscreen. We stop, both of us looking up at the bird above us. We get a really good view.

'Oh my god. It's a snake.' Andy says. He winds up the window quickly.

The bird has the snake in one of its talons, barely gripping, while the snake squirms and wriggles to get away. I panic. I hate snakes (thanks to an unfortunate incident with an adder in my grandfather's garden a long time ago) so the last thing I want is a snake dropping on to the windscreen of the van. Now I am the one who is squirming. I stop the van again. The bird flies up and lands on the top of a telegraph pole on the opposite side of the road. We see the snake writhing as the bird looks around for a few moments and then takes flight again. Andy gets off a shot just in time, but before he can snap again the bird has flown and is heading for a large plantation. We lose sight of it.

We wait for a few moments to see if it will fly again back out of the cover of the forest but, we assume, it may have preferred a bit of privacy to have its dinner. I find my bird identification book and we flick through the pages

looking to make a positive ID. Was it an eagle? An osprey? Disappointingly we identify it as a buzzard, one of Scotland's more commonly found birds of prey. Even so, it was an exciting moment to witness, even though we now speculate about what might have happened had it dropped the snake on the van.

'Snakes in a van!' says Andy.

'Snakenado!' I reply.

'Buzzardsnakeapocalypse!'

We drive on, buzzing about a rare encounter with nature on a quiet back road somewhere in the Borders. We consider ourselves to be lucky in the extreme. During this trip we have seen red squirrels, red deer and now a snake taken by a buzzard. As usual, Scotland delivers.

We continue on this heavenly trip to Langholm. En route we encounter a Buddhist retreat, a community-owned restaurant and a circle of standing stones.

It's been another amazing trip on the slow roads of Scotland.

THE DRIVING

This route is all about the slow road. It'll get you not only from A to B but via C, D and E too. And that's the point. Taking the slow road is about journeys, albeit slow ones that will transport you to somewhere better than a soulless service station on the M74. Halfway along this road, at Eskdalemuir, we found the Old School Café Bistro, where we stopped to have a bowl of soup, a huge pot of tea and a look at some local artwork. The Old School is a community development project that is owned and run by the local community to provide a space for events as well as offering services to passing trade. I absolutely loved it; it is what being on this journey is for. A carrot and coriander soup served by smiling people in a non-corporate environment. What could be better?

If you are heading back down south from Edinburgh then this route is a great way to do it. From Edinburgh head south on the A703 to Peebles and then on to the A72, following the Tweed Valley south-east towards Selkirk. At Selkirk find the B7009 and head towards Ettrickbridge. It's a tiny road that winds its way up Ettrick Water to the pass at Foulbog along a beautiful valley.

The river meanders downstream as you meander up the valley, climbing gently towards the apex of this route at what the Borders Forest Trust calls

the 'wild heart of southern Scotland', and the Ettrick Marshes. Before you reach the marshes, and the narrow, scrub-filled valley and its head, you'll need to take a left turn at Ettrick on to the B709 and into the forest. At Foulbog (great name, interesting upland country) you'll hit the peak. Then you'll start dropping as you enter Eskdale. This is when it feels as if you are entering a hidden valley. What begins as a narrow and steep-sided vale soon turns into a flat-bottomed and seemingly perfect valley of mature trees, fields and stone farmhouses, guided by a gently rambling river and surrounded by forested upland. It feels Elysian, like a Shangri-La hiding beneath wild spaces, a secluded valley paradise, hidden in plain sight.

And in some ways, to some, it is. Just before you reach Eskdale you'll pass the striking Kagyu Samye Ling Monastery and Tibetan Centre. Interestingly, this is the first Tibetan monastery to have been founded in the West. It is possible to visit, enjoy the beautiful gardens and stop for a cuppa. It might seem incongruous when you come across a golden shining Buddha in Scotland but, now I am writing this, it makes perfect sense. Andy and I decided this valley was special before we passed the monastery. There must be something in that.

Once you arrive at Eskdalemuir you join the Eskdale Prehistoric Trail, a route that takes in nine prehistoric sites between the village and Bentpath.

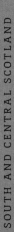
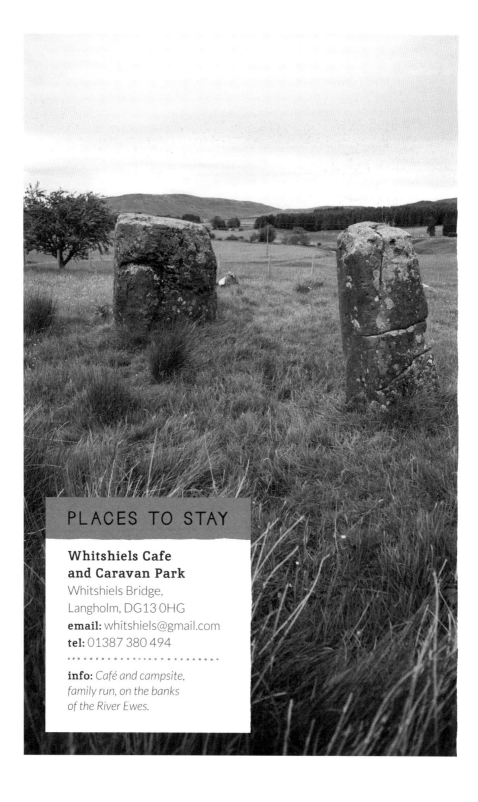

PLACES TO STAY

Whitshiels Cafe and Caravan Park

Whitshiels Bridge,
Langholm, DG13 0HG

email: whitshiels@gmail.com
tel: 01387 380 494

info: *Café and campsite,
family run, on the banks
of the River Ewes.*

Soon after Eskdalemuir on the B709 you'll encounter the Loupin Stanes, a peaceful, small stone circle of 12 stones near another larger ring, the Girdle Stanes. Both circles sit on the river bank in lush, damp, peaty meadows of marsh grass and buttercup, surrounded by grazing sheep. It is all rather pastoral – a perfect image of what countryside should be – and it's easy to imagine why our ancestors chose to live, love and worship here in this quiet Arcadia.

The route finishes at Langholm, a lovely historic market town that somehow feels very English, but I am sure the locals would have something else to say. It is elegant and tidy, stone built and ordered, with half the town constructed on a grid system and half organically chaotic.

IN THE AREA

Eskdale Prehistoric Trail
Nine prehistoric sites linked by a waymarked route between Eskdalemuir and Bentpath. Easy to drive, modest amount of walking. Lovely countryside.
• www.langholmwalks.co.uk

Nearest van hire

Lowland Motorhome Hire, Newtongrange
• www.lowlandmotorhomehire.co.uk

Roseisle Luxury Campervans, Whitecraig
• www.roseislemotorhomehire.com

Kagyu Samye Ling Tibetan Monastery and Centre for World Peace and Health
Tibetan Buddhist monastery and retreat in Eskdale. Striking place in a seemingly incongruous setting.
• www.samyeling.org

Old School Café and Bistro
Located in the old schoolhouse at Eskdalemuir, run by the Upper Eskdale Development Group, and part of the local hub. An inspiring place, run by nice people in a lovely setting with lovely community-based ideals. • www.eskdalemuir.com/oldschoolcafébistro

EAST COAST AND CAIRNGORMS

The Cairngorms and the east coast are simply beautiful, of course. And with Deeside, Tayside and Speyside offering long distance routes to follow from the peaks to the coast, there is much here for the camper vanner, especially if you like mountains, views and high passes. For those looking to challenge the old girl with a gradient or two there are two of the UK's favourite passes, at Glenshee and Lecht, while the mountain scenery is incredible wherever you point your wheels. The Moray Firth is spectacular too, with a series of beautiful villages, while many would kill for a hot smokie straight off the barrel in Arbroath.

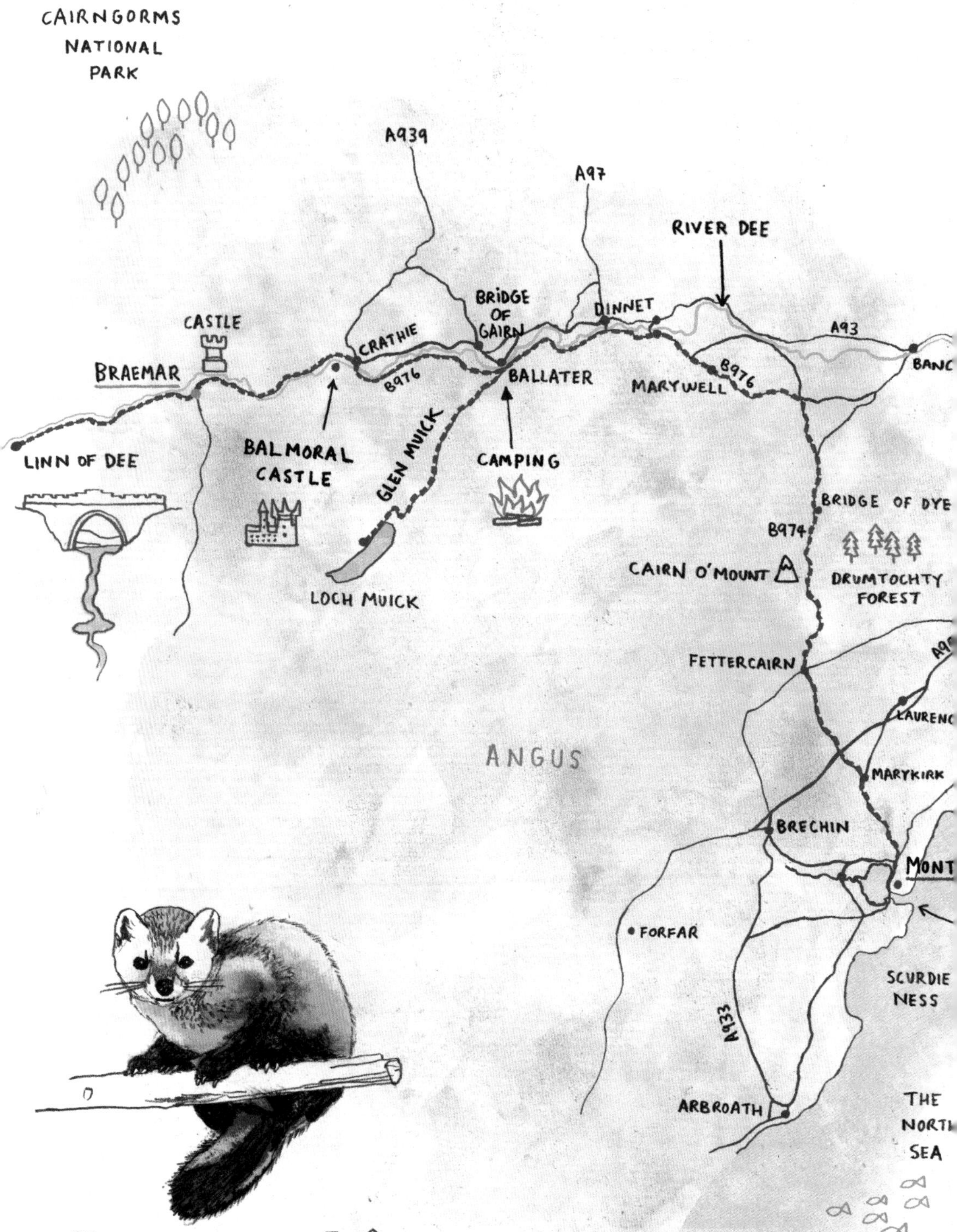

CAIRNGORMS
NATIONAL
PARK

A939

A97

RIVER DEE

CASTLE

BRAEMAR

CRATHIE

BRIDGE
OF
GAIRN

DINNET

A93

BANC

LINN OF DEE

B976

BALMORAL
CASTLE

GLEN MUICK

BALLATER

MARYWELL

B976

CAMPING

LOCH MUICK

ANGUS

BRIDGE OF DYE

B974

CAIRN O'MOUNT

DRUMTOCHTY
FOREST

FETTERCAIRN

A9

LAURENC

MARYKIRK

BRECHIN

MONT

FORFAR

SCURDIE
NESS

A933

THE
NORTH
SEA

ARBROATH

ROUTE 16

THE LINN OF DEE TO MONTROSE

ROYAL DEESIDE TO THE COAST

Follow the course of the River Dee as it rumbles and tumbles through the stunning Dee Valley. But don't go the easy way. Take a turn over the Brunel Bridge at Balmoral and follow the course of the river from its southern bank, then take a detour to Glen Muick, a little aside along a curvaceous single track to Loch Muick, where you may be lucky enough to catch a glimpse of the herd of red deer. It's a slow and stupendous route, with epic vistas over the lovely valley as it meanders towards the coast, with a final, breath-taking last hurrah before you descend to the coastal plains.

BEST FOR:
Taking a look at Royal Deeside

START:
Braemar

END: **Montrose**

MILEAGE:
70 miles (113 kilometres)

DAYS TO
EXPLORE: **2–3**

OS LAND-
RANGER MAP:
43, 44, 45

EAST COAST AND CAIRNGORMS

229

I park in the trees at the Linn of Dee. It's the farthest west into the Cairngorms I shall get on this journey from the top of the Dee to the coast road near Montrose. The road ends here, besides, so I couldn't go any further if I'd wanted to. I change into my walking boots, fill my rucksack with essentials for a walk and then set off, on foot this time, down to the Linn of Dee, a deep gorge straddled by a stone-arched Victorian bridge. The ground is soft underfoot as I descend the gorge, save for the roots of the tall and straight Caledonian pines that criss-cross the pathway. It feels spongy, hollow somehow, as if I am walking on a forgiving crust of peat and moss and pine needles.

The canopy is dense but there is little undergrowth save for a carpet of young-season myrtle berry bushes fighting for attention with dark and woody heather. It's too early for the myrtle, I think, as I check for berries by brushing the serrated top leaves aside and looking underneath. The young leaves are bright green. As they grow they will become waxy and dark before they bear the tiny, bitter berries I remember from childhood forays in the Alps with pen pals I could never understand.

Occasionally, between the low bushes, new shoots of mountain ash reach for the sky, their frondescent leaves shooting upwards, aiming high, against all odds.

The gorge is spectacular. It is narrow, forcing the peaty brown water into gushing rapids and whirling pools. The rock, shaped

by thousands of years of the same pressures, follows the flow of the water into half-moon-shaped bowls. I wonder how I'd fare if I jumped or fell in. I find a memorial to a couple who did just that in 1927. Probably not very well, it seems.

I walk downstream to find a couple of waterfalls marked on my OS map. The path is easy since it follows the steep bank, only occasionally rerouting around muddy streams or to navigate a difficult root system. Here the Dee widens and becomes fast flowing and shallow. Despite the colour it's clear and I can see slabs of rock below the surface creating standing waves and chop. It's noisy close to the water.

As I walk I find the remains of camp fires on the banks. Perhaps the result of a night's fishing or of Scotland's Land Reform Act that gives rights to roam, and therefore wild camp, in places that are beautiful, such as this. I love this, for the moment. That we can go into the wild and camp is a great freedom that should never be squandered. Allowing fires to burn the ground isn't great though, I think. People who love nature should know better than to light fires on pine needles and on top of peat. But then that's people, isn't it? No clue sometimes.

I walk on, to where the Dee meets Lui Water. It starts raining, lightly at first. Here, at a little clearing in the woods, I find a half-collapsed tent. It's a cheap pop up 'festival tent' and it looks abandoned. Something is weighing it down, stopping it from blowing into the water, bulging out one side of the bright green and grey nylon. What's inside? For a moment my mind goes off on a rocky track. What if there's a body inside? I know it's unlikely to be anything sinister but I have found a body before, while kayaking down the River Torridge in Devon. So why not here, in a remote part of the Highlands?

I pull open the rip in the fabric to see inside. Relief. It's a couple of full bin bags. Someone has spent the night here and then tidied up, put everything in bin bags and then placed them inside the tent so that it won't blow away, and then walked off. I am disgusted.

And yet I still walk away, carrying on as before, up the Lui Water to find those waterfalls. As I go along a peaty path by the side of the river I recognise Scots pines, larch and birch. The forest is different here. It's less ordered, more unplanned than by the side of the Dee, some 100 metres (yards) behind me. I hope that I have stumbled into Caledonian forest but I can't be sure. If I am right then I am in Scotland's ancient rain forest, a rarefied habitat

that once covered vast areas and was home to wolves, bears, beavers and wild cats but now hosts equally rare pine martens and red squirrel.

It's raining more heavily now and my hair is wet. I pull out my waterproofs from my rucksack and stop to put them on. I am furious about the disrespect shown by the wild campers to this beautiful, precious place. It won't leave me. I wonder about what made someone want to do that. They have been granted the right to camp by the side of the Dee and yet they are prepared to squander that right by desecrating the place they came to enjoy. I don't understand. Why can't we leave these precious places be? As I walk away, cross a stone bridge and stomp on to another deep gorge, I try to make sense of it. And I ask myself why I didn't act and just pick it up? I tell myself it would be too heavy, too bulky, too dirty to do on my own. I tell myself the rangers will find it and clear it up.

And now I am furious with myself too. I figure that if I do nothing then I am no better. What right do I have to write about the Land Reform Act or wild camping or the joys of waking in wild places if I simply let this pass? The answer is that I have no right.

I return to the bridge. The track isn't far from the campsite, so I resolve to make this right. I turn and head for the car park. It takes me ten minutes to walk back and only about a minute to drive to the bridge. It takes a few minutes to walk to the tent, less than two to work out how to fold up it up and five minutes to haul the two bags and the tent back to the van. I check there's nothing left behind. There isn't. The clearing looks how it should do, apart from the small patch of scorched earth where the fire had been. It will recover, I think to myself. I hope the same can be said for the Caledonian forest. Will it survive man's inability to live side by side with nature?

I drive away and leave the tent with a ranger who says he can get rid of it and will sift through the litter to recycle what he can. Also perhaps get an address. That would be good.

I get back in the van and drive away, back down the road towards Braemar, Balmoral and Royal Deeside where things are decidedly tidier and more ordered than the chaotic, natural forest. Even so, it's a stunning drive.

THE DRIVING

The start point for this drive has to be Braemar, because the road to the
Linn of Dee is a no through road. The Linn of Dee is not the end of the road,
however, as it continues on for a few miles to the Linn of Quoich on the Dee's
northern bank. However, this is the point where it extends the farthest to the
east, so I count it as the start.

The Linn of Dee, once you get there along the Mar Lodge Estate road, is a
popular beauty spot where the Dee rushes through a narrow gorge and into
pools before descending through a steep-sided valley of beautiful pine forest.
Some of the UK's last remaining Caledonian pine forests are on the estate
and it's an important area for natural woodland and conservation.

Cross over the bridge that was built by the 5th Earl of Mar and opened
by Queen Victoria in 1857 and begin your route at the National Trust for
Scotland car park, which is almost hidden in the forest on the northern
bank. This is the point from which walkers and cyclists head out into the
Cairngorms or to see Derry Lodge, a 19th-century shooting lodge.

Obviously, as you begin your route you'll be retracing your steps, back
across the bridge and along the southern shore of the Dee. It's a single-track
road although you will find coaches and plenty of traffic. It's popular because
it's a great drive. You'll pass through the pine and larch forests, past estate

houses and meadows before the road swings inland and the Dee drops away from you. Then, as the road rises you'll get your first big vistas of the wide, fast-flowing river in the flat-bottomed valley below you.

With the broom in bloom and distant mountains of the Cairngorms in front of you, while the river gushes and meanders below you, the parking spot opposite the Linn of Quoich offers some of the loveliest, most perfect views you'll see today. It's not dramatic like the Linn but it is picture perfect: a fluvial idyll.

Braemar is the spot that's worth stopping off for, where the Highland Games take place every summer. It's a lovely, neat and tidy town and is the hub of Royal Deeside. From here you take the snow roads south to Glenshee or follow, as I did, the Dee towards Aberdeen. Braemar has a couple of small restaurants, a supermarket, hotels and a large touring park, as well as a fantastic mountaineering shop and cafe that sells great Bakewell tart.

From Braemar head east on the A93, following the course of the Dee until you get to Balmoral Castle, royal summer residence and former country pile of Queen Victoria. Here, take a right and cross the Albert-commissioned Brunel bridge (1857) on the B976. This takes you to the south side of the Dee and the better of the two banks along which to drive. It's much quieter, prettier and, of course, slower because it weaves its way along the river, so it's a much more pleasant drive. At places where the bends in the road meet the bends in the river you can enjoy views of the open banks and beats of the Dee. Fisherman, fly casting from the bank or letting their fly drift downstream while thigh deep in waders, are often seen along this stretch. The Dee, of course, is a famous angling hotspot.

Just after Marywell, the B976 takes a turn to the south, offering a single-tracked diversion through the Forest of Birse to the Forest of Birse Church along the side of the Water of Feugh. A right-hand turn along the Old Military Road (B974) towards Montrose then takes you on a magical mystery tour of the Drumtochty Forest, over the Bridge of Dye (the Old Bridge lies by its side) and high up towards Cairn o'Mount, one of the highest points for a while. Coming out of the forest and up the steep road towards the pass is surprising, but it's not as good as the moment you crest the hill and see the coast, and Montrose, beyond. There is a parking place and viewpoint on the seaward side that's worth a stop. The vistas over the North Sea and the coastal plain below are staggering.

From here it's a steep drop down to the coast, past the famous Clatterin Brig Restaurant, and then giving you an easy run through the lovely, stone-built, whisky-producing village of Fettercairn before hitting the A90 Aberdeen to Perth Road.

PLACES TO STAY

Motorhome Parking Balmoral Castle

Balmoral, Ballater, Aberdeenshire, AB35 5TB
web: http://motorhome parking.co.uk/scot.htm

info: *There are six motorhome parking spaces at Balmoral. They are close together, but free. Great if you plan to visit the castle but I can't see why else you'd want to use them. Not level.*

Braemar Caravan Park

Glenshee Road, Braemar, Aberdeenshire, AB35 5YQ
web: www.braemarcaravanpark.co.uk
email: info@braemarcaravan park.co.uk
tel: 01339 741 373

info: *A big, popular site on the road to Glenshee.*

Silverbank Caravan Club Site

North Deeside Road, Banchory, Aberdeenshire, AB31 5PY
web: www.caravanclub.co.uk
tel: 01330 822 477

info: *Situated on the banks of the Dee, although you'd not necessarily know that. Well set out, open site. Pitches are spacious but pitch properly or else.*

IN THE AREA

Balmoral Castle If you happen to be at Balmoral on one of the days when it is open to visitors then you can go and have a wander around the grounds, breathing in the same rarefied air that once wafted past Victoria. There are winter walking tours on certain dates, as well as winter safari tours, but otherwise there isn't that much else to see – some estate vehicles from yesteryear, some pre-shot and stuffed animals, a wooden corgi that was given to the Queen once, and the ballroom – where you'll discover the Queen's ideal seating arrangement.

Braemar Castle Run by the local community to preserve the interiors and story of this historically relevant monolith, Braemar Castle has an interesting past. It was used as an elaborate, large-scale hunting lodge as well as stronghold for local Jacobites and place for tea during the time of Royal Deeside.
* www.braemarcastle.co.uk

Nearest van hire

Deeside Motorhomes, Torphins
* www.deeside-motorhomes.co.uk

Deeside Classic Campers, Finzean
* www.deesideclassiccampers.com

Cairngorm Campers, Boat of Garten
* www.cairngormcampers.com

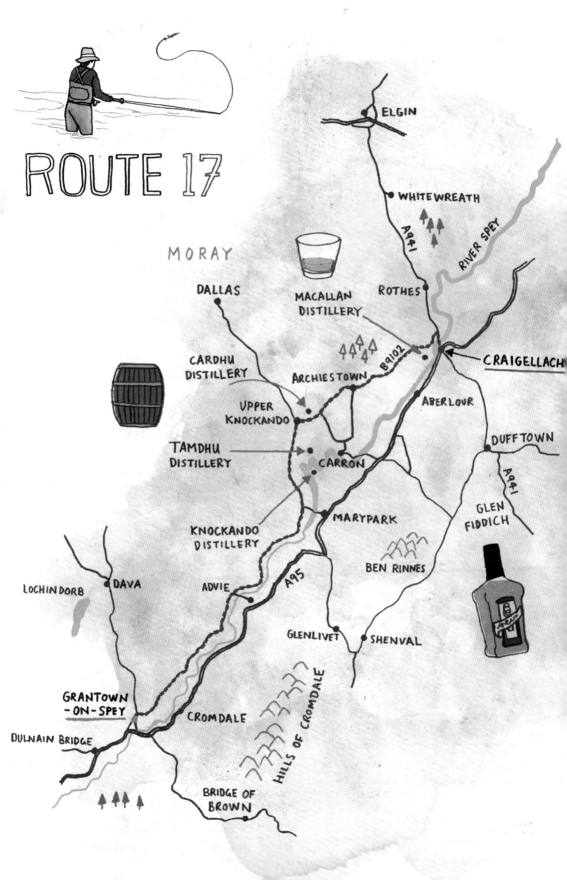

ROUTE 17

MORAY

ELGIN

WHITEWREATH

A941

RIVER SPEY

DALLAS

MACALLAN DISTILLERY

ROTHES

CARDHU DISTILLERY

ARCHIESTOWN

B9102

CRAIGELLACH

UPPER KNOCKANDO

ABERLOUR

DUFFTOWN

TAMDHU DISTILLERY

CARRON

A941

GLEN FIDDICH

KNOCKANDO DISTILLERY

MARYPARK

BEN RINNES

DAVA

A95

ADVIE

LOCHINDORB

GLENLIVET

SHENVAL

GRANTOWN -ON-SPEY

CROMDALE

HILLS OF CROMDALE

DULNAIN BRIDGE

BRIDGE OF BROWN

GRANTOWN-ON-SPEY TO CRAIGELLACHIE

THE NORTH BANK OF THE SPEY

A sublimely pretty route that follows the River Spey along its north bank through fly-fishing and whisky country as it meanders towards the coast at Spey Bay. A perfectly lovely and laid-back slow road alternative to taking the A95 which follows the south bank of the Spey and gets you there much quicker. But that's not the point, is it?

BEST FOR:
Whisky, fishing, views

START:
Grantown-on-Spey

END:
Craigellachie

MILEAGE: **25 miles (40 kilometres)**

DAYS TO EXPLORE: **2**

OS LAND-RANGER MAP: **28, 36**

EAST COAST AND CAIRNGORMS

241

For the first time in ages I wake with no real plan, apart from needing to get to Fraserburgh. There's no route marked on my well-used route map of Scotland. The road from Fraserburgh to Inverness is marked up, but that's just about it. From my pitch at Grantown-on-Spey I could drive north to Elgin and pick up the A96 to take me quickly to the furthest point east on the Moray Firth. I pack up the van and drive out of the wide main street of Grantown-on-Spey. I think how nice and ordered it is as I pass the green spaces at the side of the road so it doesn't surprise me that it is a planned settlement dating back to the 18th century. The buildings are granite, with square sandstone lintels over the doors and windows. It's raining, not helping the look of the houses. In this weather they appear dour and cross.

As I drive, the buildings soon give way and, eventually, at the end of a row of what looks like 1930s social housing with large wide gardens I stop to take a closer look at a cast-iron fingerpost on a black-and-white striped pole. I park up to take pictures and stroll over to look more closely at the sign.

It's intriguing, with both fingers pointing towards Elgin. I had intended to follow the road north but check my map and see that the road that points east follows the course of the River

Spey towards Craigellachie. It's a tiny road on my map, but, intriguingly it is marked with green shading. On my map that means it's got something about it that's picturesque. I decide to change my half-made plans and follow this little route east, along the Spey, to see what I find.

I get back into the van and point it down the little road, driving past a school and golf course and into the trees. On one side of the small single-track road there is a low wall built of stone and, behind that, spacious forestry of Caledonian pines with a bright mossy floor. It's a dark forest but not as dense as a lot of the forestry I have seen along the way. The road weaves its way through the forest, passing occasional fields but always, it seems, remaining in the cover, even though it's spacious and open. At times the understorey of the forest is birch, at other times purple heather fills the space between the pines.

Eventually the forest begins to clear and I can see that I am in a wide river valley, with a flat floor, presumably flood plain for the River Spey. The forestry gives way to deciduous woodland of silver birch, pine, ash and sycamore. It's a lovely pastoral drive and the countryside is perfect. Every

so often I get glimpses of the river to my right as it weaves its way along the valley. It's tantalising but there's no clear view of it. I see tiny lanes leading off to beats with signs declaring private fishing. I see expensive cars parked on the banks and wader-clad men in tweed casting flies on to the water.

After a few miles I come to a stretch where the road undulates gently through a series of rounded rolling mounds punctuated by mature silver birches, their branches weeping and swaying in the wind. The road rises and then, at the top of a hill, I see a perfect-looking whitewashed farmhouse on my right. It must have amazing views I think. A little further on the trees give way to a section of road high above the river, giving me, for the first time, an open view of Speyside. I stop.

There are grey clouds hugging the hillside opposite, partly shrouding dark forests of fir on the opposite bank of the river, a couple of miles away. The road is wet, but as I step out of the van and into the verge to get a better angle the sun comes out for me. Immediately I feel its warmth. Patches of sun now punctuate the valley below me, lighting up fields of bright-green grass and coppices of young tree. The river, black with peat from the moors, now glints and shimmers in the sunlight. The road begins to steam a little. It's perfect, about as lovely a landscape as I could ever hope to find on my travels. It isn't dramatic or rugged or wild. It's gentle and benign, hardly a leaf out of place. Below me in the river an angler casts his fly hopefully and the scene is complete.

Just lovely.

THE DRIVING

The B9102 is an easy, perfect slow-road drive along the north bank of the Spey. The A95, the main road to Keith, runs on the south bank, but I bet that this road is quieter, slower and much more interesting. It starts at Grantown-on-Spey and runs for just over 20 miles (32 kilometres) through some lovely countryside. Along the way you pass the Advie Bridge, a concrete structure linking the north and south banks of the River Spey at Advie, as well as Archiestown, an 18th-century planned village that was originally based on weaving. Today, though, it's almost impossible to ignore the presence of whisky in the area. Just about everything, it seems, in the town is made from whisky barrels, including signage, planters and tables outside the Archiestown Hotel.

This is part of the whisky trail, then, and the Cardhu, Knockando, Tamdhu and The Macallan distilleries are nearby.

The route is partly forested and partly farmland with native mountain ash, birch and pine giving light relief from forestry. Between the coppices lie meadows and rolling farmland.

The road is well tarmacked and undulating, with plenty of twists and turns but no surprises. It's well worth a detour if you are heading north-east or looking for a nice ride into the Cairngorms.

PLACES TO STAY

Grantown-on-Spey Caravan Site
Seafield Ave, Grantown-on-Spey,
Highlands, PH26 3JQ
web: www.caravanscotland.com
tel: 01479 872 474

info: *A popular, tidy park on the edges of Grantown-on-Spey, with great views from the loos on the park's lofty edges.*

Speyside Camping and Caravanning Club Site
Archiestown, Aberlour,
Moray, AB38 9SL
web: www.campingand
caravanningclub.co.uk
tel: 01340 810 414

info: *A leafy, level site at the eastern end of this pretty little route. Handy for distilleries nearby.*

IN THE AREA

The Whisky Trail The Whisky Trail runs along Speyside and the B9102 is a big part of it, particularly around Archiestown, where there are number of famous distilleries, most of which offer tours if you are so inclined. There are more distilleries in this area than anywhere else in the world, so if you like whisky, this is the one for you. Sadly I am driving.

• http://maltwhiskytrail.com

Nearest van hire

Happy Highland Campers, Inverness
• www.happyhighlandcampers.co.uk

OutThere Campervans, Inverness
• www.outtherecampers.co.uk

Lossiemouth Campervan Hire, Lossiemouth
• www.lossiemouthcampervanhire.com

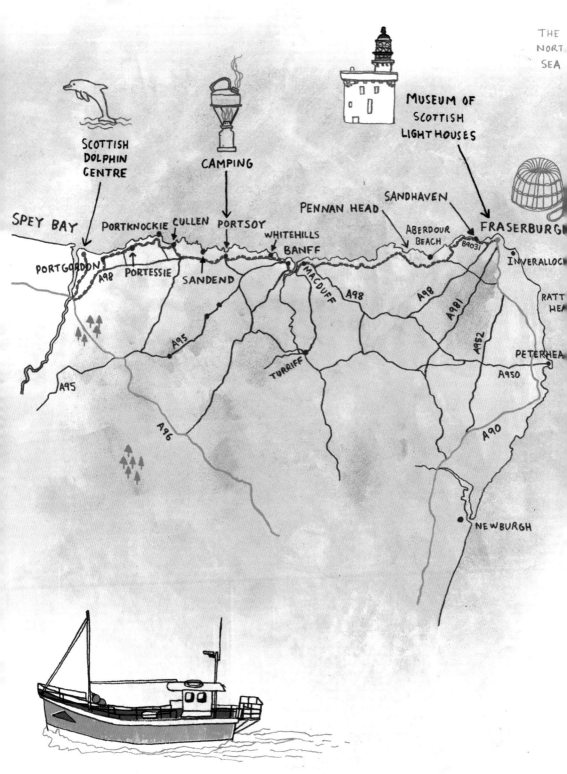

THE NORT SEA

SCOTTISH DOLPHIN CENTRE

CAMPING

MUSEUM OF SCOTTISH LIGHTHOUSES

SPEY BAY

PORTKNOCKIE CULLEN PORTSOY

SANDHAVEN

PENNAN HEAD

ABERDOUR BEACH

FRASERBURGH

PORTGORDON A98 PORTESSIE

WHITEHILLS

BANFF

B9031

INVERALLOCH

SANDEND

MACDUFF

A98

A98

A981

RATT HEA

A95

A952

PETERHEA

TURRIFF

A950

A95

A96

A90

NEWBURGH

ROUTE 18

MORAY FIRTH

FROM THE BLACKENING
INTO THE LIGHT

The eastern end of the Aberdeenshire
Coastal Route that follows the coast for
43 miles (70 kilometres) from Fraserburgh
to Spey Bay takes in some truly lovely
beach towns, quaint harbours, gorgeous
beaches and some of Scotland's best
locations for watching cetaceans.

BEST FOR:
Fishing
villages, seals,
odd rituals

START:
Fraserburgh

END: Spey Bay

MILEAGE: 50
miles (80
kilometres)

**DAYS TO
EXPLORE: 2**

**OS LAND-
RANGER MAP:**
28, 29, 30

EAST COAST AND CAIRNGORMS

249

I arrive in Fraserburgh from the south-east on the A98. I follow signs for the harbour, avoiding the town centre. As I drive down a narrow road towards a corrugated warehouse I can tell immediately that this is a working port. The unmistakable aroma of seafood fishery pervades the van and betrays the truth about Fraserburgh before I see it for myself. The smell of old lobster pots, of smokeries, of grease and shellfish gets stronger the closer I get to the water. I take a left down Shore Street and see, for the first time, the shape

of Europe's largest seafood port. There is a sailor's mission, a chandlery, harbour office and rowdy looking pubs on one side of the road and the port itself on the other. Here, behind giant stacks of lobster pots and coils of rope, lies *The Fleet* at anchor, a colourful antidote to the drab grey granite buildings and peeling whitewash on the harbour side.

The harbour has four or five sections, with each occupied by different sizes of vessels. At the north end, by the warehouses and smokers, lies a collection of some of the biggest fishing boats I have ever seen. These are the pelagic trawlers, the ocean-going giants that scoop up the contents of our seas so we can eat fish fingers and fishy bites whenever we fancy.

To the south, the tubs of the inshore fisheries are waiting patiently for a break in the weather or tide. As with all ports it's an alluring mix of senses-assaulting smells, sights and sounds. Ropes lie coiled on the quayside, funnels tip gently backwards and forwards, masts clank and gulls squawk.

I smell the local smoker on the breeze, a reminder, if ever there was one, that we aren't that far away from Arbroath, the home of the smokie. One or two men in oilskins tinker with fishing or sailing gear on their boats while a couple eat fish and chips in their car watching the comings and goings of this hardworking, but cheery little spot.

I carry on driving and find myself behind the warehouses, on a forgotten no through road with weeds growing through the cracks in the concrete and broken glass on the pavement. It's the kind of place you wouldn't want to be after dark. I round a corner and see a tipper truck adorned with spray-painted sheets and balloons. I can make out the names Amy-Jo and Jack on the sheet facing me and then a date. It's in a couple of weeks' time. There are about ten people sitting in the truck, mostly women, I think. They are covered

from head to toe in something that looks like powder paint and are wearing boiler suits, with filthy knotted handkerchiefs on their heads, smiling with white teeth through faces dripping with colour. A couple, dressed in what look like a suit and a dress, stand in the back of the truck, laughing. A woman, also wearing a filthy boiler suit, leans into the cab's window and bangs on the door, signalling something to the driver. It looks like the worst carnival float ever, put together in a panic the day before the big parade, a parody of something dying on its arse and so very home-made that it should end up here, at the forgotten end of a working harbour. I drive past and then turn around, not really sure what I have just seen. I take a few turns before pulling out on to Fraserburgh high street. Ahead of me I see the flat-bed tipper again, this time caught up in traffic. I pull up behind.

The people in the truck are now banging wooden spoons on saucepans. Surprisingly, I think, passers-by stop to smile and wave. Some cheer. Cars going the opposite way beep their horns. Despite it being the worst carnival float ever, I think to myself, everyone seems to be enjoying it. When the lights change and we both get caught up I stop the van, grab my camera and fire off a few shots. I want to remember this, whatever it is. When the lights change the truck goes left and I go right.

Later, at the Scottish Lighthouse Museum I ask the receptionist about the spectacle. Without any need to think about what I describe she tells me

it's a 'blackening', a unique Scottish wedding tradition. Based on an ancient tradition whereby a bride and groom had their feet blackened by coal to bring them good luck in their forthcoming nuptials, it's been bastardised and taken to its extremes: the bride and groom are captured, sometimes even tarred and feathered before being paraded around town in a horse and cart. Today, it's tamer, perhaps, and uses the internal combustion engine for propulsion, but things haven't changed that much.

I guess that this couple got lucky. They look more like they got lost on the way home from India's Holi festival than people who have been tarred and feathered. Perhaps they will get tied to a lamp post later, as tradition dictates. I don't hang about to find out.

I take the B9031 to Sandhaven to begin my trip along the Aberdeenshire Coastal Route. I had hoped for colour here, among the dour granite of Fraserburgh, and I wasn't wrong. Colour is everywhere, if you know where to find it. Or, more to the point, where to stumble upon it.

THE DRIVING

Fraserburgh is a fantastic place to start a journey. On a practical level it's at the north-eastern tip of Aberdeenshire, and is therefore one of the furthest points east on the Moray Firth. It is one of the largest towns in the area and has supermarkets galore behind its lovely, dune-backed beach. The sand is golden and the sea is clean, but of course, this is the far north and it's bound to be colder than it looks. I didn't dip enough to find out. I was keen to leave the crowded little town and head out along the tiny roads making up the Aberdeenshire Coastal Trail.

Fraserburgh has a number of hidden gems. The Museum of Scottish Lighthouses might look austere and foreboding from the outside but inside it's full of fabulous Fresnel glass with crystalline reflections focusing beams of light and shade here, there and everywhere. If you are interested in how and why lighthouses came to be symbols of hope and guidance, this is the place to come. I love lighthouses so it was wonderful to be able to peer through the lenses of lights that saved lives all over Scotland. The cost of entrance includes a visit to the old Fraserburgh lighthouse, a light that was built through the middle of a 16th century castle. Views are lovely. The stories of lighthouse keepers, storms and unending service enthral.

Leaving Fraserburgh is easy, thankfully. Follow the brown signs for the Coastal Route west, with a right on to the B9031 towards Sandhaven, a tiny fishing village a minute or so along the coast road from Fraserburgh. With a small stone harbour and cottages gathered around it, Sandhaven sets the mood for the rest of the ride. It reminds me of the North Yorkshire Coast, but without the idyllic beauty. There is underlying beauty here, but it's somehow been tarnished by hard work. It's the same at Rosehearty, where a collection of motorhomes sits on the seashore in the local caravan park. We are still within sight of Fraserburgh on low-lying land and the state of the villages somehow reflects this. It's tough here on the Moray Firth coast.

The coast rises from Fraserburgh towards Aberdour Bay and Pennan Head. Here, the flat fields of the hinterland drop off in high cliffs or collapse down steep-sided, meandering river valleys to tiny harbours below. Access is more difficult, streets narrow and driving ill advised in some places, such as Pennan, for larger vehicles. Even so, the villages I encounter along this stretch are lovely, largely untouched, it seems, by the kind of second-home

gentrification and abandonment you'd find down south, with a measure of holiday mixed with a stolid work ethic, if that were possible.

Troup Head, a little way along from Pennan Head is a recommended point from which to spot dolphins, porpoises and seabirds. It's an RSPB reserve with high cliffs so makes a good place to look out for the famous Moray Firth dolphins. Cullen is also another recommended spot, but in reality any cliff along this coast is good, as long as the conditions are right. That means calm conditions and good light.

Pennan I like very much. It sits at the bottom of a red sandstone cliff, with a pretty little harbour and net drying racks on the harbourside. The cottages are tiny but well kept and someone has been using discarded fish crates to plant flowers. It is delightful and I take lots of pictures. There are tourists here too, like me, following the Coastal Trail. The jolly mood continues as I drive onwards through Banff and Macduff, both reminding me of jolly Cornish towns with a little less whitewash. That's a good thing.

I spend the night at Portsoy, on a grass pitch a few feet above the beach. It's one of the best-located pitches I have ever been on. With my back to the caravans behind it could have been wild camping here, such is the beauty of the surroundings. There is a pub in the village but I opt to sit on the low grassy cliff and watch the seabirds. When I clean my teeth the next morning I realise my basin has one of the best views I have ever seen from a toilet block.

I am blown away again as I continue west along the B9139 and enter first Sandend, then Cullen. Sandend, another tiny spot with one road in and out, has a small campsite and a glorious sandy beach, as well as a harbour,

pub and collection of cutesy cottages, drying racks and bobbing boats in the harbour. A couple sit outside their house drinking coffee, enjoying the sunshine, watching over the beach, which is metres away across the road.

At Cullen I find a working town with a beautiful harbour and sandy beach sitting in a crucible below the cliffs, crossed by an impressive railway viaduct that was built in 1884 because a local landowner refused to grant permission for the track to cross their land. The railway closed at the hand of Dr Beeching but the viaduct was saved and now provides great views for a cycle route.

After Cullen the route takes you to Portknockie, another lovely little spot, and Portessie, before heading along the coast just a few metres above the shore to Portgordon, where I saw seals basking very close to the shore. This section offers a true coastal road. You can stop the van and step straight on to the dunes or the sea wall, watch seabirds or take pictures of seals without even leaving your vehicle.

From here the route goes inland before winding its way out to the Scottish Dolphin Centre at Spey Bay and my final stop. The dolphin centre is a one of the best places to see dolphins along this coast. There are great walks along the beach and estuary here, as well as a cafe and interpretation centre for those who want to find out more. A great place to stop and set yourself up for the next route.

PLACES TO STAY

Portsoy Links Caravan Park
Links Road, Portsoy, Aberdeenshire,
AB45 2RQ
web: http://portsoylinks.org
email: contact@portsoylinks.org
tel: 01261 842 695

info: *Portsoy Community Enterprise runs this great little campsite right on the beach at Portsoy. I stumbled upon it while looking for a decent spot and felt I had really lucked out.*

Sandend Caravan Park
Sandend, Portsoy, Aberdeenshire,
AB45 2UA
web: www.sandendcaravanpark.co.uk
email: sandendholidays@aol.com
tel: 01261 842 660

info: *Gorgeous fishing village with a fantastic sandy beach. The campsite is right on the beach and highly recommended.*

IN THE AREA

Museum of Scottish Lighthouses An interesting museum with a fascinating range of optics on the site of Scotland's oldest lighthouse.
- http://lighthousemuseum.org.uk

Scottish Dolphin Centre Cafe, shop and information centre at the mouth of the River Spey in an 18th-century salmon fishing station. It is a popular site for spotting dolphins and learning about them, as well as for seeing other Morayside wildlife. • http://dolphincentre.whales.org

Nearest van hire

Morayfirth Camper and Caravan Hire, Hopeman
- www.morayfirthcamper andcaravanhire.co.uk

OutThere Campervans, Inverness
- www.outtherecampers.co.uk

Lossiemouth Campervan Hire, Lossiemouth
- www.lossiemouthcamper vanhire.com

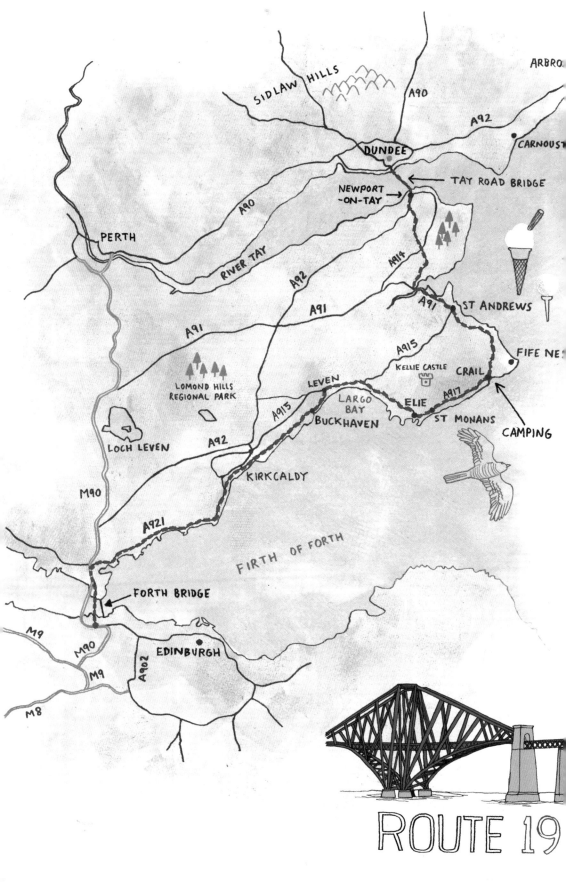

ARBRO

SIDLAW HILLS

A90

A92

DUNDEE

CARNOUST

TAY ROAD BRIDGE

NEWPORT -ON-TAY

A90

PERTH

RIVER TAY

A914

A92

A91

ST ANDREWS

A91

A91

A915

FIFE NE

Kellie Castle

CRAIL

LOMOND HILLS REGIONAL PARK

LEVEN

LARGO BAY

A917

A915

ELIE

ST MONANS

LOCH LEVEN

A92

BUCKHAVEN

CAMPING

M90

KIRKCALDY

A921

FIRTH OF FORTH

M90

FORTH BRIDGE

M9

M90

EDINBURGH

A902

M9

M8

ROUTE 19

19

DUNDEE TO EDINBURGH

A TRAIL OF TWO BRIDGES

It's easy to get from the Tay road bridge to the Forth road bridge on the M90. However, it's a much more pleasant pootle to take a coastal detour via St Andrews and Scotland's golfing country. There are a number of extraordinarily beautiful – and ancient – coastal fishing villages along the way. You'll also get a chance to visit what could be the true home of golf, not far from the home of golf itself. Confused? Go and follow the links...

BEST FOR:
Golf, and cute coastal villages

START: Dundee

END: Edinburgh

MILEAGE:
70 miles (113 kilometres)

DAYS TO
EXPLORE: 2–3

OS LAND-
RANGER MAP:
54, 59, 65, 66

EAST COAST AND CAIRNGORMS

261

We clear up our breakfast, a couple of Arbroath smokies cooked on the seafront in Arbroath (where else?), and head south. We've got St Andrews in our sights, but not for golf. Far from it. Andy is my travelling companion on this trip. We have been laughing our way around the Cairngorms and now we are on our way home to England and back to our respective lives.

Our mission is to avoid Dundee, Perth and the M90 and instead take the slow road between the bridges over the River Tay and the Forth Road Bridge to South Queensferry and Edinburgh. It'll be a big moment for me to cross the Firth of Forth again, the first time for Andy. My first crossing was in 2010 when I eventually did it in a classic VW after failing miserably previously; a few years before I had attempted a trip to Scotland in my 1981 T25 but got only as far as the Avonmouth Bridge near Bristol because the drive shaft sheared off.

Some people have to cross bridges every day, but I don't, which makes using them all the more special. Crossing bridges is crossing vast divides, joining one land mass to another. In some ways, bridges are the ultimate in positive human endeavour because their purpose is only for good (when used properly). We use bridges because we need to be connected.

We cross the Tay Bridge and head south towards St Andrews on the A914. We mooch about at the start of the Old Course, the official 'home of golf'. We watch the golfers, walk on the beach and, eventually, find the harbour – a pretty little port with multi-coloured houses and a few fishing boats. A gorgeous tub of a boat is in dry dock on the quayside, the owner shaping bits of wood for repairs. People watch, licking ice creams while sitting in chairs outside the harbour cafe as he saws planks into submission.

We drive on, finding Crail, another place with a rich golfing history, in an area called the East Neuk. It is believed, as I read later, that a form of golf was played here before 1492, which could well pre-date what is claimed by St Andrews. But we're not here for a golfing-history lesson, although it makes fascinating reading. Oh how poetic it would be – to me – if the home of golf wasn't the home of golf at all, but a tiny town little further down the coast.

We park in a back street, outside a higgledy-piggledy house with stone steps leading up to a faded red door on the first floor. It's made of red sandstone, set off by fiery red nasturtiums growing up the wall that makes up the outside of the steps. The house, like many of the others in the street, has a roof of faded clay pantiles and crow-stepped gables, making them look like they don't belong here. Down at the quayside, where the dates on the houses show some were built in the 17th century, there is more of the same. It reminds me of Staithes in Yorkshire, but then why wouldn't it? Dutch traders often traded their telltale S-shaped clay tiles, which were used as ballast in ships plying trade up the east coast. The stepped gables are a part of that heritage too, creating a very beautiful vernacular in this part of Scotland and the east coast.

It's a steep road that leads to the harbour. There are a few teashops and galleries here, as well as working boats and a shellfish seller. It's a very pretty place and we walk around admiring the stonework, the carved lintels and door jambs and the little gardens, made all the more colourful by geraniums growing in pots outside the tiny front doors.

We stop on a seat above a steep, cliff-top meadow to look out to sea and eat our sandwiches. The sea is blue and the sun is shining. Although the wind is chilly we are sheltered by a wall of red sandstone. Directly in front of us a sparrow hawk hovers over the meadow, spotting something. We watch it for a moment.

'Good here, isn't it?' says Andy.

'Yes,' I reply.

'Famous for golf apparently,' says Andy, 'fancy a game?'

'Not really,' I reply, 'I am happy here.'

'Good point. No reason to spoil it.'

THE DRIVING

The Tay Bridge, which marks the start of this journey, carrying the A92, is unusually, perhaps disappointingly, uninspiring. It was built between 1963 and 1964 and is 1.4 miles (2.25 kilometres) in length. Whether or not you like the very functional design, the bridge takes you from Dundee to Newport-on-Tay and saves a round trip of more than 43 miles (70 kilometres) via Perth. Once over the bridge it's a pleasant drive, though not spectacular, on the A914, then the A91 to St Andrews. Rounding St Andrews bay provides nice views over the North Sea, but it isn't until you get into St Andrews that the journey starts to come alive.

St Andrews is, predictably, stately, genteel and pretty. The beach is lovely and the buildings are elegant. It's just that the whole place is full to the brim with golfers, golfing shops, golf-themed cafes and golf hotels. There is more tartan here than at a Highland fling. The harbour, on the plus side, is really pretty, with a nice beach and dunes. It's just below the cathedral.

From St Andrews the A917 heads out of town to the south-east, heading first to Boarhills before arriving in Crail. It then follows the coast – its best

PLACES TO STAY

Sauchope Links Caravan Park
Westgate North, Crail, Fife, KY10 3XJ
web: https://largoleisureholidays.co.uk
email: info@largoleisure.co.uk
tel: 01333 450 460

info: *Heated outdoor pool, sea views and walking distance to Crail.*

stretch for views – until Upper Largo when the road turns into the A915, which heads inland just before Kirkcaldy. However, if you pick up the A921 you'll have a run along the coast all the way to the M90, which will take you on to the Forth Road Bridge.

Crossing the Forth Road Bridge is exciting because it runs parallel to the Forth Bridge, one of the world's most beautiful structures, if you like bridges. It is truly an icon (and I don't use that word very often) and we are bound to make talk about how they never finished painting it. Although they did, in 2011, when a new long-lasting paint job was finally put to bed.

If you think about it, crossing a bridge means you can't actually look at the bridge, so crossing the road bridge is a rare chance to see another great bridge from a different perspective. It's a great finish to this route, too!

IN THE AREA

Scotland's secret bunker Beneath a farmhouse in Fife there lies a once-secret nuclear-fallout shelter, which lay hidden for more than 40 years during the Cold War. It's a bizarre place, with air-raid sirens going off every so often and all kinds of scary stuff. Go and find out how the other 1 per cent would have lived.
• www.secretbunker.co.uk

Fife Coastal Path Superb coastal trail that links up the cute coastal villages along this route. • www.fifecoastalpath.co.uk

St Andrews Cathedral The remains of Scotland's largest and most impressive medieval church. Visit the museum, and St Rule's Tower for great views over the town.
• www.historicenvironment.scot/visit-a-place/places/st-andrews-cathedral/

Nearest van hire

View from the Slow Lane, Arbroath
• www.viewfromthe slowlane.com

Angus Motorhome Hire, Arbroath
• www.angusmotorhome hire.com

Fantastic Campervans, Dairsie
• www.fantasticcamper vans.co.uk

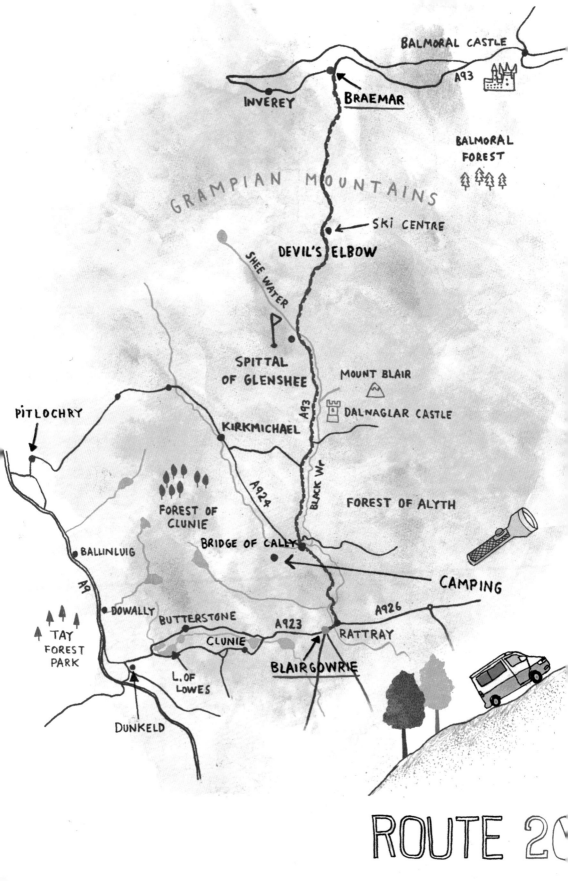

BALMORAL CASTLE

INVEREY

BRAEMAR

A93

BALMORAL FOREST

GRAMPIAN MOUNTAINS

SKI CENTRE

DEVIL'S ELBOW

SHEE WATER

SPITTAL OF GLENSHEE

MOUNT BLAIR

A93

DALNAGLAR CASTLE

PITLOCHRY

KIRKMICHAEL

A924

Black Wr

FOREST OF ALYTH

FOREST OF CLUNIE

BALLINLUIG

BRIDGE OF CALLY

CAMPING

A9

DOWALLY

BUTTERSTONE

A923

A926

RATTRAY

TAY FOREST PARK

CLUNIE

BLAIRGOWRIE

L. OF LOWES

DUNKELD

ROUTE 20

GLENSHEE

THE DEVIL'S ELBOW

This diverse and beautiful drive through the eastern Cairngorms takes you over the highest public road in Britain along the old military road, the A93 and the A939. It includes some of the loveliest countryside in Britain as well as wild landscapes well above the treeline.

BEST FOR:
Britain's highest main road

START:
Blairgowrie

END: Braemar

MILEAGE:
35 miles (40 kilometres)

DAYS TO EXPLORE: 2

OS LAND-RANGER MAP:
43, 53

I leave Pitlochry heading south on the A9. I've been driving up and down the B8079 to the north of the town trying to find a place to spend the night. I don't necessarily want to camp wild, but equally I don't want to stay on a big corporate site with acres of mobile homes and touring pitches. It's been a big effort to drive this far from home and I'd prefer not to squander the opportunity to wake up somewhere lovely. I have water, food and gas, so I don't necessarily need a campsite. I just have that feeling that I need to stop driving soon. However, each site I find seems to have more plastic than grass. I move on.

The beauty of being in a motorhome or camper van is that you can just pull off the road and relax. But of course it's never as simple as that. As a considerate wild camper I need somewhere to be properly suitable before I stop. That means it needs to be discrete, flat and away from the road. I don't want to be disturbed or moved on or to upset anyone. I am fussy, just like I am about any other campsite.

I take a left off the busy A9 and follow the A923 towards Blairgowrie for the start of my next drive, up to Glenshee. The A923 is a lovely low-altitude road that winds up into the hills and then follows a small river valley, skirting lochs as it goes. At the turn-off for Clunie I go in search of a quiet spot by the side of the loch. I find a pull-in where it seems as if others have camped before. With a little tidying it could be great. The sun is low and clouds of insects play on the still, glass-like water. Further on a man flicks a fly on to the surface of the loch. I notice lilies and the charcoal from a fire by the water's edge. I also notice a sign nailed to a tree over the road. It's the message from the local community saying that there have been issues here and requesting no fires, overnight parking or sleeping in vehicles. It's a blow, to be honest, especially since the day is starting to wear on. The light goes in a few hours. I have no choice but to reluctantly drive on.

For the next few miles I bemoan the fact that I can't find anywhere suitable, until, of course, serendipity strikes.

As I round a bend I see a track turn up steeply to the left, almost back on itself. As I whizz by I catch sight of a small white-and-blue sign at the entrance to the lane. It looks like … but it can't be. I stop too late to turn in and reverse back up the road. As I suspected it's a CL, a Certificated Location, which means it's a small campsite with no more than five pitches. I drive up the lane and arrive in a farmyard with a sloping lawn leading away from semi-derelict outbuildings. I see a pond on the left and a chicken run. The lawn is neatly cut, with five pitches already containing caravans. I wonder if they have any space. I stop the van and get out, following a home-made sign for the warden's 'office', another caravan, as it happens, recumbent beneath a huge copper beech. I am informed there are no pitches apart from some space at the back of the site, away from the other pitches, in the meadow. I take it and drive through the site, past a colourful stone-built border filled with roses, foxgloves, ferns and a couple of tall birches. The border bends around to the left and leads me to a little track on to a half-mown field. I park and set up.

It's perfect. My view is of nothing but the meadow, the fields behind and the fields on the valley sides opposite. Swallows dart about, delirious, I presume, at arriving back home. Rabbits hop about a little further up the field and cows moo restfully in the field behind.

I walk to check out the rest of the site, and the loo. The sign leads me to one of the roofless sheds. As I enter, swallows dash in and out of the doorway and disappear into nests in the rafters, changing course at the last minute as I enter.

The toilet is at the back of one of the barns. Like everything here it's a little ramshackle but tidy, like the hand-painted signs in new, if a bit squiffily painted, shiny gloss British racing green and Ferrari red. These are the kind of colours, and the kind of hand lettering, that my granddad would have done if he'd owned a campsite. What it lacked in skill would be made up for with care and enthusiasm. It's a good way to be.

There's no shower, but I don't care. The sun is shining and it's going to be a beautiful warm evening and I am happy. I have a spot in a meadow that I never imagined I'd find, just when I'd almost given up. The birds are flying, catching insects. The other campers are making their dinners. It's quiet.

Everything's home, the way it should be.

Tomorrow I set out for Glenshee and Britain's highest public road. I shall be ready. But first a supper, a glass of wine and a long, deep sleep.

THE DRIVING

You can't drive The Devil's Elbow, a notorious double hairpin bend on the A93, any more: it was bypassed when the A93 was upgraded with a safer, new stretch of road in the 1970s. However, that doesn't detract from the thrill of driving Britain's highest main road.

The route starts at Dunkeld on the A9, now the major route north for people wanting to rush from Perth to Inverness. However, for those of us who wish to dawdle, the A93 provides a welcome relief from the frenzied lorries and Mondeo-driving sales reps. If you wanted to take it the whole way it'd give you an alternative route to Aberdeen, or you could take a left at Balmoral (who wouldn't) and crack on over the tops to Tomintoul and then on to Inverness.

However, for our purposes we are heading as far as Braemar, home to the Braemar Gathering in September that is traditionally attended by the British Royal Family (if you wanted an autograph or something).

From Dunkeld take the A923 to Blairgowrie and Rattray. It's a gorgeous country road that winds its way past forestry before opening up as it follows Lunan Burn past six lochs in a gentle, pastoral kind of a glen with gently sloping sides and lots of agriculture. Of course it's all very pretty and provides a lovely lead-in to the main event, which is the A93. It departs Blairgowrie and Rattray unassumingly enough at first and then winds up to become something truly special by the time it gets to Bridge of Cally, passing through avenues of beautiful deciduous trees. Copper beeches, maples, chestnuts and beeches line the route as you climb up the River Ericht valley.

After Bridge of Cally you enter the 'wow' country as the road takes on a number of elegant sweeping bends, rising above the trees and following the meandering Black Water towards The Devil's Elbow. The valley here is sublimely beautiful. It could have been art directed. Wonky telephone poles take the place of the beeches, poking out of crumbling stone walls as the road passes a series of small plantations in a rounded, wobbly landscape. To your right the river meanders in a series of sharp turns with rocky beaches at each bend offering a stark change to the green of the fields and the darker green of the fir trees.

At the Spittal of Glenshee you'd be forgiven for being brought back down to earth by the deserted ski lodge on the old road. If you don't stop you may not need to dwell on it too much. This spot marks the end of the treeline and the transition into Glenshee 'proper', the road that rises to 670m (2,200ft) above sea level. It's great driving with lovely bends and a final uphill straight that levels out at Glenshee Ski Centre. Not bad! Not bad at all. But now we have to get down again.

The cruise down into Braemar is another lovely drive, with not much in the way of bends or hairpins to get in the way of a good, old-fashioned dawdle. Once you get close to Braemar it's worth taking a left turn at a little stone bridge that'll take you along the very pretty west side of Clunie Water. Unlike the main road this is a single-track affair with passing places, allowing you to mooch along admiring the traffic on the A93. From there it's just a question of parking up in Braemar and stopping at the excellent Braemar Mountain Sports Café for a cuppa and a little bit of peck.

PLACES TO STAY

Braemar Caravan Park
Glenshee Road, Braemar,
Aberdeenshire, AB35 5YQ
web: www.braemarcaravanpark.co.uk
email: info@braemarcaravanpark.co.uk
tel: 01339 741 373

info: *Caravan and Motorhome Club-affiliated site within walking distance of Braemar Village.*

Quarryhill Caravan and Motorhome Club Certificated Location
Kinloch, Blairgowrie, Perthshire
& Kinross, PH10 6SG
web: www.caravan
club.co.uk
tel: 01250 884 222

info: *Lovely, quiet certificated site on a working farm. Peace and tranquillity.*

IN THE AREA

The Braemar Gathering The Princess Royal and Duke of Fife Memorial Park in Braemar hosts the annual Braemar Gathering on the first Saturday in September. Even if you don't get there on that day it's worth having a wander to the site of the games: it's a bit like something out of *Harry Potter*.
www.braemargathering.org

Braemar A lovely little village that suffers from extreme temperatures in the winter and a bit of drizzle every time I visit. But don't let it put you off. There is a fantastic mountain equipment shop here with a cafe as well as chippy; the Invercauld Arms Hotel (good pizza); and a few eateries and nick-nack shops, plus a Co-Op.

Balmoral Castle and Braemar Castle
See route 16 on page 239 for more information.

Nearest van hire

Pitlochry Motorhome Hire, Pitlochry
• www.pitlochrymotorhomehire.co.uk

Deeside Classic Campers, Finzean
• www.deesideclassiccampers.com

Big Tree Campervans, Bankfoot
• www.bigtreecampervans.com

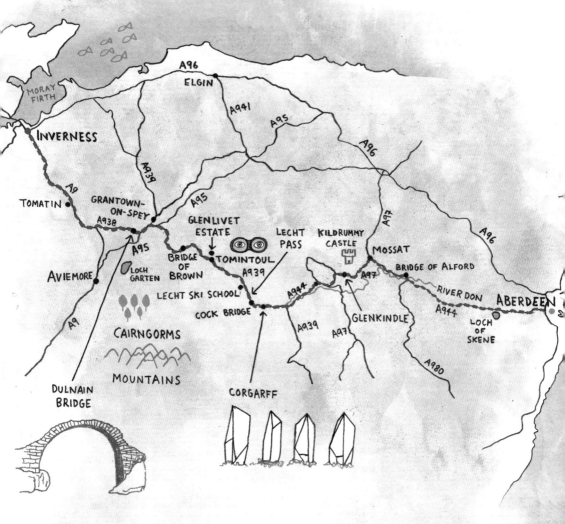

MORAY FIRTH

A96
ELGIN

A941

A95

A96

INVERNESS

A939

A9

TOMATIN

GRANTOWN-ON-SPEY

A938

A95

A95

GLENLIVET ESTATE

LECHT PASS

KILDRUMMY CASTLE

MOSSAT

A97

BRIDGE OF ALFORD

A96

AVIEMORE

LOCH GARTEN

BRIDGE OF BROWN

TOMINTOUL

A939

A944

A97

GLENKINDLE

RIVER DON

A944

ABERDEEN

A9

LECHT SKI SCHOOL

COCK BRIDGE

A939

A97

LOCH OF SKENE

A980

DULNAIN BRIDGE

CAIRNGORMS

MOUNTAINS

CORGARFF

ROUTE 21

ABERDEEN TO INVERNESS

TAKE THE SNOW ROADS

A long cut (as opposed to a short cut) that takes a direct route between Aberdeen and Inverness but that's not going to do it quickly. Taking in some incredible roads, this is part of the 'Snow Road' route, which includes one of Britain's highest public roads and a couple of fabulous new sculptures.

BEST FOR:
Bridges, forest, cycling, wildlife

START POINT:
Aberdeen

END POINT:
Inverness

MILEAGE:
64 miles (100 kilometres)

DAYS TO EXPLORE: 2–3

OS LAND-RANGER MAP:
26, 36, 37, 38

EAST COAST AND CAIRNGORMS

I am having a stand-off. Standing in the middle of a forest, a middle-aged man dressed in Lycra, wheeling a bike, I can't go forwards or backwards. My path is blocked, and, if I retreat I shall have to return to the van, my tail between my legs, intention denied.

Black eyes, glinting a little with the soft reflected light of a cloudy March afternoon, stare at me, unblinking from the path. I dare not breathe, for fear of upsetting the creature that's right in front of me. It moves, a fraction, then dashes for the nearest tree. I remain as still as I can. I know that if I go for my camera it will disappear completely.

Motionless, it continues to stare at me, as if willing me to back away. Its bushy tail is still, tufty ears pricked, revolving ever so slightly. It's a red squirrel, a native of these parts. I am not used to seeing them and I want the encounter to last as long as possible, so I remain still. I will not be the one to back down. It's only the first or second red squirrel I have ever seen, and it's a feisty one at that.

Before my slow-road adventures I had only ever seen the three stuffed red squirrels my grandfather 'kept' in a cabinet in his living room. Their black glass eyes glinted in the living room lights, but their ears never picked up the sounds of the world outside their Victorian glass case. I wonder where they are now.

So I know what red squirrels look like, but I don't often see them moving. Mind you, this one, standing his ground in front of me, isn't moving much. I am an invasive species in Lycra, coming from the south, and he clearly doesn't like it. If he was a lobster he'd be 'giving it all that', as the joke goes.

The Glenlivet Estate, a part of Crown Estate Scotland, owns a vast tract of land to the north of the A939 at Tomintoul. A lot of this land is given over to outdoor activities and some of it is semi-native birch forest. I passed through beautiful river valleys of this birch forest on my way here, to the Glenlivet Mountain Bike Trailhead from the A938 near Tomintoul. I stopped to admire the open, grassy understorey between the mature weeping birches and to take pictures. Unlike the dense, industrial-scale forestry I see so much of in Scotland, this kind of forest is light and open and full of possibility. It makes me think of afternoons by the river, of picnics and walks, sheep grazing beneath the birches and the river gurgling gently around its snaking curves.

By contrast, it's darker here at the head of the trail. I have 5½ miles (9 kilometres) of Blue Route to begin and my adversary, the red, is still staring at me. I make a move to get on my bike and he scuttles up the tree, along a branch and then on to another tree. He stops for a moment, to check I am not chasing him I suppose, and then finally disappears into the labyrinthine criss-crossing branches of the pine forest.

The track stretches out before me, winding its way into the forest as a wavy reddish line between the trees. I set off, on a 4-mile-long (6.5-kilometre-long) downhill that will see me twist and turn around berms, over hump and bumps and around hairpins in the silent, dark forest. I needed to get out of the van and get some air in my lungs after a long day exploring the Cairngorms and this is the perfect way to do it.

I hope my red friend is comfortable with it.

THE DRIVING

Leaving Aberdeen on the A944 takes you upstream, along the River Don to Mossat. It's a great drive, on a great road that's easy, simply because it follows the floodplain through spurs of hills on tree-lined curves and groves of chestnut and beech. In the distance, dark plantations of forestry land cover the hillsides, while the valley floor is made lighter by agriculture.

The Don takes a sharp left at Mossat, changing course to head south towards the Cairngorms. There's a left turn to take yourself, on to the A97, which starts to get really good, following the river as it heads upstream into the mountains. The further on you go the better the drive gets here until you reach the section around Glenbuchat when the river runs quickly, wide and lovely, right next to the road. Soon after Glenkindle there is a right-hand turn for Dinnet and Deeside that will take you straight into the mountains and a very beautiful stretch of road – if you wanted a very beautiful detour

before taking one of Britain's highest main roads. In fact, following the A97 south will bring you out at the A93 on Deeside, in itself an awesome road. Turning towards Braemar will carry you along the river until the Bridge of Gairn when the A939 will take you back towards Cock Bridge and the major attraction on this route, the Lecht Pass. This is where you join 'The Snow Road', an initiative that creates a route between Blairgowrie and Grantown-on-Spey.

Before you rise up the full height of the Lecht Pass, to its magnificent 645m (2,116ft) or more above sea level, there is a stop that must be made, at a sharp bend in the steep approach to the main climb, at Corgarff. This is 'The Watchers', an inspirational art installation commissioned by the Scottish Government's Scenic Routes initiative and designed by John Kennedy. The view from the piece is just lovely and it's a great place to stop and take pictures or marvel at the mountains. It's only at viewpoints like this that you can begin to see how the land lies. A white farmhouse stands out starkly from the hills, with a green field protecting it from the constant threat of rewilding from the rock and heather. Rivulets from the peaks form deep gullies and spurs as the water, the source of the Don, tumbles ever downwards.

Once you've admired the view, it's time to tackle the pass. It's a straightforward affair with a long steep run up to the top and no challenging bends or hairpins.

At the top you reach the ski centre at Lecht and almost immediately drop down a steep-sided glen with dark forest to your left and open moorland on the right. At the bottom there is a sharp left-hand bend and a place to stop on the right. This will take you to Lecht Mine (on foot), a short-lived iron ore and manganese mine. From here the road is sometimes referred to as the Old Military Road. It was built in 1745 following the Jacobite revolution.

Then it's on to Tomintoul and another artwork, 'The Still', this time by Angus Ritchie and Daniel Tyler. This is a square arch with reflective sides that allows you to get amazing views over the Cairngorms. It's well worth a stop.

This is where the Glenlivet Estate has its influence. The new road bypasses the old Bridge of Avon but you can still cross it on foot. It's a lovely spot and warrants a leg stretch at the very least. This is also the point where you can turn off for the Glenlivet Mountain Bike Trailhead.

Continuing on from Tomintoul you'll come to a spectacular valley and pretty bit of road at Bridge of Brown. The roads drops into an open valley of birch and pine, winding past cottages and the Bridge of Brown Tearoom, before turning sharply in a hairpin and then climbing up and out of the treeline again. A few miles on you'll come to the junction with the A95.

Turn left and follow the main road for a couple of miles before taking a detour on the A938 through Dulnain Bridge, if only to see the old packhorse bridge at Carrbridge before you hit the A9 and the last run into Inverness.

The bridge is a remarkable arch of stone that is the oldest stone bridge in the Highlands. It crosses a fast-flowing river gorge that couldn't be crossed when the river was in spate, delaying funerals at the church at nearby Duthil.

IN THE AREA

The Glenlivet Estate There's lots to do in this Crown Estate-owned part of the Cairngorms, including gorge walking, mountain biking, wildlife spotting and, of course, whisky tasting at Glenlivet and Tomintoul.

• www.glenlivetestate.co.uk

Pitfichie Forest Trails and White Hills Stone Circle
A series of walks and trails in lovely forest. Interesting stone circle too.

• http://scotland.forestry.gov.uk/visit/pitfichie

PLACES TO STAY

Haughton House Holiday Park
Montgarrie Road, Alford,
Aberdeenshire, AB33 8NA
web: www.haughtonhouse.co.uk
email: enquiries@haughtonhouse.co.uk
tel: 01975 562 107

info: *A large holiday park in the Haughton Country Park.*

Glenlivet Hall Caravan Site (Caravan Club Certified Site)
Glenlivet Village Hall, off the B9008
web: www.glenlivetestate.co.uk/
accommodation-food/camping-caravans
tel: 01807 590 207

info: *A quiet certificated site behind Glenlivet Village Hall.*

The Bowling Club Caravan Site
10 Tomnabat Lane, Tomintoul,
Ballindalloch, Moray, AB37 9EZ
web: www.glenlivetestate.co.uk/
accommodation-food/camping-caravans
tel: 01807 580 201

info: *Five hardstanding pitches in Tomintoul with toilets.*

Nearest van hire

**Cairngorm Campers,
Boat of Garten**
• www.cairngormcampers.com

Deeside Motorhomes, Torphins
• www.deeside-motorhomes.co.uk

HIGHLANDS AND THE NORTH

The North Coast 500 is one of the world's best
coastal driving routes and rivals even the Wild Atlantic Way,
Ireland's epic drive. It takes you on a huge loop along the Great
Glen, Scotland's great fault line, to Inverness, then up the east coast,
along the very top of Scotland and then down the west coast with
stop offs at Applecross and Ullapool. There are natural wonders here,
as well as a lot of incredible driving, lovely beaches and out-of-the-
way adventures. Walk into remote Sandwood Bay, visit Smoo
Cave or make yourself the most northerly person on the
great British mainland on this slow road
adventure to Britain's extremes.

CAVE

STRATHY POINT

CASTLE OF ME~

DUNNET
HEAD

MURKLE
BEACH

HOLBORN
HEAD

DOUNREAY

DURNESS

SANGOBEG

RABBIT
ISLANDS

TORRISDALE

PORTSKERRA

DUNNET

STR~

A838

FARR KIRTOMY

A836

THURSO

CASTLETOWN

LAID

LOCH ERIBOLL

BETTYHILL

MELVICH

GOLVAL

B976

ERIBOLL

COLDBACKIE

LOCH
CALDER

TONGUE

CAMPING

A897

A9

LOCH
HOPE

KINLOCH
LODGE

BEN
HOPE

A836

BEN
LOYAL

LOCH
LOYAL

ROUTE 22

DUNNET HEAD TO DURNESS

ON THE TOP OF THE WORLD

From mainland Britain's most northerly point to its most north-westerly settlement, the drive from Dunnet Head to Durness is spectacular, taking in some of Europe's best surf spots as well as a handful of extraordinary beaches and some lovely villages.

BEST FOR:
Surf, beaches, wilderness

START:
Dunnet Head

END: Durness

MILEAGE:
75 miles (120 kilometres)

DAYS TO EXPLORE: 4–5

OS LAND-RANGER MAP:
9, 10, 11, 12

HIGHLANDS AND THE NORTH

I am woken by my phone ringing. For a moment I don't know where I am. I slept well and, as a consequence of waking unnaturally, take a little time to gather my thoughts. I hear the sound of rain on canvas and smell the mustiness of a damp tent. It takes me to exactly where I am and why the phone is ringing. I answer. It is Elena, a radio producer at Heart FM, who has rung me to talk about camping on Jamie Theakston's Breakfast Show. Apparently Mr Theakston is going glamping at the weekend, is afraid of bears and is looking for reassurance from a camping expert. I explain that I am more into camper vans than tents, but they bill me as a 'camping expert' anyway and push on with the interview. I agree to talk about camping disasters.

Jamie asks me where I am. I think about it. I am in a tiny tent in a tiny campsite at a tiny place called Melvich, on the north coast of Scotland. The campsite is attached to the raucous and friendly Halladale Inn, very near to a lovely sandy beach that's also a very good surf break. It's about halfway between Dunnet Head and Durness, a few miles over the border that

separates Sutherland, once the last hunting grounds of the wolf in Britain, from its neighbour to the east, Caithness. I got here by hire car, after flying from home in Cornwall, because I have a few things to research before I complete this section on the North Coast 500, and not enough time to drive up here in the van. As it's August Bank Holiday all the camper van- and motorhome-hire companies are fully booked too, so I have had no choice but to do my research by car.

I feel a bit of a fraud. Flying meant I had to pack everything – my tent, sleeping bag, sleeping mat, cooker and cooking stuff – into a bag to go in the hold. Unable to put a gas canister on to the flight, and unable to find one since I left Inverness airport, I am without any way of making a cup of tea or cooking dinner. Last night I ate in the pub. Later on the trip I resort to cooking pasta in a hotel kettle, but we'll leave that for another book. In my tiny tent I am suffering for the lack of space, unable to even sit up and write on my laptop (first-world problems, I know). I have pitched on a slight slope and so, despite sleeping well, I have slid down the sleeping mat until my sleeping bag has been forced against the inner lining of the tent, which has pushed the lining against the fly sheet. I have broken the first rule of camping to never touch the fly sheet when it's raining. My sleeping bag is very wet.

Now I remember why I don't like camping.

The night before, I was chatting to the person on the next pitch to me, a lady driving the North Coast 500 in a rented Type 2 Volkswagen camper, a Devon Moonraker. We joked about how it chugs up the hills and doesn't drive in a straight line, but secretly I am so very envious. As she said goodnight and closed the sliding door, leaving me to crawl into my tent, I wished I could be in my van. I remembered why I love camper vans and motorhomes and deeply missed the space and the light, the ease with which you can boil a kettle or make dinner, the way a rock and roll bed converts in seconds into a comfy bed, the way a set of chocks and a spirit level can always give you a level night's sleep and the way you can draw back the curtains in the morning and drive away. You can't do any of that in a tent.

Jamie Theakston is wary of camping, apparently. He's afraid of wild animals, of being out of his comfort zone. He wants to know what it's like to be in a tent.

'It's raining outside but I am cosy inside,' I say. 'I am warm. I have food. I have everything I need right here, even a phone signal and passable 4G.'

He laughs. 'I am warming to you,' he says, 'but what about bears? How am I going to avoid being eaten in the night?'

'This is the UK. There are no bears or wolves, even in this part of Scotland. The biggest danger you face on your camping trip is yourself.'

That gets a laugh. And, happily, for the radio audience, I am an 'expert camper', speaking from a tiny tent in a tiny campsite in Northern Scotland, and signing off.

It's time to pack up and hit the road. I have some driving to do before my flight leaves at 9am tomorrow morning. The rain comes down still, getting heavier with each passing minute, soaking me as I pack my stuff into the boot of the car. It soaks the inner tent too, as I try to take the sopping-wet fly sheet off without making everything else wet as well. I make a cack-handed job of it, which results in the fly sheet sticking to the inner tent. By the time I have bundled the whole lot into the car, all of it is dripping with rainwater. Thinking about the night ahead of me, I try to spread the inner tent across the back seat of the hire car so that it will dry off as I drive. I turn the heating to full and drive away, hungry, wet and steaming in the dampness of an August deluge.

Again I feel like I am a terrible fraud. I have just about – I think – managed to pass myself off as an 'expert camper' at exactly the time when I am making a complete mess of it. I take a last look at the old VW that is still pitched up next to the space my tent was in and wish I was driving something like that.

I would do anything right now to chug up hills in second gear, to worry every time I had to start the engine and to be able to drive away knowing my bed would always be dry and warm. To have the freedom to park up wherever I like and put the kettle on, to cook up a feast on my little two-ringed stove and to draw the curtains at night would be a gift I would never take for granted.

I am an 'expert camper', apparently, but I wish I was in a van.

THE DRIVING

The north coast of Scotland is many things. It can be drab but it can also be beautiful in the extreme. It can be windy and rainy and very cold. And yet on the day I drove from Dunnet to Melvich it was warm and clear, with hazy orange light fading into a star-filled night. No one was on the road and there were no people on any of the beaches I stopped at. Who would want to be anywhere else on nights like these?

Dunnet Head is the most northerly point on the Great British mainland. There is a lighthouse with a compound and a few bits of forgotten concrete – all that remain of the Second World War radar station – and not much else. It's low, flat, scrubby land, but it has high, vertical cliffs.

The B855 winds around Barifa's Hill and Long Loch and Many Lochs before it reaches farmland at Brough and then goes on to meet the A836 at Dunnet. This is where you'll encounter the first of your north coast beaches, Murkle Beach. It's a huge arc of pale pinkish sand, with a Caravan and Motorhome Club Site right in the dunes. From Murkle it's just a few twists and turns and a long straight into the region's biggest town, Thurso. Surfers talk about the place with reverence because the east side of the River Thurso is home to one of Europe's best waves. Breaking in peaty water over a shallow reef, it's both terrifying and exhilarating and brings business to Thurso all year round. The town was 'redeveloped' in the 18th century on a grid system (said to be the inspiration for New York) and built from local pink stone. It's regimented and not very quirky, seeming to hide away from the sea that gave the town its prominence as a port and shelter.

Thurso is the last big stop before Durness, so this is the place to get your bits and pieces (there is a Tesco, but also lots of local shops in the high street) before venturing west. The A836 meets the A9 for part of its final journey to the port of Scrabster before turning back into the A836 again just west of the town and heading out across farmland towards Dounreay, Sandside (lovely,

if a bit nuclear, harbour and beach) and then into the moorland on the winding way up to Melvich.

After Melvich things change. You'll drive over moorland between lush green glens as you pass through Strathy, Armadale, Farr and on to the lovely village of Bettyhill, where there is a swimming pool, cafe, shop, campsite and the unbelievably lovely beach at Torrisdale at the mouth of the River Naver. The road follows the river inland and then weaves its way to Coldbackie (incredible white-sand beach with caves and waterfalls) before following the Kyle of Tongue south and over the causeway towards Loch Eriboll. There is a small road that takes a short cut just before Tongue that brings you out along the side of the water that is just gorgeous. Big motorhomes won't make it but the more nimble camper will cruise it. Great picnic spots or opportunities for wildlife spotting.

The 'jewel in the crown' of this route, for want of a better phrase, is the little island Ard Neackie, which must be one of the most photographed

places in Scotland. Connected to the mainland by a narrow strip of machair and beach, it's stunningly beautiful and the views of it from the layby on the road are magical. Calm, clear water, sandy beaches, heather and mountains behind make an absolutely idyllic landscape. Mind you, it's not disappointing to get back in the van and continue onwards. The drive around Loch Eriboll is sublimely beautiful, with lots of twists and turns and perfectly appointed painted houses, moorings and 'to die for' vistas along the way. This is the place you'd like to move to, if only you had the nerve and Tesco would deliver this far out. It's the same for me. To look out of the window and see Loch Eriboll would never, ever get boring.

Once you are done with the views, the drive into Durness is a formality, with just a couple of gorgeous beaches and sands at Sangobeg to distract you. Or you could fly like an eagle on the zip wire above it and see the lie of the land from a different perspective. Either way you'll soon have landed at Durness, the oasis in the north, and your final stop on this leg.

PLACES TO STAY

Dunnet Bay Caravan Club Site
Dunnet, Thurso, Highlands, KW14 8XD
web: www.caravanclub.co.uk
tel: 01847 821 319

info: *Top of the world! A neat and tidy site on the machair above the beach at Dunnet Bay.*

Thurso Bay Caravan and Camping Park
Smith Terrace, Scrabster Road, Thurso, KW14 7JY
web: www.thursobaycamping.co.uk
email: stay@thursobaycamping.co.uk
tel: 01847 892 244

info: *A handy site for Thurso town and the beach, with views over the bay.*

Sango Sands Oasis – See route 23, page 317.

IN THE AREA

Pool and Fitness Suite at Bettyhill If you need a scrub, a sauna or even a workout, this is your only chance to do so for miles.

- www.northcoastleisurecentre.org.uk

The Castle and Gardens of Mey Once owned by the Queen Mother, this is Britain's most northerly inhabited castle. The Queen Mum saved it from demise following the death of King George VI in 1952 and spent a lot of time there before her death. She bequeathed it to the castle trust in 1996.

- www.castleofmey.org.uk

Led Zep fans Phillips Harbour at Harrow, a little to the east of Dunnet Head, was opened by Jimmy Page of Led Zep when restoration works were completed in 1979. Go find the plaque that commemorates the event, if you can't get enough of Jimmy's love.

Smoo Cave and **Golden Eagle Zip Lines, Durness** See route 22, page 308.

RSPB Dunnet Head Free-to-enter RSPB site, with no facilities, but opportunities for spotting puffins, fulmar and guillemot. • www.rspb.org.uk/reserves-and-events/find-a-reserve/reserves-a-z/reserves-by-name/d/dunnethead/

Nearest van hire

Happy Highland Campers, Inverness
- www.happyhighland campers.co.uk

OutThere Campervans, Inverness
- www.outthere campers.co.uk

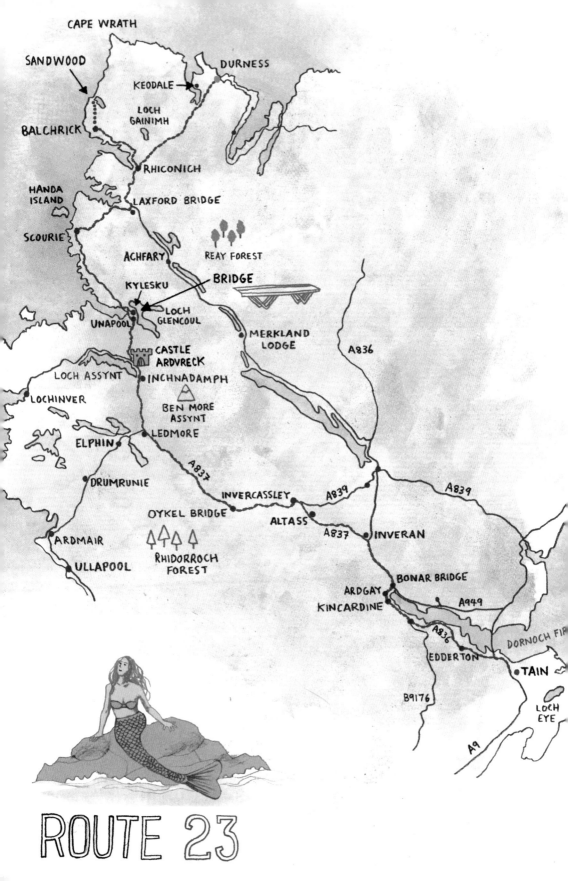

CAPE WRATH

SANDWOOD

DURNESS

KEODALE

LOCH
GAINIMH

BALCHRICK

RHICONICH

HANDA
ISLAND

LAXFORD BRIDGE

SCOURIE

REAY FOREST

ACHFARY

BRIDGE

KYLESKU

UNAPOOL

LOCH
GLENCOUL

MERKLAND
LODGE

A836

CASTLE
ARDVRECK

LOCH ASSYNT

INCHNADAMPH

LOCHINVER

BEN MORE
ASSYNT

ELPHIN

LEDMORE

A837

DRUMRUNIE

INVERCASSLEY

A839

A839

OYKEL BRIDGE

ALTASS

A837

INVERAN

ARDMAIR

RHIDORROCH
FOREST

ULLAPOOL

BONAR BRIDGE

ARDGAY

A949

KINCARDINE

A836

DORNOCH FIR

EDDERTON

TAIN

B9176

LOCH
EYE

A9

ROUTE 23

23

DURNESS TO TAIN

CROSSING THE LAST WILDERNESS

A spectacular Highland route from Durness, the last outpost on the north coast that takes you as close to wilderness as you'd care to get by road, then follows the west coast south as far as the magnificent bridge at Kylesku and then follows the lovely, ever-changing Glen Oykel to Dornoch Firth and the A9 at Tain.

BEST FOR:
Highland wilderness

START:
Durness

END: Tain

MILEAGE:
100 miles (160 kilometres)

DAYS TO EXPLORE: 2

OS LAND-RANGER MAP:
9, 15, 21

HIGHLANDS AND THE NORTH

307

I have all I need on my back for a night under the stars. I have a tent, a sleeping mat, some food and water and a sleeping bag. Unusually for me I have abandoned the van and have decided to tent it overnight, if conditions stay good, because I have an inkling that I want to find out what it's like to be as remote as possible, even if it's just for one night.

I park the van in the tiny car park at Blairmore, change into my walking boots, load up my pack and head across the road to the path that leads to Sandwood Bay. It's a bright, if cloudy day and there is a touch of mugginess to the air. It's July. As I put one foot in front of the other and walk along the path, past the last fences I will see in a while, I think of what lies ahead.

I am walking into one of Britain's most remote beaches. It is also said to be one of Britain's most beautiful, if not the most beautiful. It's a tough one to call so I have decided to go and see for myself. But of course there is more to it than that. In visiting Sandwood Bay on this slow-road adventure I will be fulfilling another of my life's ambitions: to visit the UK's extremities. My original plan had been to carry a board with me and surf but after a stern warning from the doctor in Durness that I should keep a perforated eardrum dry for at least 48 hours, I decided it would be a foolish thing to do. Besides, I am alone and would be 4 miles (6.5 kilometres) from help if anything happened while in the water. I think of the distance to the next slice of land from Sandwood and shudder. The nearest place to Sandwood, heading west, is probably the eastern seaboard of Canada, if not the southern tip of Greenland. With unpredictable and unknown currents, surfing here alone would be beyond foolish.

Sandwood Bay is one of those places that inspires, simply because of its isolation and the myths and legends that have been built up around it. As the first beach on the western side of the mainland after Cape Wrath, it is said Vikings drew their longships up here to launch them on Sandwood Loch. Remnants remain under the sands, they say. There are also said to be remains of Pictish settlements near here. So people have always been here, but it's been a lonely place since 1847 when the land was cleared of crofters and the Gaelic-speaking poor to make way for sheep farming. Death has a place here, too, as many ships were lost in the area before the lighthouse at Cape Wrath was built in 1828. On stormy nights the ghost of a sailor, wrecked on the beach, is reputed to knock on the door of the bothy that's around a mile inland from the sands. In January 1900 a local farmer claimed he saw a mermaid of ravishing beauty languishing on the rocks, and maintained this firm assertion until his death. Aeroplanes have ditched here, too, and there is apparently a Merlin engine from a Spitfire buried in the sand somewhere on the beach.

It's 4 miles (6.5 kilometres) to the beach from the car park. And it's not a terribly interesting walk. I follow the well-worn path over the open, flat, boggy landscape, crossing peaty rivulets on stepping stones, skirting the southern tip of Loch na Gainimh and passing close to three other small lochs before rounding the hillock on the south side of the bay.

As the bog gives way to tufty grassland the beach reveals itself in one glorious sweep of pink sand. In a few steps my view is transformed. One minute I am looking over loch and bog, the next I am laying my eyes on a beach of sublime beauty and of such a grand scale that it's hard to take it all in. The beach is a mile long and is backed by dunes and Sandwood Loch. A few ruins dot the hinterland. At either end there are huge sea cliffs, rising vertically from the grasslands at the south end and from the river that joins Sandwood Loch to the sea at the northern end. In the middle of the bay are a couple of rounded and pitted rock islands jutting out of the sand like huge walnuts. A thin line of dark seaweed marks the high tide. To the north the headlands of Cape Wrath, partly shrouded in low cloud, jut out into the sea.

I walk on towards the sands and enter the dunes. They are huge, with steep drops down to beach level. It's hard to know where to walk to reach the beach so I walk along the ridgeline of one dune and then half slide and half run down it and on to the sand. It is then that I see the Am Buachaille sea stack for the first time. At 65m (213ft) tall it is equally impressive and daunting at the same time and shows me just how huge this landscape is. I feel tiny, insignificant, alone. There are just a couple of other people on the beach, but they soon drift away and I am left to my own devices among the marram grass.

I walk up and down the beach, eat my packed lunch and contemplate the night ahead. The beach is magical, of course, but it also has an atmosphere that I can't put my finger on. There is something about it that's unsettling,

longing, sad, deeply melancholy. I think of all those who were forcibly removed from here, of those who ended their lives here and of those who landed here.

I feel spots of rain on my skin as I sit on a rounded grey-pink rock overlooking the loch. It's coming from the south, beyond the sea stack, where dark clouds are brooding. I try to ignore it but the drops just keep on dropping: heavy, fat globules of warm summer rain landing on my bare arms.

It's mid afternoon. I see the couple scrambling up the dunes, up and away from the beach towards the path that will take them, eventually, back to their car.

The morning is a long time away, I think to myself, as I pack up my lunch stuff. I have a choice. I can either pitch up now and sit out the rain or I can walk back to the van.

It's a tough decision, but it's made easier by gusts of wind from the south, bringing fatter drops of rain. My raincoat flaps in the wind as I struggle to do up the zip, raise my pack on to my back and start walking towards the dunes. The rain is getting heavier. It's now gone from summer rain to squally downpour and I am about to make a decision I know I'll regret for years to come.

I trudge out of the dunes, across the machair and into the bog. There is no shelter and I am soaked through in minutes, heading south, straight into the rain. An hour later I am still wet, still trudging into the rain, still wishing I'd had the nerve to stay and pitch up. But for the moment I have one mission: get back to the van, get dry and get a cup of tea on.

It happens soon enough and before long I am back on the slow road, slightly unfulfilled but also deeply humbled by Sandwood Bay. Ambition part complete, it's enough for me today. I vow to return to this magical, mysterious, deeply moving place.

It's only four miles.

THE DRIVING

At Durness there is a petrol station that is automated and therefore available 24 hours a day. It's popular and you might have to queue, since there is only one pump, but don't miss your opportunity to fill up. While you have come a long way to get here from Thurso or Wick, you still have a long way to go to get back to the A9 or, if you detour south and carry on down the west coast, to Ullapool.

But no matter. If you fill up at Durness you'll be fine. You might need to fill up on all kinds of other stuff at Durness, too. Food, water, pubs with views and maybe even company. You are in the very north-west of the UK here and about to head south on the A838 down the Kyle of Durness and around the MOD firing range and wilderness that is Cape Wrath. If you have the time and can make the boat and minibus that'll take you out to the lighthouse then do it. Pick it up from Keodale (times vary according to the tide and ferry). Sadly my timetable didn't allow it. Instead, I walked in – and not even to – the really wild bit. At Balnakeil Bay, a lovely sweep of pale-yellow sand facing the wilderness, there is a sign that explains what the MOD do at Cape Wrath. They shell it, sometimes from ships. Don't be alarmed. And it's all done under the auspices of a 'responsible' land ownership.

It's remarkable, but departing from Durness really does feel like you are stepping out into the unknown, even if you encounter cars and motorhomes all along this route.

As you leave Durness and head down the east side of the Kyle you will see a view as huge as one you'll ever encounter in the UK. The sky is big. The hills are big. The Kyle is big. There are big standing stones erected at the side of the road for you to stop at. The bends are big. It's all massive, exciting, fantastic. And it's easy to drive. Take your time and enjoy not having to pull over every two minutes to let someone pass. However, it doesn't last long.

At the head of the Kyle there's a steady ascent on a straight-ish road that follows the River Dionard upstream for a while before it veers left into the wild and you are left following a tributary up to Loch Taebhaidh and on to Rhiconich. Here you can pick up the B801 that'll take you to Blairmore and the path to Sandwood Bay. It's a lovely road in itself and follows Loch Inchard for much of the way.

The A838 continues south through low-level(ish) Highland scenery to Laxford Bridge, past the bay at Scourie and then on to Kylesku. It's lovely scenery here, and you notice the change. It's not on such a big scale and yet it's still brilliant, undulating, twisted, fantastic countryside, with water and rock meeting in dramatic fashion at every turn. I loved driving this section and especially enjoyed pulling in at the car park above the Kylesku Bridge, even though it was hammering with rain. The bridge was completed in 1984, saving drivers a ferry journey, or, if the weather was bad, a very long round trip via Lairg. The bridge is an award winner, is supposed to be among the world's most beautiful and is always worth a stop.

There's more to come past Kylesku too. The A894 becomes the A837 just before Ardvreck Castle, a stunning wreck on an island in the middle of a loch, connected by a small sandy causeway. Get your camera out...

At Ledmore Junction the A837 meets the A835 in open moorland, with the latter heading west and then south to Ullapool. By following the A837 instead of taking the A835 I am going off the North Coast 500 and taking a very pretty and ever-changing diversion back to Inverness. The road follows Loch Borralan close to the shore before heading further up into the open

moorland. The route climbs a little at first, ending up on moorland with big skies and big vistas, before peaking out at 176m (577ft) above sea level just before joining Glen Oykel. From here the landscape changes rapidly as the river gains pace on its journey towards Dornoch Firth. The valley floor becomes wider and ever more used for agriculture from here, changing the feel of the road from wilderness to benign highway snaking along a glen towards the sea. It's a feeling of coming down off the wild stuff and into the trees.

At the junction with the B864 at Inveran there is a welcome diversion to the Falls of Shin, a famous salmon leap. It's a spectacular spot with a viewing platform enabling a clear view of the leap. It is remarkable how far these things can jump!

A little further down stream and you hit the Kyle of Sutherland, crossing over to the south side of the Dornoch Firth at Bonar Bridge. Thereafter is a really lovely low-level drive alongside the water until you reach the A9 just after the Dornoch Bridge.

PLACES TO STAY

Loch Clash Stopover

Loch Clash Pier, Kinlochbervie, Sutherland, IV27 4RR

web: https://klbcompany.wordpress.com/loch-clash-stopover

email: grahamandlynn@theuphouse.co.uk

info: *A great spot on the quayside at Bervie.*

Scourie Camping and Caravan Site

Harbour Rd, Scourie, Lairg, Sutherland, IV27 4TE

web: www.scouriecampsitesutherland.com

email: info@ scouriecampsitesutherland.com

tel: 01971 502 060

info: *A nice site adjacent to the pub and lovely beach.*

Sango Sands Oasis

Sango Bay, Durness, Sutherland, IV27 4PZ

web: https://sangosands.com

email: keith.durness@btinternet.com

tel: 07838 381 065

info: *Amazing views and direct beach access. Best campsite for miles and miles.*

IN THE AREA

Smoo Cave A very impressive sea cave, combined with a freshwater cave in Durness. Tours of the cave are available in season but it's still impressive enough if you simply stroll in, and free. It's a big visitor attraction in these parts as it's a truly natural wonder. ▪ http://smoocavetours.weebly.com/

Golden Eagle Zip Line A zip line across Rispond Beach east of Durness that is 227 metres (yards) long and 30 metres (yards) above the ground. Looks like fun. ▪ www.facebook.com/goldeneagleziplines

Nearest van hire

Happy Highland Campers, Inverness
▪ www.happyhighlandcampers.co.uk

OutThere Campervans, Inverness
▪ www.outtherecampers.co.uk

Falls of Shin Community Project Salmon leap viewing platform, walks in the woods, cafe and play park. Run by the Kyle of Sutherland Development Trust.
• www.kyleofsutherlanddevelopmenttrust.org/current-projects/falls-of-shin-community-project/

Sandwood Bay Beautiful and remote, this bay is owned and managed by the John Muir Trust. Accessible by foot from Blairmore.
• www.johnmuirtrust.org/trust-land/sandwood

Cape Wrath Scotland's most north-westerly point, this is accessible only by boat across the Kyle of Durness and then by minibus on its only road, 11 miles (17 kilometres) from the ferry, unless you plan to walk. There is a cafe too. • www.visitcapewrath.com

ROUTE 24

CAMPING

MALLAIG

LOCH NEVIS

MORAR

TARBET

LOCH MORAR

ARISAIG

A830

LOCHAILORT

ROSHVEN

GLENFINNAN

KINLOCHEIL

DRUMSALLIE

LOCH EIL

STRATHAN

B8005

LOCH ARKAIG

ARDECHIVE

LAGGAN

LOCH LOCHY

A82

GAIRLOCHY

BANAVIE

CORPACH

SPEAN BRIDGE

B8004

A82

TORLUNDY

FORT WILLIAM

LOCH SHIEL

SALEN

A861

LOCH SUNART

CORRAN

INCHREE

ONICH

INVERSANDA

CAMPING

BEN NEVIS

LOCH LEVEN

KINLOCHLEVEN

GLENCOE

BALLACHULISH

A82

KINGAIRLOCH

LOCH LINNHE

A828

PORTNACROISH

GUALACHULAIN

DALNESS

GLEN ETIVE

RANNOCH

BEN STARAV

BLACK MOUNT

ACHALLA

LOCH TULLA

BRIDGE OF ORCHY

LOCH ETIVE

A85

A82

24

HARRY POTTER TRAIL

CHASING POTTER

If you need an excuse to see the lochs and glens around Fort William, this is it. From the well-visited Glenfinnan Viaduct and monument to the lonely shores of Loch Arkaig and the vast expanses of Rannoch Moor, there is much to see on a slow road through 'Harry Potter country'. At the very least it offers another way to look at the countryside through the lens of a famous movie. For kids who have grown up with Harry, Hermione and Ron, it's magical.

BEST FOR:
Chasing Harry Potter locations and seeing the glens and lochs

START:
Loch Tulla Viewpoint

END: Corran Ferry

MILEAGE:
150 miles (240 kilometres)

DAYS TO EXPLORE: 4–5

OS LAND-RANGER MAP:
41, 33 (34)

HIGHLANDS AND THE NORTH

It's almost 11am. I am standing ankle deep in dark, black, oozing, peaty mud. It's a precarious spot, halfway up a hillside, about 6m (20ft) above a pathway and rocky outcrop that is an 'official' viewing point. People of all nationalities are sharing the hillside with me, excited, agitated, all eager to get a good spot. Some prefer to stay dry and clean on the viewing point while others, like me and my girls, Maggie and Charlie, have climbed a little further up the muddy hillside to get a clearer view, away from the selfie sticks and tripods. From the mud and the ooze it's clear we aren't the first people to come here and stand in this place. There must have been thousands before us. Maggie's feet squelch next to me. She's taking pictures of the mud that is threatening to engulf her boots.

It wasn't an easy climb to where we are standing but the view is much better. Behind me is the Glenfinnan Monument, an 18m (59ft)-high tower that was built in 1815 to remember those who lost their lives in the Jacobite Uprising. Behind that is Loch Shiel, stretching away to the south-west for 17 miles (27 kilometres). It is strikingly beautiful, idyllic. Spurs jut out into the water along its length, each one slightly milkier than the last as they fade into the distance in a perfect example of colour perspective. Like a child would draw a house with a door and four windows, this is how I imagine a painter would draw a Scottish loch.

Despite the beauty of the loch, and its relevance to why we are here, all have their backs turned to it. Instead, they face another marvel, the Glenfinnan Viaduct. At 380m (1,247ft) long, with 21 arches and a beautiful curve carrying a single railway line 30m (100ft) from the valley floor, it is an impressive piece of engineering and definitely a man-made marvel. It's beautiful too, straddling the glen elegantly, its curves never looking out of place.

But of course we haven't come here at this time to see an immovable object. We've come to see the Jacobite, a steam train carrying hundreds of Harry Potter fans, as it passes over the viaduct at 11 on the dot. It's the next best thing to securing a ticket to ride on the 'Hogwarts Express', the tourist steam train with 'Harry Potter-style' carriages that carries would-be wizards and witches from Fort William to Mallaig in the summer months. The highlight of the journey is crossing the viaduct, which appears

in four of the Harry Potter films and was the location for the famous flying-car sequence in *Harry Potter and the Chamber of Secrets*.

Of course, with Harry Potter being famous the world over, tickets for the train are hard to come by, which is why we're ankle deep in mud waiting for the Jacobite to arrive. I had to admit defeat with the tickets but promised the girls a much better alternative, in the way that hapless dads try to make up for their ineptitude. I convinced myself – and them – we'd get a better view of the train and the viaduct and, besides, we wouldn't have to sit on it for four hours as it chugged from stop to stop. They took it well, although I am sure that the Harry Potter fans inside them would have loved the experience. My advice? Book early.

The viaduct is just a small part of the route we are taking to link up several of the locations used in the making of the Harry Potter film franchise. It's a good reason to visit the glens and lochs around Fort William and a great way to entice teenagers to Scotland for a mini slow-road holiday. We have seen some truly wonderful places, camped in some lovely locations and remembered and discussed parts of our favourite films. It's a nice chance to enjoy some family togetherness. We have much to thank JK Rowling for.

My attention is taken away from thoughts of happy camping trips with my girls – and the midges and the mud – as the Jacobite comes into view. The industrial, coal-black engine is pulling six or seven carriages as it moves slowly across the arches. But there's something wrong. There's no smoke or steam. It doesn't look right. What is a steam train without hissing stream and white smoke rising in a trail behind it?

Then, as if by magic (what else?), smoke billows from the chimney, along with the steady chuff chuff we expect to hear from a coughing, spitting beast of steam and fire. We hear a steam-powered whistle too, and we are transported. For a moment we are seeing the Hogwarts Express puff its way from Platform nine and three-quarters to the finest of the 11 schools of witchcraft and wizardry. Disbelief is suspended for a moment and a few people around us gasp in delight. A lot of camera shutters click, selfie sticks waved and smiles smiled. I look at my girls smiling, smiling myself.

Then we're done, and it's time to turn and head for the van, which is parked half a mile away, on a verge on the A830, the road that follows the railway from Fort William. When we got here, at about 10.15am, we were surprised to see so many people waiting for the train. We really didn't expect the passing of the Jacobite over the viaduct to be such a major event. Instead, we found that the car park was full and the roadway was coned off for hundreds of yards either side. People in rental compacts scoured the verges in a frenzied and chaotic effort to find a space. The train, they know, waits for no one.

We turn and begin to trudge to the car park and the road that will take us back to the van. It is then that we are able to turn our attention to Loch Shiel. We've got time to admire it now. It's familiar, of course, as it doubled as the Black Lake in the Harry Potter films. I can see why it would turn a director's head. It is, like the Harry Potter locations we've been chasing for the last couple of days, just lovely.

We are passed by a coachload of tourists from Japan. They have just disembarked in the car park and are frantically climbing past us to the viewpoint. They have worried looks on their faces. They see that most of the crowd is now leaving and fear the worst. Their coach driver has brought them here too late to see the Jacobite. Nevertheless, they continue up the steps. A few minutes later, when Maggie, Charlie and I are cleaning the mud off our boots in Loch Shiel, we hear a high-pitched cheer. A diesel train is passing across the viaduct and the tour group has their picture. With a little extra imagination it could be the Jacobite parading as the Hogwarts Express. We smile. You have to get up early to catch the Hogwarts Express (and you have to plan a lot earlier if you want to ride it).

Our next stop, the island that was used as Dumbledore's final resting place on Loch Eilt, is nearby so we must press on towards Mallaig. We walk

back to the van and set off again on this enchanting slow road that is giving me an excuse to show my lovely girls some of Scotland's finest scenery. I feel blessed to have time with them before they go back to school at the end of the summer. I have caught them before the magic wears off, too. I hope it never does, of course, but they are growing fast and soon they may not want to traipse around the Highlands with me in a camper van. We belt up, put on the music and tootle off in the direction of Loch Eilt.

'That was cool, Dad,' says Maggie. 'Thank you for bringing us.'

'My pleasure.' I reply.

Magical.

Book early to avoid disappointment.

THE DRIVING

This route focuses on Fort William but begins on the A82 heading north from Loch Lomond after the Loch Tulla Viewpoint. This is when it reaches Rannoch Moor, the first 'location' on our Harry Potter Tour. It was in this wilderness, near Corrour Station, that the Death Eaters boarded the Hogwarts Express in the film *Harry Potter and the Deathly Hallows: Part 1*. The road, while one of Scotland's main routes, is a joy to drive. The landscape is vast, empty and impressive. A worthy place to encounter a Death Eater or Dementor or whatever else you fear most.

Just after the Glencoe Mountain Resort, take a left turn in the middle of nowhere to Glen Etive. This single-track road with passing places follows the path of the river feeding Loch Etive. There are waterfalls and mini gorges, with native birch and, later, as you get closer to Loch Etive, oak and pine. It's a beautiful landscape that looks, in parts, as if it were designed by a calendar maker. Dark peaty waterfalls tumbling into narrow pink-sandstone gorges with purple heather and birches clinging to the rocks make it sublimely brilliant.

The road to Loch Etive is a no through road, with a car park at the end so you'll need to retrace your steps back to the A82 for the descent into Glencoe through the gorge and into a wide, open glen. There is much history and horror here and people say it's foreboding because it's surrounded by mountains. You could be locked in here. But as soon as you turn the corner into Glencoe village, the world opens up again with Loch Leven and then on to the southern bank of Loch Linnhe, over the Ballachulish Bridge (staying on the A82) and on to Fort William, the focus of this area. It's the place to stock up on mountain gear and food if you are heading out to the peninsulas. Our route takes us through Fort William and on to Spean Bridge, past the Nevis Range mountain centre (have a ride on the gondola) and out into the wide scrubby 'flats' of the Great Glen, Scotland's great rift. Just after Spean Bridge the route takes a left down a small, undulating single-track road just after the Commando Memorial, the B8004. This takes you to Gairlochy, a tiny hamlet where you turn right on to the B8005 towards Loch Arkaig. The first left to Arkaig takes you along the west bank of the dramatic Loch Lochy, past the beautiful Eas Chia-aig waterfall, which was used as a location in the 1995 film *Rob Roy*. A little further on you come to Loch Arkaig, a location that was used as backdrop for Dumbledore's final resting place.

After exploring Loch Arkaig (the road follows it for more than 12 miles/20km) follow the B8004 back to Gairlochy, staying on the north side of the River Lochy and the Caledonian Canal to Banavie and on to the A830 towards Mallaig and Glenfinnan. The B8004 is a lovely winding single-track road that passes through forest on the slopes of the Great Glen. It is the perfect antidote to the busy A82 that follows Loch Linnhe through Fort William.

The A830 is a fast, good road, but the scenery it passes is spectacular, of course. It winds its way to Glennfinnan and Loch Shiel, and the Glenfinnan Railway Viaduct, the site of the famous flying-car incident. The road follows the railway track all the way, which, in turn follows the banks of Loch Eil past the end of Loch Shiel and up and over the pass to Loch Eilt and the sea Loch Ailort. Eilaean na Moine, at the eastern end of Loch Eilt, is the island used as Dumbledore's final resting place, although it was superimposed on to Loch Arkaig.

Arisaig, just before Mallaig, is a great place to camp as it has a number of beachside sites set on white-sand beaches with dark rocks in a shallow and calm sea. It is possible to camp yards from the sea here. Loch Morar, a little further along the A830, was also used for Hogwarts Lake.

Fort William can be gridlocked on occasion and tends to be a bottleneck at busy times. This just gives us an excuse to take a perfect slow-road diversion along the A861 that takes you on a beautiful single-track road along the southern shore of Loch Eil, through the hamlets of Duisky, Blaich and Achaphubuil. The views of the loch are outstanding as you pass just yards from the water or tootle along between forest and narrow strips of meadow where sheep graze. We saw a red squirrel here, dashing across the road from one patch of forest to another. At Achaphubuil the road takes a right turn and follows the northern shore of Loch Linnhe. Here, you are directly opposite Fort William, enjoying an open road while others sit in traffic with all the caravans, lorries and holidaymakers less than a mile away. Here, you'll find a peaceful community of bungalows overlooking the water with the occasional neatly mown lawn leading to the road, and ultimately to the water. There are pull-ins and quiet spots, too, although avoid the 'no overnight parking' signs if you see them.

At Corran you'll need to take the ferry across the loch back to the A82 to complete the loop.

PLACES TO STAY

Invercaimbe Caravan and Camping Site
Invercaimbe Croft, Arisaig, PH39 4NT
web: www.facebook.com/invercaimbe-caravan-
site-256438287736152/
email: invercaimbe@btinternet.com
tel: 01687 450 375

info: *Awesome campsite right on the sea at Arisaig.*

Bunree Caravan Club Site
Onich, Fort William, Highlands, PH33 6SE
web: www.caravanclub.co.uk/club-sites/scotland/
highlands/bunree-caravan-club-site
tel: 01855 821 283

info: *Absolutely stunning location on the shores of Loch Linnhe. Fish from your pitch!*

IN THE AREA

Ben Nevis Range Britain's only mountain gondola will take you to up to Aonach Mòr, to a height of around 600m (2,000ft) above sea level. The views from the top are stunning, of the Great Glen, Loch Lochy and Loch Linnhe. In summer you can find your way down by bike if you have the nerve, although it's for experts only. Other bike trails go from here and in the winter it is a major centre for winter sports.
• www.nevisrange.co.uk

Glenfinnan Viaduct The viaduct that was famous before – thanks to its architecture – but that has since become world famous thanks to Harry Potter and his flying car. • www.visit scotland.com/info/towns-villages/ glenfinnan-p236571

Glencoe There's a lot to this tiny village on the shores of Loch Leven, including opportunities for watersports, cycling, walking (of course) and mountaineering.
• http://discoverglencoe.scot

Nevis Gorge and Falls Another Harry Potter location (where he fought the dragon in *Harry Potter and the Goblet of Fire*) that offers a steady and spectacular low-level walk through the Nevis Gorge to Scotland's third-highest waterfall.
• http://ben-nevis.com

Nearest van hire

Western Isles Campers, Fort William
• www.westernislescampers.co.uk

Four Seasons Campers, Loch Lomond
• www.fourseasonscampervanhire.com

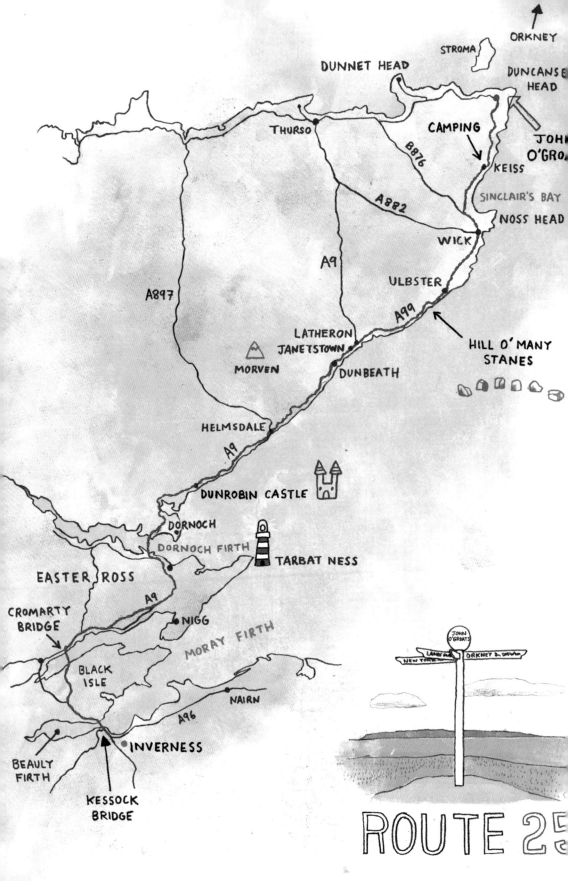

ORKNEY

STROMA

DUNNET HEAD

DUNCANSBY HEAD

CAMPING

JOHN O'GROATS

KEISS

THURSO

B876

SINCLAIR'S BAY

A882

NOSS HEAD

WICK

A9

ULBSTER

A897

A99

HILL O' MANY STANES

LATHERON
JANETSTOWN

MORVEN

DUNBEATH

HELMSDALE

A9

DUNROBIN CASTLE

DORNOCH

DORNOCH FIRTH

TARBAT NESS

EASTER ROSS

A9

CROMARTY
BRIDGE

NIGG

MORAY FIRTH

BLACK
ISLE

NAIRN

A96

INVERNESS

BEAULY
FIRTH

KESSOCK
BRIDGE

JOHN
O'GROATS

LANDS END   ORKNEY & SHETLAND
NEW YORK

ROUTE 25

A9 TO JOHN O'GROATS

THE FINAL RIDE NORTH

This is the final push, the last mile, the zenith, nadir and climax of any Scottish adventure. It's not the prettiest, but it is one of the most significant, simply because of the destination, John o'Groats. People shed blood, sweat and tears to get here so it's our duty to follow them on our slow-road adventures with a lovely coastal tootle up Scotland's low-lying north-east coast to the last signpost on mainland Britain. A must.

BEST FOR:
Coastal vistas and castles

START:
Inverness

END: John o'Groats

MILEAGE:
111 miles (179 kilometres)

DAYS TO EXPLORE: 3–4

OS LAND-RANGER MAP:
26, 21, 17, 12

HIGHLANDS AND THE NORTH

I am excited. I am on the North Coast 500, Scotland's 'alternative to Route 66', heading north, to the point that's widely accepted as the furthest point north on the British Mainland, but actually isn't. It's the point that everyone aims for, or sets out from, on an epic cycle, run, walk or drive of 874 miles (1,406 kilometres) to or from Land's End. For me it's the final leg of an epic trawl around the islands, highlands and lowlands of Scotland. It is the zenith, both spiritually and (almost) geographically of a year-long odyssey to cover as much of the country as I can. I have driven alongside lochs and glens, taken ferries, cable cars and causeways, and crossed rivers and high passes to discover some of the best slow roads in Scotland. I have been guided by maps, made-up themes and a little bit of lore along the way, taking routes that are well known and beautiful as well as discovering routes for myself that are lesser known but just as worthwhile.

Finally, 771 (1,241km) miles from home, I am about to reach a finish line of sorts with a stop-off at John o'Groats before I wind my way along the north coast to Durness and then head south via the Kyle of Tongue and the fabulously curly bridge at Kylesku. I shall not complete the North Coast 500 route because I have done most of it in chunks, but I will still make a giant loop with the start and end point as Inverness. I left this bit until last, and I am glad I did.

John o'Groats might be the acknowledged 'most northerly point on the British mainland', but it isn't. That's because 11 miles (18 kilometres) to the north-west lies Dunnet Head, the lonely spot with the lighthouse that's a little further up, but probably not as far from Land's End to warrant being

the final stop. Besides, as far as I remember there's nowhere to get an ice cream there, if you needed one after such prodigious wanderings.

As usual I'm a cheat. I live near Land's End and yet I've done this the slow way around, via all points of the compass. I haven't the legs to do it in one go, so I hardly feel worthy of any kind of welcome or celebration. Besides, I know from visiting the Butt of Lewis and Lizard Point that Britain's extreme places are rarely thronging with people. Mostly they are lonely, out of the way and a little threadbare, unloved even. A side effect of being at the edge I suppose.

John o'Groats, I imagine, will be similar. The drive up from Inverness has been interesting and, in places, beautiful, but unlike a lot of the driving I have encountered in this epic country there have been few 'wow's. Instead, I have been smiling the whole of the last 80 miles (129 kilometres), at the thought of the finish line, but also of driving with the sea constantly out of the driver's window. The sea, shimmering blue in the August sunshine, has been my constant companion, as it has been my entire adult life. I feel at home with it as my wingman.

The last few miles to John o'Groats take me along unbending roads on the flat, undulating A99 from Wick over peaty bog, through small

bungalowed settlements and across
low-level farmland where huge bales
of hay sit in the late-afternoon sun.

I pull into the car park. It's about
5pm and there are people milling
about, looking across the water to
Orkney and sipping coffee outside
a ramshackle coffee shack. It's
tidier than I imagined, thanks to
improvements made since 2010.
Then it was voted as the most dismal place in Scotland,
prompting a flurry of investments and improvements that have seen the
once-abandoned hotel turn into apartments, a remodelling of the area,
a new signpost and a general chivvying along.

Today, John o'Groats isn't windswept nor rainy nor dismal at all. The
campsite is full and the people are happy. Accents appear to be from the
USA, Germany, France, Australia. There's no melancholic moan in the breeze
or sheets of rain in the darkening sky. Paint isn't peeling in the golden glow

of the afternoon sun. It's hot and still and sunny. Bikers take turns to get their picture taken at the 'most northerly' point, the famous John o'Groats signpost that points to Edinburgh, Land's End and New York.

I wait my turn in the queue, take a self-conscious selfie and leave it to a group of Russians, who have biked here from who knows where. It seems a rather insignificant moment in the scale of things. There's no fanfare or slap on the back. I don't even buy an ice cream. Instead, I bask in the joy the bikers are showing at reaching the end. They smile, take a photograph and make this last post a most significant spot on their journeys.

Across the water, no more than a few miles away, lies Orkney and all the riches it promises. I had wanted to go there but my plans wouldn't allow it. I wanted to go to Skara Brae, to visit Scotland's most important Neolithic site and to stand in the places where it is thought the cult of the stone circle emerged. I stand and stare at the islands, across the clear blue sea, wondering. I shall have to save that for another slow-road adventure.

As I walk back to the van I realise that now I am on the last leg home, the final descent. I have much driving still to do. And all of it is downhill.

THE DRIVING

Depending on where you begin, this could be the first leg of the NC 500 from Inverness. As such it's an easy coastal drive that skirts the North Sea for almost 100 miles (160 kilometres). A lot of the way is flat, but there are times when the mountains encroach, forcing the road to take sharp hairpins into steep-sided coastal valleys, around sweeping bends high above the cliffs and through forests. Most of it is completed on the A9, the main road from Stirling that passes through Perth, Pitlochry and Aviemore before arriving at Inverness and heading north along the coast to Latheron, turning north-west to Thurso.

Of course, getting to the top of the world would never be easy. The first obstacle to overcome is the Beauly Firth, an inlet of the mighty Moray Firth, which it does rather marvellously via the Kessock Bridge. It's a glorious cable-stayed construction of over a kilometre in length that crosses Scotland's great divide, the Great Glen. It's a great bridge to drive as its apex, at around 30m (100ft) above sea level, gives great views of the Beauly Firth, the Black Isle, the isthmus to the north of Inverness and the Moray Firth to the east.

In total contrast is the bridge at the northern side of the Black Isle, the Cromarty Bridge, which carries the A9 across the firth a few metres above sea level in an unremarkable sweep. The road then follows the banks of the firth before heading inland towards Dornoch and the bridge over the Dornoch Firth. Cromarty Firth, and the Port of Nigg, is a base for the oil industry so it's not unusual to see oil rigs at anchor off shore. The port itself has one of the biggest dry docks in Europe and almost a kilometre of deepwater quayside, allowing the world's largest ships to dock.

After the Dornoch Bridge the A9 starts to behave like a true costal route. At Dunrobin Castle it begins to hug the coast, rarely straying far from it for miles. It's a beautiful drive, especially on a bright afternoon, and the views over the North Sea are lovely. Inland, mountains drop from heights of around 500m (1,640ft) to the coast, reminding us that the Highlands are ever present. At times, at places such as Helmsdale and Berriedale, they come close, making the road take tight turns in narrow river valleys. There are the parts of the drive that are a real joy, with chugging ascents and the occasional descent that feels like it's going to deposit you straight into the sea.

At Latheron the A9 heads north-west, leaving us to take the A99 towards Wick and beyond, skirting Sinclair's Bay and Freswick Bay before taking the level route to John o'Groats.

PLACES TO STAY

Motorhome Stopover, Keiss
Sinclair Hotel, Main St, Keiss, KW1 4UY
tel: 01955 631 233

info: *A few hardstanding pitches in Keiss, opposite the Sinclair Hotel, if you need 'leccy and an empty.*

John o'Groats Caravan & Camping Site
John o'Groats, Caithness, KW1 4YR
web: www.davidbody.co.uk/JohnoGroatsCampsite
email: info@johnogroatscampsite.co.uk
tel: 01955 611 329

info: *A nice site adjacent to the signpost with great views towards Orkney.*

Stroma View Caravan & Camping Site
Huna, Wick, KW1 4YL
web: www.stromaview.co.uk
email: john@stromaview.co.uk
tel: 01955 611 313/07340 112 774

info: *A weeny site with room for 8 motorhomes. Handy for John o'Groats and Orkney.*

IN THE AREA

Hill O' Many Stanes Stanes is how they write stones in Scotland. And there are many at this curious site just outside Ulbster – more than 200 in fact – arranged in rows in a fan shape. No one knows why or how or when. Go see. Great views of the coast. • www.ancient-scotland.co.uk/site/179

Dunrobin Castle A 'fairy tale' castle with pointy bits and lots of rooms (189) that has been continuously occupied since the 13th century. Home to the Earl of Sutherland it was remodelled into the Scottish Baronial style in 1845 by Sir Charles Barry. • www.dunrobincastle.co.uk

Castle Sinclair Girnigoe Unlike Dunrobin, this castle is a proper ruined pile, a World Monument and something truly special. It was once impregnable – and it's easy to see why – although you can go and see it on its precarious promontory a few miles north of Wick.
• www.castlesinclairgirnigoe.org

Glenmorangie Whisky Tour
I haven't focused on whisky much in this book, partly because you're driving (I am all heart) but if you must, perhaps you should consider this one. Tours take place every day for the connoisseur.
• www.glenmorangie.com

Nearest van hire

Happy Highland Campers, Inverness
• www.happyhighlandcampers.co.uk

OutThere Campervans, Inverness
• www.outtherecampers.co.uk

CAMPER VAN AND MOTORHOME HIRE

ADVENTURE WAGONS
Grannie's Park Industrial Estate,
Edinburgh Road, Dalkeith, EH22 1JY
Website: www.adventurewagons.com
Email: info@adventurewagons.com
Name: Gary/Nikki Jack
Telephone: 07874 113 930/07828 663 913
Info: 4 camper vans – VW T5 Transporter,
2 x VW Caddy Maxi, 1 x Mazda Bongo

ANGUS MOTORHOME HIRE
17 Robert Street, Arbroath, Angus, DD11 3AT
Website: www.angusmotorhomehire.com
Email: office@angusmotorhomehire.com
Name: Bruce Duncan
Telephone: 01241 433 553
Info: 1 x Baileys Approach Advanced 665

ATLAS MOTORHOME
AND CAMPERVAN HIRE
Glasgow Headquarters, 104 Hydepark
Street, Glasgow, G3 8BW
Website: www.atlashiredrive.co.uk
Email: info@atlashiredrive.co.uk
Name: Richard Offord
Telephone: 01413 742 126
Info: 45 mixed motorhomes and camper vans

AWESOME CAMPERS
Website: awesomecampers.co.uk
Email: hire@awesomecampers.co.uk
Name: Janet Baxter
Telephone: 07967 275 962
Info: 1 x VW T5 California

BC MOTORHOMES
Heathfield Road, Ayr, KA8 9HE
Website: www.bcmotorhomes.co.uk
Email: enquiries@bcmotorhomes.co.uk
Name: Craig Main
Telephone: 01292 272 277
Info: Selection of motorhomes

BIG TREE CAMPERVANS
Birch House, Church Lane, Bankfoot,
Perthshire, PH1 4BD
Website: www.bigtreecampervans.com
Email: simon@bigtreecampervans.com
Name: Simon and Sarah Yearsley
Telephone: 01738 788 056/07785 320 074
Info: 8 x vans: 4-berth camper van or a
2-berth camper van

BONNY SCOTLAND CAMPERS
2 Southhook Road, Kilmarnock, KA1 2NN
Website: www.bonnyscotland-campers.co.uk
Email: info@bonnyscotland-campers.co.uk
Name: Jack Wilson
Telephone: 07725 975 561
Info: 6 x vans: mix of motorhomes and camper vans

BUNK CAMPERS
Ligget Syke Pl, Broxburn, EH52 5NA
Website: www.bunkcampers.com
Email: enquiries@bunkcampers.com
Telephone: 02890 813 057
Info: 9 x vans: from compact campers, VW
camper vans, to large 6-berth motorhomes

CAIRNGORM CAMPERS
Birch View, Kinveachy, Boat of Garten,
Inverness-shire, PH24 3BT
Website: www.cairngormcampers.com
Email: enquiries@cairngormcampers.com
Name: Jo-Ann Clark
Telephone: 07492 704 140/01479 831 202
Info: 3 x Toyota Alphard 2–4-berth
camper vans

CALEDONIAN CAMPERS
AND CONVERSIONS LTD
582 Glasgow Road, Clydebank, G81 1NH
Website: www.caledoniancampers.co.uk
Email: info@caledoniancampers.co.uk
Name: Isla Bisset
Telephone: 0141 952 5399/07877 564 822
Info: 6 x vans – VW T6 SWB and LWB

CALEDONIAN TOURERS
26 Matthews Drive, Almondlea Estate,
Perth, PH1 2UR
Website: www.caledoniantourers.co.uk
Email: info@caledoniantourers.co.uk
Name: Andrea and Russell
Telephone: 07756 079 445
Info: 1 x luxury Swift Escape (6-berth,
5 seat belts)

CARBERRY CAMPERS
Springwood Cottage, Carberry,
East Lothian, EH21 8PZ
Website: www.carberrycampers.co.uk
Email: carberrycampers@gmail.com
Name: Angus/Gillian
Telephone: 07854 858 284
Info: 2 x 1960 classic VW split-screen vans

CLASSIC CAMPER HOLIDAYS
22 Buccleuch Street, Hawick, Scottish
Borders, TD9 0HW
Website: www.classic-camper-holidays.co.uk
Email: info@classic-camper-holidays.co.uk
Name: Ian and Becca Anderson
Telephone: 08435 235 723
Info: 3 x VW camper vans

CLIPPERTREK MOTORHOME HIRE
Station House, 4 Station Road, Oakley,
Fife, KY12 9QF
Website: www.clippertrek.co.uk
Email: info@clippertrek.co.uk
Name: Michelle Wallace
Telephone: 01383 851 133/07831 458 985
Info: 1 Peugeot Bailey 6-berth motorhome

DEESIDE CLASSIC CAMPERS
Crann Dearg, Drumhead, Finzean,
Aberdeenshire, AB31 6PB
Website: www.deesideclassiccampers.com
Email: office@deesideclassiccampers.com
Name: Claire and Martin Page
Telephone: 01330 850 555/07790 356 660
Info: 5 x vans – Hamish 1976 Westfalia, Fergus
1974 Camper, Murdo VW T6 and Angus and
Srchie split-screen buses

DEESIDE MOTORHOMES
Annesley Steading East, Fareview, Torphins,
Aberdeenshire, AB31 4HL
Website: www.deeside-motorhomes.co.uk
Email: info@deeside-motorhomes.co.uk
Name: Helen Cowie
Telephone: 01339 882 065
Info: 3 x vans – 2-, 4- and 6-berth motorhomes

FANTASTIC CAMPERVANS
Main Street, Dairsie, Fife, KY15 4SR
Website: www.fantasticcampervans.co.uk
Email: Dauto@btinternet.com
Name: Saul Hain
Telephone: 01334 870 271
Info: A wide selection of camper vans,
including seasonal variations

FOUR SEASONS CAMPERS
Gallangad Lodge, Merkins, Alexandria,
West Dunbartonshire, G83 9LX
Website: https://fourseasonscampers.com
Email: liz@fourseasonscampers.com
Name: Liz and Ivan
Telephone: 01389 830 602
Info: A mix of 2017 T6 VW camper vans
and 2016 T6 VW camper vans

HAPPY HIGHLAND CAMPERS
Unit 8, Canal Road, Muirtown Locks,
Inverness, IV3 8NF
Website: www.happyhighlandcampers.co.uk
Email: enquiries@happyhighlandcampers.co.uk
Name: Neil Dickinson
Telephone: 07796 675 639
Info: 4 x VW vans – including original 1971
Westfalia and 1978 bay window camper and
a 1978 Devon conversion

HARRIS CLASSIC CAMPERS
Unit 2, Seilebost, Isle of Harris, HS3 3HX
Website: www.harrisclassiccampers
Email: harrisclassiccampers@yahoo.co.uk
Name: Alan and Ellen McDougall
Telephone: 07920 748 852
Info: 3 vans: 1967 VW split screen (Californian
Roadrunner), 1979 VW bay window (Devon),
1963 Renault Estafette

ISLE OF MULL CAMPERVANS
Tobermory, Isle of Mull, PA75 6QF
Website: www.mullcampervans.co.uk
Email: info@mullcampervans.co.uk
Telephone: 01688 400 388/07909 680 285
Info: 3 x vans – Rimor Katamarano motorhome,
Toyota HiAce Regius, Mazda Bongo

KOMBI CAMPERS LTD
Unit 96 C, Murray St, Paisley PA3 1QT
Website: www.kombicampers.co.uk
Email: smile@kombicampers.co.uk
Name: Andy and Norma
Telephone: 0141 889 6156
Info: 5 classic VW camper vans, 2 VW California,
1 converted VW T5

LOSSIEMOUTH CAMPERVAN HIRE (LOSSIE CAMPERS)
Strathlene, Commerce Street, Lossiemouth,
Morayshire, IV31 6BW
Website: www.lossiemouthcampervanhire.com
Email: lossiecampers@gmail.com
Name: Magnus
Telephone: 07915 606 517
Info: 1 van – T5 LWB campervan

LOWLAND MOTORHOME HIRE
Yard 3b, 3 Newbattle Road, Newtongrange,
EH22 4RA
Website: www.lowlandmotorhomehire.co.uk
Email: info@lowlandmotorhomehire.co.uk
Name: Iain Peacock or Karen McWilliams
Telephone: 0131 629 1920
Info: 5 x coach-built motorhomes (they also have
a caravan and motorhome maintenance business)

MORAYFIRTH CAMPER AND CARAVAN HIRE
51 Farquhar Street, Hopeman, Elgin, IV30 5SL
Website: www.morayfirthcamperandcaravanhire.
co.uk
Email: info@morayfirthcamperandcaravanhire.
co.uk
Name: Joanna Saville and Malcolm Brown
Telephone: 07500 117 427
Info: 16 x vans – mix of Classic VW T2 – Sally,
3 VW T5s – Ruby, Sylvie and Blossom, 6-berth
Autoroller motorhome, 4-berth Tribute
motorhome, 2 x 4-berth touring caravans

MOTORHOME ADVENTURE SCOTLAND LTD
10 Clashburn Way, Kinross, KY13 8GA
Website: www.motorhomeadventure
scotland.co.uk
Email: info@motorhomeadventure
scotland.co.uk
Name: Liz Jeffrey
Telephone: 01577 864 795/07770 823 478
Info: 3 x vans – mix of Swift Escape,
2–4-berths and 6-berths

MOTORHOME HIRE SCOTLAND
5A Houston Mains, Dechmont,
West Lothian, EH52 6JU
Website: www.motorhomehire-scotland.co.uk
Email: info@motorhomehire-scotland.co.uk
Name: David, Nicola and Rebecca Gill
(family business)
Telephone: 01506 243 111/03332 001 663
(free call)
Info: 12 x vans – luxury Bailey 3-, 4- and
6-berth motorhomes (expanding fleet)

OPEN ROAD SCOTLAND
Unit 12 Airlink Industrial Estate, Inchinnan
Road, Paisley, PA3 2RS
Website: www.openroadscotland.com
Email: info@openroadscotland.com
Name: Andy McCluskey
Telephone: 0141 634 8444
Info: 20 x vans – mix of 2–6-berth motor-
homes and 2–4-berth VW camper vans

OUTTHERE CAMPERVANS
Willowvale, Tradespark Road, Nairn, IV12 5NF
Website: www.outtherecampers.co.uk
Email: info@outtherecampers.co.uk
Name: Jennifer and Neil Watson
Telephone: 07802 843 309
Info: 5 vans – mix of motorhomes and
camper vans

PITLOCHRY MOTORHOME HIRE
9 Castlebeigh Park, Pitlochry, PH16 5QH
Website: www.pitlochrymotorhomehire.co.uk
Email: info@pitlochrymotorhomehire.co.uk
Name: Ewan and Tracey
Telephone: 07943 481 102
Info: 2 x Auto-Roller motorhomes

ROCKIN VANS
62B Galston Road, Kilmarnock, KA1 5HY
Website: www.rockinvans.co.uk
Email: info@rockinvans.co.uk
Name: Katie Bassett
Telephone: 0141 404 8384
Info: 35 x vans – mix of 2-person camper
vans, 4-person VW camper vans, mid-size
motorhomes, large 6-berth motorhomes

ROSEISLE LUXURY CAMPERVANS
34 Whitecraig Road, Whitecraig,
Musselburgh, East Lothian, EH21 8NE
Website: www.roseislemotorhomehire.com
Email: campers@roseisle.com
Name: Emanuel Maxim
Telephone: 0131 653 5023
Info: 40 camper vans and motorhomes – mix
of VW California, VW Westfalia, Compact
Plus, medium 2-berth, medium 3-berth,
deluxe, deluxe plus and deluxe family

SPACESHIPS CAMPERVAN RENTALS UK AND EUROPE
The Workshop, Union Street, Kelty, Fife,
KY4 0EF
Website: www.spaceshipsrentals.co.uk
Email: tom@spaceshipsrentals.co.uk
Name: Tom Lanauze
Telephone: 020 8573 2300
Info: 50+ mix of 2- and 4-berth camper vans
and 4- and 7-berth motorhomes

THE TARTAN CAMPER COMPANY
9 Hogarth Avenue, Saltcoats, North
Ayrshire, KA21 6BY
Website: www.thetartancamper.co.uk
Email: info@thetartancamper.com
Name: Stuart Shepherd/Gavin Stevely
Telephone: 07590 876 381/01294 446 016
Info: 7 vans – mix of VW T25, VW T4
Automatic and VW T5 (all wrapped in Royal
Stewart tartan)

VIEW FROM THE SLOW LANE
Campion Cottage, Leys of Boysack,
Arbroath DD11 4RP
Website: www.viewfromtheslowlane.com
Email: info@viewfromtheslowlane.com
Name: Samantha Lockhart-Mure
Telephone: 07935 010 978
Info: 2 x vans – 1975 and 1972 VW T2
camper vans

WEST COAST VW CAMPER HIRE
Cambridge Crescent, Airdrie, ML6 7HF
Website: www.vwcamperhirescotland.co.uk
Email: info@vwcamperhirescotland.co.uk
Name: Brian or Emma Carlin
Mobile: 07824 555 124/07824 556 863
Info: 2 x vans – VW Californias

WESTERN ISLES CAMPERS
Ben Nevis Industrial Estate, Fort William
PH33 6RU
Website: www.westernislescampers.co.uk
Email: info@westernislescampers.co.uk
Name: Matthew and Isadore
Telephone: 07833 372 583
Info: 5 x vans – motorhomes, VWs and Bongos

INDEX

Entries in **bold** are featured routes.

ACKNOWLEDGEMENTS

THE UNSUNG HEROES

Books don't happen by themselves. And without the following
people this one would never have happened.
And so, grateful thanks to...

The vanbelievers: Jenny Clark, Penny Phillips and
Sutchinda Thompson at Bloomsbury, Austin Taylor in Bristol,
David Broadbent in Brighton, Sonja Brodie in Leswalt.

Team Tim: my agent Tim Bates and the team at PFD.

Cover story: Claire and Martin at Deeside Classic Campers
for the loan of Hamish.

Creature comforts: Andy Brand and Emma Franklin at
Marquis Motorhomes for the loaners.

Snorkeltastic: Noel Hawkins at the Scottish Wildlife Trust.

Get in the van: Andy Price for the cover shots and gags.

Dustbin lids: Maggie and Charlie for their constant love and
companionship.

Barra boy: Ben, who guided me to the waves in the Outer Hebrides.

Botanical bearings: Kevin Reid at the Royal Botanic Garden
Edinburgh for showing me the way.

PR Powerhouse: Nikki at the Caravan and Motorhome Club
for invaluable support.

Gaelic Guru: Andrew Ditton for his tweets and advice.

Disposable duds: Bernie for dishing out the sweets and the advice.

Fort holder: Nicky Green for flying the flag while I was out.

Back office: Jamie Harper, always there with the words.

Wing girl: Dolly, for looking out for me from a very long way away.
And finally,

Nice Kona: Lizzy for showing me that it's OK to be ten again.